ROUTLEDGE LIBRARY EDITIONS: WORK & SOCIETY

Volume 10

REPERCUSSIONS OF REDUNDANCY

REPERCUSSIONS OF REDUNDANCY

A Local Survey

HILDA R. KAHN

LONDON AND NEW YORK

First published in 1964 by George Allen & Unwin Ltd.

This edition first published in 2024
by Routledge
4 Park Square, Milton Park, Abingdon, Oxon OX14 4RN

and by Routledge
605 Third Avenue, New York, NY 10158

Routledge is an imprint of the Taylor & Francis Group, an informa business

British Library Cataloguing in Publication Data
A catalogue record for this book is available from the British Library

ISBN: 978-1-032-80236-7 (Set)
ISBN: 978-1-032-81698-2 (Volume 10) (hbk)
ISBN: 978-1-032-81701-9 (Volume 10) (pbk)
ISBN: 978-1-003-50094-0 (Volume 10) (ebk)

DOI: 10.4324/9781003500940

Publisher's Note
The publisher has gone to great lengths to ensure the quality of this reprint but points out that some imperfections in the original copies may be apparent.

Disclaimer
The publisher has made every effort to trace copyright holders and would welcome correspondence from those they have been unable to trace.

REPERCUSSIONS OF REDUNDANCY

A Local Survey

by

HILDA R. KAHN

B.SC.(ECON.), PH.D.

Lecturer in Social Administration
University of Hull

FOREWORD BY CHARLES MADGE, M.A.
Professor of Sociology, University of Birmingham

London

GEORGE ALLEN AND UNWIN LTD

FIRST PUBLISHED IN 1964

PRINTED IN GREAT BRITAIN
in 10 point Times Roman type

FOREWORD

Surprisingly little is known about what actually happens to men and women who are declared 'redundant' in modern industrial society, how they adapt themselves to the situation, what difficulties they encounter, and whether the long-term effects of the change are harmful, beneficial or neutral in human and in economic terms. Yet redundancy seems to be a recurrent feature of the industrial scene, against which existing institutions and insurances provide inadequate protection.

The survey made in such painstaking detail by Dr Hilda Kahn refers to a large-scale redundancy that took place as long ago as 1956. But since that time no work of equal thoroughness has been done on this problem, and Dr Kahn's findings remain relevant today. They will, I am sure, be carefully studied by all those for whom redundancy remains an issue of practical importance.

The survey is also of great methodological interest to the social scientist, especially to the practitioner of *applied* social science.

Seldom if ever have the results of a survey based on personal interviews been so rigorously and methodically checked and counter-checked. I agree with Dr Kahn that this intensive scrutiny leaves one with uncomfortable doubts about the validity of many of the hit-and-run, pre-coded interview studies which currently pass as 'scientific'. If rapid, relatively inexpensive surveys are needed by policy makers and administrators, then it is high time that more searching tests should be applied to methods now in general use, so that more adequate and accurate techniques can be developed.

Dr Kahn would not claim, I am sure, that her study is the last word on redundancy. What makes it important is that it is very probably the only study in this field which offers a sound basis for an appraisal of the social impact of large-scale simultaneous dismissals in a time of full employment.

CHARLES MADGE
Professor of Sociology
University of Birmingham

PREFACE

The present work contains the results of the Birmingham Redundancy and Re-employment Survey, which took shape following a suggestion by the then Minister of Labour—the Right Honourable Iain Macleod, M.P.—that the sudden and large-scale dismissals occurring in the Midlands in mid-1956 were worthy of 'academic' attention. After a meeting with the Minister, Professor Charles Madge, Professor of Sociology at the University of Birmingham, accepted responsibility for the project, to be carried out within the Faculty of Commerce and Social Science of the University. The Survey was sponsored by the National Institute of Economic and Social Research, and has enjoyed the support of the Ministry of Labour, the Engineering and Allied Employers' Association, the Birmingham Trades Council and affiliated trade union bodies, as of all the firms and overwhelming majority of the men and women approached.

The principal object of the Survey was to study the experience of redundant workers, by examining all relevant facts about their industrial and domestic history in the period following dismissal; the main method of inquiry has been that of the personal interview. In this type of research—more, perhaps, than in any other—the investigator is dependent on the co-operation of numerous individuals and organizations; as Head of Research of the project I have been conscious throughout of the calls made on the time and good will of others. It is the assistance received from so many quarters which alone made my labours possible.

First, I would express my appreciation to Professor Madge, through whose initiative the Survey was launched; equally so to the National Institute of Economic and Social Research for sponsoring the study. Next, I wish to thank those making various preliminary investigations, on which I was able to draw on taking up my post. Much gratitude is also due to many officials of the Ministry of Labour—in particular, at its Midland Regional Office—for their extremely valuable help.

The paths of this project were materially smoothed by the very effective support of Mr J. Hope, Secretary of the Engineering and Allied Employers' Association, and of Mr H. Baker, Secretary of the Birmingham Trades Council, and his colleagues. Several members of the Birmingham business community and trade union movement supplied most useful information.

For facilities to draw samples, for providing essential background data and for putting up with a host of queries, the Survey is heavily indebted to Brigadier B. Walton and Mr C. J. Horton of the Austin Motor Co. Ltd., to Mr A. L. Toye of the Birmingham Small Arms Co. Ltd., to Mr B. L. Mackie and Mr W. R. W. Randall of Messrs Fisher and Ludlow Ltd., to Mr R. E. March and Miss G. Roberts of Messrs Joseph Lucas (Electrical) Ltd., to Mr C. L. Coade of Messrs Morris Motors (Tractor and Transmissions) Ltd., and to Mr N. Coatsworth and Mr H. R. Bennett of Messrs Nuffield Metal Products Ltd. It is a pleasure to pay tribute to the unfailing courtesy and promptness of all the above and their staffs.

The most crucial partners in any social survey are the men and women whose experiences form its subject matter. By allowing us into their homes, by giving us of their time, and by letting us into some of their secrets, they have earned the unreserved gratitude of all those associated with this inquiry.

The bulk of interviews were completed by Mrs J. Gardner, Miss J. A. Hawes, Mr M. A. Johnson, Mr A. Milligan, Mrs P. Luckett, Mrs M. Watkinson and Mr R. A. Woodhouse, and I gladly here attest to their skill and resourcefulness. But perhaps the biggest compliment that can be paid to them is to say that they survived the many frustrations that are of the lot of interviewers, and that they successfully coped with the intricacies of the document reproduced in Appendix C.

I am much obliged to Dr J. Wise who acted as statistical adviser to the study; special thanks are likewise due to Miss J. M. Bellamy, Mr J. P. Davison, Dr A. H. Halsey and Dr N. S. Ross. I am grateful to Mrs M. Watkinson for her services as research assistant for one year, and to Mrs L. Butcher who was a most useful clerical assistant. The majority of calculations were undertaken by Mrs B. E. Tatlow and Mrs B. Taylor. The brunt of research chores, however, fell on Mrs P. Luckett: no words of mine could do justice to her truly splendid assistance.

Before I conclude, I would record my sincere appreciation to the Faculty of Commerce and Social Science of the University of Birmingham for the support given to this project. I should like to express my particular thanks to Professor H. S. Ferns, Dean of the Faculty.

Finally, it is with a deep and very special sense of gratitude that I here acknowledge the immense debt which I owe to Mrs June Norris, who helped me to sort out countless problems—large and small—on all aspects of the Survey. Her experience, judgement and advice were altogether invaluable to me. To both Mrs Norris, and to Dr E. W. Evans of the University of Hull, I am also extremely grateful for reading the manuscript in draft and making numerous pertinent suggestions.

For the contents of the following pages—including all errors of fact or interpretation—no one but myself is in any way responsible.

H.R.K.

Department of Social Administration
University of Hull
November 1963

CONTENTS

LIST OF TABLES*

* Key: R=redundancy; RJ=firm/job from which made redundant

Chapter 1

INTRODUCTION

The essence of redundancy as applied to human beings is an excess or superfluity of labour, due to a change—however caused—in some aspect of the market situation. It can perhaps be defined as the initial process of laying off workers that may or may not give rise to unemployment. It is in this sense that redundancy is not identical with the latter, and can in fact be said to have crystallized as a 'problem' since the achievement of a full employment economy.

Just as redundancy overlaps but is not identical with unemployment, so it also differs from the ordinary processes of labour mobility—of which it nevertheless forms part. Thus a declared or *de facto* decision by firms in a given industry in a given area to suspend further recruitment may induce a sizeable movement of school-leavers to other trades/localities in search of work, but no redundancy would be involved because no one had been dismissed. A shift of similar dimensions caused by the actual discharge of personnel would clearly amount to redundancy.

There are two main reasons why redundancy has been felt to be a problem only in the post-war period—and in the latter part of that period in particular. For as long as there was an overall deficiency of demand in the economy, any fresh lay-off was bound to lead to unemployment—not necessarily of those immediately affected, but of some workers somewhere in the system. Redundancy was thus overshadowed and dwarfed by the general phenomenon of unemployment. Then, with the advent of labour shortage during and since the war, the emphasis swung to the other extreme, and discussion tended to focus on those aspects of mobility which stemmed from the initiative of the worker. In other words, it was the latter's propensity to bid adieu to his boss rather than the reverse which primarily attracted attention.

While, speaking in broad terms and taking the country as a whole, full or near-full employment has been maintained, and while the problem of rapid labour turnover has remained with us, there is now no longer—as Mrs Jefferys found in the early 'fifties—'a tendency to ignore the fact that full employment does not mean an unchanging distribution of employment opportunities between undertakings'.[1]

[1] M. Jefferys with W. Moss, *Mobility in the Labour Market* (Routledge, 1954) p. 11.

This is because in the more recent period sizeable redundancies have occurred in a number of important industries—such as textiles, shipbuilding, vehicles and other consumer durables. At the same time, smaller ones have taken place in many other fields, while currently major ones are in progress on the railways and in the pits. The regional incidence of these dismissals is another serious complication.

The problems that arise are of several kinds. First, there is the truism that, unless the economy is to stagnate, there must be movement between industries, occupations and areas; though labour turnover may be wasteful, some labour mobility—in practice the two are rather awkwardly interlinked—is an essential concomitant of economic change. However, in a society with full employment on the one hand and a high standard of living on the other, geographical mobility is at a discount. Pay differentials, which in theory should effect the ideal distribution of labour, themselves lose of their attractive force, quite apart from the fact that for a variety of reasons actual wage relativities are not necessarily of a shape as would bring about such optimal deployment. The question thus is whether redundancy is one of the tools needed to achieve the requisite distribution of labour.

At the same time, we cannot be certain that redundancy is an efficient method for this purpose. While the laying off of workers can be expected to produce some redeployment of manpower, we cannot automatically assume that this will be in a direction such as to benefit the economy. Further, there is the possibility that a waste of resources might result, either through prolonged spells of unemployment on the part of those laid off, or because, even in the absence of the latter, there is a loss of capital in terms of acquired, but potentially still useful, skills.

Next, there are the social problems generated by redundancy, and a country committed to both full employment and a welfare state cannot simply take refuge in the cosy comfort provided by favourable overall unemployment statistics. In other words, whether or not some redundancy is essential for the efficient functioning of the economy, it behoves a modern democracy to ensure that the price paid in social terms is not excessive. This, among other things, raises the crucial issue of identifying the ultimate beneficiaries of redundancy—with a view to an equitable sharing of the overall cost of the operation.

The social and economic aspects of the subject are not, of course, distinct, for the fear of redundancy is a potent factor that has soured industrial relations in many spheres. And more serious than the tangible outcome of this—such as the strikes which have occurred over this issue—is the subtle brake that this fear imposes on productivity. Clearly, if increased effort is liable to mean working oneself out of a job, prudence dictates that one should drag one's feet, even though such personal prudence may jeopardize national growth. The terror of the 'sack' is also bound to create suspicion of new techniques—automatic and other—something, again, which the country can ill afford if it is not to fall behind in the industrial race. Further, the fear of redundancy is becoming more acute as a result of the increasing exposure of national economies to the forces of international competition.

The question of redundancy thus commands attention for both economic and social considerations, as well as for reasons grounded in that large indeterminate territory where the two are inextricably intertwined. Problems, however, cannot be solved in the absence of policies, and the latter cannot be formulated in the absence of knowledge. One of the noteworthy features of the present situation is that we have little specific knowledge about important facets of the problem of redundancy.

This inquiry did not, however, come about to provide all the answers; it took shape with the more modest aim of throwing light on one particular corner of the problem. In brief, as indicated in the Preface, it owes its birth to the suggestion that the sudden and large-scale dismissals, which occurred in the Midlands in mid-1956, deserved to be studied. The chief object of the survey has been to investigate the actual experience of redundant workers, and the accent has been on the impact of redundancy—industrial and social—on those personally its victims, rather than on its wider economic causes or effects. The project is thus concerned with one aspect only of the subject—and it is a case study of one particular redundancy which took place in one particular area at a particular point of time. Nevertheless, it is from the detailed and the specific rather than from the broad sweep of generalization that knowledge, in the last analysis, is built.

II

On Wednesday June 27, 1956, the British Motor Corporation announced that as from Friday, June 29th there would be an overall reduction in personnel in its various factories, affecting some 12½ per cent of its total labour force, or approximately 6,000 employees. So large a number to be dismissed by one combine, at one fell swoop and with such negligible prior warning, was unprecedented as far as post-war Britain was concerned, and it came as a rude shock to the nation.

The recession in the car industry, which led to this dramatic turn of events, had not in itself been sudden. 1955 had been a record year for the industry, with the number of vehicles produced about 19 per cent up on 1954, while the British Motor Corporation itself had improved on its 1954 output to the tune of nearly 27 per cent. However, the normal seasonal downturn during the winter and spring months of 1955–56 was aggravated by a severe decline in car exports, as well as by a significant fall in sales on the home market—following the purchase tax increases introduced by the Chancellor of the Exchequer's autumn budget, and the credit squeeze and analogous measures announced in Parliament in February 1956. The situation was at first marked by extensive short-time working and a small amount of redundancy in the Coventry and Birmingham areas, the situation being made more difficult by the (then) Standard Motor Company's plans for the laying off of some 2,600 workers due to the re-tooling of its Coventry tractor plant.[1] It was only later, as the recession developed, that the B.M.C. dismissals took place.

In the statement issued when the discharges were made public, the British Motor Corporation recalled that the expansion programme embarked upon three years previously envisaged a production rate for 1956 of 12,500 units weekly, there being every indication at the earlier date that world markets would absorb this output. While the number of vehicles currently sold abroad was higher than in the corresponding period of the preceding year and while B.M.C. had increased its share of the home market, anti-inflationary policies adopted in various overseas countries were beginning to take their toll, whilst at home enhanced purchase tax, new hire-purchase restrictions and heavier costs had led to a rise in the price of vehicles, resulting in a contraction of demand. The Corporation added that although other car manufacturers had raised prices in October 1955, it had postponed similar action until forced, by the March 1956 revision of engineering wages, to follow suit. Meanwhile, other factors had militated against expansion abroad—in particular, a substantial curtailment of export outlets in Australia and New Zealand, the former for many years the Corporation's biggest overseas customer. It was also subsequently pointed out that the labour force of the works concerned had been stepped up by 16 per cent between January 1954 and March 1956.

The 6,000-odd workers to be discharged by B.M.C. were spread over eight different units, with a combined labour force of about 42,700. Of those made redundant, about 100 were employed in South

[1] The number dismissed as a result of the re-tooling operation was rather smaller in the event than that initially announced. However, a further 1,000 workers were discharged by the Company at end-August 1956 in view of the decline in car sales.

Wales (Llanelly), nearly 1,000 in Cowley and Oxford, and the remainder in Birmingham.

Strong criticism of the 'profoundly disturbing' course pursued by the Corporation in announcing the redundancies at such short notice was expressed by the Minister of Labour in the House of Commons the following day. The Minister added that it would not be possible for all the dismissed to secure employment in their own localities, and that at his request the Ministers of Transport and of Fuel and Power had asked the British Transport Commission and the National Coal Board to accelerate their rate of labour intake so as to help men find jobs. The Coal Board had agreed to send special recruiting teams to the Birmingham area for this purpose.[1]

The suddenness of the lay-off and the lack of prior consultation with union officials and shop stewards caused deep resentment among many B.M.C. workers—with threatened or actual strike action at several of the plants affected. On July 4th trade union leaders—who had been restive since the introduction of short-time at the beginning of the year—met B.M.C. representatives to discuss the situation. However, the encounter proved fruitless, the Company stating that there was no possibility of re-employing the discharged men in the immediate future, and rejecting—because of the national issues involved—the unions' suggestions as to monetary compensation. Further attempts to call a strike at Longbridge failed, but after the Corporation had issued another statement repeating its earlier stand, a meeting of union leaders in London unanimously resolved to recommend strike action at all B.M.C. factories as from July 23rd, unless their demands had meanwhile been conceded.

After further exchanges, the fifteen trade unions concerned decided to ask the Minister of Labour to convene an immediate meeting of the parties, and separate talks were consequently held between the Ministry's Chief Industrial Commissioner and representatives of the two sides. However, they were unsuccessful. The strike accordingly took place, though the response to it was mixed, with only about half of the Corporation's remaining employees 'coming out'. Efforts were likewise made to extend the dispute to those indirectly engaged in the handling of B.M.C. products, the strike also having drastic, though short-lived, repercussions at a Ford subsidiary at Dagenham.

On July 25th the Minister of Labour appealed to the two sides to use the breathing-space afforded by the annual fortnight's holiday—due to commence the next day—to try and find a solution of their differences. The Engineering Employers' Federation thereupon indicated its willingness to examine with the unions all problems

[1] June 28, 1956, H.C. Deb. 555, 704–12.

connected with the redundancy, and informal discussions began at the Ministry of Labour on August 1st, the issue being narrowed to the question of compensation. A settlement was finally reached on August 10th, the chief provisions of which were, first, that the British Motor Corporation repeated its undertaking to offer re-engagement to its ex-employees in appropriate vacancies which might arise. Secondly, on the crucial subject of compensation, the Corporation agreed to make what were officially described as 'payments in lieu of longer notice' to those dismissed men who had been employed continuously for three years or longer. These were to be of the order of one week's wages for those with from three to ten years' service, and of two weeks' remuneration for those with ten or more years to their credit—at the appropriate consolidated time rate in each case. The strike was thereupon called off, and work was resumed when the holidays ended on August 13th. Everything was thus back to normal —except for the redundant men.

III

An attempt to put the mid-1956 redundancies into 'statistical perspective' comes up against the difficulty that comprehensive statistics on the topic do not exist. It is with some trepidation, therefore, that we set out the following summary figures:

TABLE 1

Redundancies Notified to Employment Exchange Managers mid-1955 to mid-1957*

	Midland Region		*Great Britain*	
	Motor Vehicles, etc.	*All industries*	*Motor Vehicles, etc.*	*All industries*
	No.	No.	No.	No.
July–December 1955	550	1,600	770	16,100
January–June 1956	12,760	15,900	16,890	62,300
July–December 1956	7,690	9,900	15,070	42,100
January–June 1957	2,770	8,600	8,430	51,000

* These and subsequent redundancy statistics were made available by courtesy of the Ministry of Labour, who were good enough to draw the writer's attention to many of their limitations. It is because of these that more detailed breakdowns are not being given.

The limitations of redundancy statistics arise from the fact that they represent the sum-total of dismissals reported by firms to local employment exchanges. The data are supplied on a purely voluntary basis; they are not derived from any statutory series as are, for example, the 'L' returns dealing with labour turnover. Nor are they the product of a specific and regular survey in which employers voluntarily co-operate—as are, for instance, the Ministry of Labour's half-yearly earnings inquiries. These, notwithstanding their non-statutory character, provide valuable and reliable information on the earnings of the majority of manual workers.

While the relation between individual exchange managers and local industry is no doubt satisfactory in most cases, the accuracy of the figures is nevertheless liable to vary with the ability and experience of individual managers, as well as with the nature of the area's industry. It is the smaller dismissals, in particular, which may frequently not get reported, so that almost certainly the figures understate the facts. The position is less serious regarding major redundancies, both because the larger concerns have normally more dealings with exchanges, because such discharges are likely to find their way into the local press, as well as because some of those affected are bound to register as unemployed.

One reason why firms may feel disinclined to notify redundancies is a simple commercial one. An enterprise having to lay off a sizeable proportion of its labour force is obviously in difficulties; it may not be keen for its competitors to know of this, and may therefore try to conceal the extent of the discharges. Another ground for lack of enthusiasm in divulging the relevant details is that employers may prefer not to cause trouble on the trade union front.

A further point—and it is not merely an academic quibble—is that the definition of 'redundancy' is not clear, in that the term can be looked at from the point of view of the individual, that of the firm, or that of the labour market. As far as the individual is concerned, he is redundant when his services are no longer required for reasons other than disciplinary ones; however, such a one-man discharge hardly constitutes redundancy from a wider angle. Dispensing with twenty men because their services are not further needed is more tricky: if the enterprise has a pay-roll of only fifty employees, a reduction by two-fifths can be said to amount to redundancy, though in the context of the general scene, it can still be viewed as part merely of the ordinary processes of labour mobility. The time unit is another complication: staggered or 'driblet' dismissals, involving x workers per week, will equal y workers laid off at one swoop in the course of the same time-span. Again, the question of causal antecedents is one for argument. Redundancies may be due to a fall in demand, to the introduction of automation or other new techniques, to rationalization, or to bankruptcy; or they may be the result of strikes or of a shortage of materials. They may be seasonal, temporary or permanent, and here again firms must be expected to differ in what they feel inclined to report as such.

Another shortcoming of statistics in this sphere is that the figures of redundancies which are furnished to the Ministry of Labour are sometimes given in round numbers or are estimates of persons *likely* to be discharged, so that these totals may diverge considerably—and at times substantially—from those actually laid off.

We may here add that it is not possible to deduce the extent of redundancies from unemployment statistics on the one hand or from labour turnover data on the other. In so far as the former are concerned, not all those made redundant become unemployed, and those who do, do not invariably register at employment exchanges. Conversely, a person may be unemployed for several reasons other than redundancy. As for labour turnover statistics, here again there are many causes—such as retirement, disciplinary dismissal or voluntary resignation—for a man leaving his boss.

Turning now to unemployment itself, throughout 1955 the Midland Region witnessed practically none: the rate of unemployment (all workers) was 0·5 per cent, except in July and December when it fell to 0·4 per cent. These rates were consistently below those for Great Britain as a whole. The position during 1956 is set out below.

TABLE 2

Percentage Rate of Unemployment:* Midland Region and Great Britain, 1956†

	Midland Region		*Great Britain*
	Males	*All Workers*	*All Workers*
1956	%	%	%
January	0·6	0·6	1·2
February	0·6	0·6	1·3
March	0·6	0·7	1·2
April	0·7	0·7	1·2
May	1·1	1·0	1·1
June	1·3	1·2	1·0
July	2·2	1·9	1·1
August	2·5	2·1	1·2
September	1·1	1·1	1·1
October	1·0	1·0	1·2
November	0·9	1·0	1·2
December	0·9	1·0	1·4

* Number registered as unemployed (including 'temporarily stopped') expressed as percentage of the estimated total number of employees.

† Source: *Ministry of Labour Gazette*. For 'absolute' figures, see Appendix A.

It will be seen that although the boom conditions of 1955 no longer obtained, the Midland Region in 1956 saw little real unemployment; indeed, the relatively sharp fluctuations of the percentages in the middle of the year to a considerable extent reflect movements in the 'temporarily stopped' rather than in the 'wholly unemployed' component of the figures. This 'temporarily stopped' category not only comprises those laid off from their place of work on the understanding that they are shortly to return there; it also covers persons on short-time who happen to be non-working and registered for unemployment benefit on the crucial day of the Ministry's monthly count. In July and August 1956 the 'temporarily stopped' in the Midlands actually accounted for 60·4 and 60·1 per cent of the total registered as unemployed,[1] on which the official unemployment rates are calculated; the drop between August and September was chiefly due to a change of rule governing the eligibility to benefit of short-time workers.[2] However, what concerns us here is that the proportion registered as unemployed in the Midlands—even including the somewhat dubious group of the 'temporarily stopped'—exceeded 2 per cent in one month only of 1956, or in two months in the case of men.

TABLE 3

Number of Wholly Unemployed and Number of Vacancies Midland Region, 1956*

	Men, 18 years and over		*All Workers*	
	Wholly unemployed	*Vacancies unfilled*	*Wholly unemployed*	*Vacancies unfilled*
1956	No.	No.	No.	No.
January	7,084	23,050	11,214	48,382
February	7,162	22,884	11,011	47,335
March	7,223	20,991	11,143	45,277
April	7,153	20,837	11,815	43,692
May	7,230	20,041	11,647	40,915
June	7,718	19,381	12,252	39,588
July	10,434	16,028	16,051	36,273
August	10,867	15,058	17,766	31,954
September	10,901	14,298	18,720	28,749
October	10,690	14,168	18,322	27,576
November	11,025	13,020	18,341	26,474
December	11,509	10,752	18,622	24,087

* Source: *Ministry of Labour Gazette*. The unemployment figures relate to the day of the monthly count; the vacancy figures, which are collected at four-weekly intervals, relate to the nearest available date.

[1] The corresponding proportion for June 1956 was 52·2 per cent.

[2] The number of registered unemployed on September 17, 1956 i.e. was 20,915 less than in August, the 'wholly unemployed' having increased by 954 and the 'temporarily stopped' decreasing by 21,869. This resulted chiefly from the cessation of registration after August 21st of workers in the engineering industry (covered by the Guaranteed Week Agreement between the Engineering and Allied Employers' National Federation and the Confederation of Shipbuilding and Engineering Unions), who were disqualified by the National Insurance Commissioner from claiming unemployment benefit in respect of days on short-time. A new agreement early in 1957 led to a reversal of the position.

This rather encouraging picture of conditions in the Midlands in 1956 is confirmed if we compare the number of 'wholly unemployed', month by month, with the vacancies outstanding on the books of employment exchanges at approximately the same date (Table 3).

It will be seen that in the whole of 1956 the number of vacancies was larger than the 'wholly unemployed' figure in the case of all workers, though the gap narrowed throughout the year;[1] as regards men, the 'wholly unemployed' exceeded vacancies in December. For both categories the position materially worsened in the early months of 1957;[2] more generally, the outlook in the Midlands during the latter year was distinctly less propitious than in 1956.[3] At the same time, it should be pointed out that the 'temporarily stopped' have been excluded from Table 3; *some* of these were genuinely (temporarily) without a job. Similarly, the Midlands experienced a good deal of under-employment in 1956. Though the total on short-time fluctuated greatly—primarily due to developments in the vehicles and allied industries—it reached very high proportions, the average weekly figure in July being 51,250 workers. All in all, however, we can say that notwithstanding the numbers involved and the dramatic nature of the exercise, the mid-1956 redundancies took place against the background of a by no means unfavourable employment situation.

IV

Though the present project arose out of the large-scale dismissals, primarily in Birmingham, announced by the British Motor Corporation in mid-1956, the question of extending the scope of operations was subsequently considered. However, in broad terms, it was decided to stick to the original plan. More precisely, it was resolved to sample all except the smaller discharges which had occurred in Birmingham in its peak period of redundancies, i.e. June and July 1956.

The number of redundancies reported to the Ministry of Labour during these two months—by firms in the area covered by the six Birmingham employment exchanges—was 5,130 and 1,184[4] res-

[1] As well as economic factors, the revocation of the Notification of Vacancies Orders as from May 7, 1956 (S.I. 1956 No. 649) may have significantly contributed to this.

[2] By February 1957 the number of 'wholly unemployed' (all workers) had reached 29,405.

[3] The total of 'wholly unemployed' was below 20,000 during only two months of 1957.

[4] The corresponding figure for August 1956 was 194; that for each subsequent month of 1956 was less than 500. Though dismissals reported in May 1956 were also more than 1,000, a substantial proportion were caused by strike action then in progress in Coventry, and were of short duration only.

pectively, a total of 6,314.[1] The population which has been sampled for purposes of the survey covers all such discharges in so far as they involved 100 or more workers from any one firm in either of the two months although, with one exception, women have been excluded. These '100 and over' redundancies constitute the great bulk of those declared to the Ministry in the period, those involved in 'under 100' dismissals amounting to only 356 persons in all. As far as men are concerned, it is estimated that those sampled represent approximately 95 per cent of all men known to have been laid off in June/July 1956.

The reasons for not following up the small discharges were, first, that the 356 individuals in question were spread over a relatively large number of enterprises, so that the resources involved seemed disproportionate to the contribution they could be expected to make to the findings of the inquiry. Secondly, as pointed out earlier, firms are under no obligation to inform the Ministry of dismissals, and as far as the minor ones are concerned, there are certain to be gaps in the official figures. While there is no guarantee that all big ones are notified, it is improbable that redundancies of the order of 100 or more workers would escape the vigilant eye of exchange managers. It appears a reasonable assumption, therefore, that—as regards men—the sample is representative of all except the smaller lay-offs occurring in Birmingham in the period.

The number of Birmingham firms declaring '100 and over' redundancies to the Ministry of Labour in June and July 1956 was six. Four were constituent firms of the B.M.C.[2]—whose dismissals had occasioned the project—the fifth being the Birmingham Small Arms Co. (B.S.A. Motor Cycles Ltd.). The sixth, Joseph Lucas Ltd., was the only firm with, officially, a Standard Industrial Classification other than 'manufacture of motor vehicles and cycles', though the discharges were in fact directly connected with those in the car industry, all those affected having been engaged in the making of accessories.

As regards the five firms from the motor industry, a 1 in 10 sample of all men laid off in Birmingham in June and July 1956 was drawn by the Survey staff from records kindly made available by the

[1] These figures of course suffer from some of the shortcomings of redundancy statistics, discussed in the preceding section. However, they were merely used to decide precisely which months of 1956 to include in the survey programme, and to ascertain which firms had relatively large redundancies. For these purposes they were regarded as adequate.

[2] The number of B.M.C. firms in Birmingham involved in the mid-1956 redundancies was five; one of these was excluded from the interviewing programme as less than 100 individuals were dismissed who, it may be added, were all women.

managements concerned.[1] In the case of J. Lucas—where the redundancies were spread over several of the Company's factories—similar arrangements were made for extracting a 1 in 3 sample. The reason for the higher sampling fraction here was to allow of a number of detailed inter-firm comparisons—should such a course subsequently commend itself[2]—for which the product of a 1 in 10 sample would have been inadequate. In addition, a 1 in 2 sample of women dismissed by the Austin Motor Co. in the period was drawn.

There is one qualification regarding the redundant populations on which the samples are based. In the case of two of the firms, numbers respectively given as 27 and estimated as approximately 90 were re-engaged either immediately or within a few days of the lay-off; their records were taken out of the file of discharged persons, and they were no longer included therein when the sample was extracted. It is a matter of definitional preference whether these men ought to be considered as having been redundant; they were hardly so from a 'survey' point of view. The qualification, so far as the sample is concerned, is that the possibility cannot be ruled out that some others, who had their dismissal notices cancelled after a somewhat longer interval, were likewise removed from the relevant files at the time.

It should also here be made clear that the sample does not comprise any workers aged over 65 on the day of discharge, who in some instances were retired by the firm or themselves retired voluntarily at the latter's suggestion. The necessary particulars in respect of this

[1] In the case of the 4 B.M.C. firms, two 1 in 12 samples were initially extracted, one being treated as the main sample, the second being kept as a reserve. In order to increase the size of the former, a 1 in 5 sample was subsequently drawn from the reserve list, thus raising the sampling fraction of the main sample from 1 in 12 to 1 in 10.

Before the samples were drawn, the sampling frames were stratified by such factors as age (50 and over, and under 50), skill grading and length of service. The precise factors of stratification varied according to the data that were supplied with, or could readily be obtained in respect of, each list/set of record cards, though women were removed from the frames in each case. In one instance a simple random sample was drawn without prior stratification (except for that by sex and except that the list was in check number order).

In the case of the male Austin sample, stratification was by works, skill (with a subdivision of the semi-skilled into upper and lower according to their base rate of pay) and age (as above); a small number of juveniles and another small batch of cards indicating that the person had been ill since some time before redundancy were treated as separate strata. Each of the latter was arranged in alphabetical order, and the names were then drawn at equal intervals. In the case of the other firms, the standard procedure was to divide the strata into groups of 12, and to pick two names by lot from each set of 12 (see beginning of footnote).

[2] In the event, such detailed inter-firm comparisons were not proceeded with—partly because of the differential response rates achieved (see *post*), and partly because the analysis of the main data proved much more of a 'mouthful' than had been anticipated.

category could not be ascertained in all cases, and it was reluctantly decided, therefore, that it would have to be omitted from the interviewing programme.

Details of the composition of the sample and the extent of non-response are given in Table 4.

TABLE 4

Composition of Sample

	Total sample	*Inter-viewed*	*Not interviewed*	
	No.*	No.	No.	%
Men:				
Austin Motor Co. Ltd.	310	281	29	9
Fisher & Ludlow Ltd.	54	50	4	7
Morris Motors Ltd. (Tractor and Transmissions Branch)	30	29	1	3
Nuffield Metal Products Ltd.	66	57	9	14
B.S.A. Motor Cycles Ltd.	21	14	7	33
Joseph Lucas Ltd.	81	55	26	32
All men	562	486	76	14
Women:				
Austin Motor Co. Ltd.	107	100	7	7
Total sample	669	586	83	12

* Product of 1 in 10 sample in case of first five firms; product of 1 in 3 sample in case of J. Lucas; product of 1 in 2 sample in case of women.

It will be seen that the proportion interviewed varied widely being 91 per cent for the men from the four B.M.C. concerns, 93 per cent for the Austin women, but 67 and 68 per cent for the two other companies. Among several factors, this is due to relatively more of those laid off from the B.M.C. subsequently returning to their original employer; accordingly, the number who could not be traced was much smaller. Reasons for non-response—using the term in its wide sense—are shown overleaf.

As regards the questionnaires employed for the interviewing programme, useful ideas as to type of question to be put had been gained from a small number of informal (unstructured) interviews and a pilot study conducted in the spring and summer of 1957. At the same time, the 'pilot' revealed that, for purposes of the main programme, a more comprehensive schedule was desirable, which was accordingly drawn up and tested in the spring of 1958. The bulk of main sample interviews were carried out between end-June

Reasons for Non-Response

	No.	As % of total sample
Deceased	5	0·8
Left area/moved/not known by present occupier/house demolished, etc.	67	10·0
Refusal	10	1·5
Other*	1	0·1
Total not interviewed	83	12·4
Total interviewed	586	87·6
	669	100·0

* Living at some distance from Birmingham and (apparently) never at home. All other persistent not-at-homes were ultimately contacted.

and end-December 1958; as regards the 486 men, all except 22 were completed in this period.[1]

Although the questionnaires—the final version of that used for interviewing the male sample is reproduced in Appendix C—contained a considerable number of open-ended questions, interviews were nevertheless standardized as far as practicable. Thus all salvoes were to be fired in the precise order shown on the schedule, while those ending with a '?' were, as a general rule, to be put in the exact form printed.[2] Where, however, the answer was already obvious as a result of information previously supplied, interviewers were expected to 'turn'; i.e. they could change the emphasis if otherwise either question or questioner would have looked foolish. Interviewers were also free to add anything by way of an innocuous introductory preamble in order to smooth the flow of conversation or to explain items misunderstood, while neutral prompts in the case of monosyllabic replies on 'reason' or 'opinion' topics were encouraged. Questions not set out in full—such as date of birth—could be asked in whatever form was preferred. All answers were to be taken down as fully as possible, and many in fact were recorded—and are subsequently quoted—verbatim.

Interviewers were recruited both by local advertisement and recommendation. While the former evoked a quantitatively large response, it proved difficult to find persons able satisfactorily to administer the schedule. However, they were secured in the end, and comprised both men and women working full- or part-time, some

[1] These 22 were cleared during January/mid-March 1959. The schedule for women was compiled and tested during the second half of 1958, the 100 women being interviewed during December 1958/mid-March 1959.

[2] Plus missing pronouns, verbs, etc., left out for reasons of space.

being graduates and some having previous relevant experience.[1] All were given a brief training, one feature of which was the ordeal of mock-interviewing this writer; each investigator also had successfully to tackle a series of practice interviews before being launched on the main sample. All were equipped with a set of detailed notes covering such matters as the planning of visits, the treatment of refusals and 'gone-aways', and the completion of the questionnaire. Interviewers also had by them a letter from the Birmingham Trades Council—the representative body of Birmingham trade unionists—expressing the Council's support for the project.

Before fieldworkers paid a first visit, each respondent was sent a letter,[2] explaining the objects of the survey and asking for his co-operation. On calling, it was found that a sizeable proportion had moved to an address different from that initially obtained from the firm. Thus of the 586 interviewed, 186 or nearly 32 per cent had to be traced to a new home, though as we shall see subsequently, the overwhelming majority of these moves were unconnected with the redundancy. Further, the addresses of those in the sample were widely scattered, and included considerable numbers living at some distance from Birmingham in towns such as Dudley, Stourbridge and Bromsgrove. Isolated interviews took place as far afield as Coventry and Stratford-upon-Avon.

Many of the movers were caught only after a series of calls at neighbours, relatives, shops, Post Offices—and in some instances by recourse to less orthodox sources such as pubs. Not counting these ancillaries, the number of journeys to respondents' homes or presumed homes was also high: in 120 cases (20 per cent) four or more trips were necessary due—apart from the change-of-address element—to factors such as men being on shift work or overtime and the incidence of holidays and football matches. Although 69 individuals or 12 per cent were in and could be seen on first call, on the whole the fieldwork proved extremely time-consuming, a substantial part of interviewer-time having to be spent on travelling and inquiries, including efforts to track down the 'gone-aways'.

While most interviews took place in respondents' homes—day, evening or week-end according to the latter's convenience—53 or 9 per cent were conducted at the University.[3] One was held at the man's place of work (office). As to duration of interview, in the case of the 486 men this ranged from 35 minutes to 3 hours, 20 minutes,

[1] The writer interviewed in order to test successive versions of the questionnaires, but (with one exception) did no main sample interviews.

[2] See Appendix B. A letter of thanks was also sent after the interview.

[3] The proportion was 10·5 per cent for the 486 men, and 2 per cent for the 100 women.

C

the average length being 1 hour, 34 minutes. Time spent on non-formal business before or after the event—i.e. tea, chat, etc.—is included. Schedules were completed at one sitting throughout.

Wives were frequently present and often proved a distinct boon, in that they were able to supply a missing fact. Other members of the family also sat in at times, while a small handful of interviews were completed with the aid of interpreters, watched by several interested compatriots. The great majority of respondents were very willing co-operators in the project; though some required a measure of gentle persuasion, others were positively enthusiastic. There were no instances of half-finished schedules, while the questions on earnings—about which some secret misgivings had been felt—did not, with one or two exceptions, give any trouble.

Though respondents' communicativeness showed the inevitable variations, the open-ended technique on which the questionnaires were primarily based brought in a sizeable harvest of pertinent comment. Many took the opportunity to elaborate, to qualify—and sometimes to contradict—earlier statements, and enormously though this increased the problems of coding and analysis, it was felt that such material gets nearer the truth than the bald 'yes' or 'no' that so rarely fits a human situation.

In view of the wealth of data collected, this report is being confined to an analysis of 447 'male' schedules—i.e. a 1 in 10 sample of men involved in '100 and over' redundancies in Birmingham in June and July 1956. The figure of 447 is arrived at by subtracting, from the total of 486 men interviewed, 39 Lucas cases removed so as to reduce the Lucas contingent to 1 in 10 proportions.[1] By analysis is meant the presentation and discussion of both simple tabulations and appropriate cross-tabulations, relieved or illuminated, as the case may be, by some of the illustrative material gathered. All the tabulations, it may be added, were done by hand—a method which, in the event, proved very suitable. The male 1 in 10 sample of 447 men, on which the following pages are based, constitutes 89 per cent of the names originally drawn for the purpose.[2]

As to the general validity of the findings, any survey based on

[1] The redundant population (men) from J. Lucas Ltd. (3 factories) was 244. One in 10 sample, therefore, would have been 24. Minus non-response (32 per cent) = 16 'Lucas men' for purposes of 1 in 10 sample. The 16 were selected so as to reproduce, proportionally, the following characteristics of the 55 actually interviewed: (*a*) skill grading at Lucas; (*b*) age 50 and over and age under 50; (*c*) degree of difficulty in finding work after redundancy; and (*d*) response rate for each of the three works.

[2] As will be clear from p. 32, the remaining 11 per cent overwhelmingly consist of 'gone-aways'. No substitutes were drawn to compensate for these or for deaths and refusals.

interview techniques is subject to tricks of memory and lapses of accuracy, the precise incidence of which is bound to vary between respondents. On the whole, however, the standard of accuracy attained was high; the schedule contained several internal checks which by and large bear this out. The fieldwork did of course take place a considerable time after the redundancy: though for practical reasons there was no alternative,[1] it would doubtless have been of advantage if some of the questions could have been put nearer the event to which they relate. Nevertheless, the lateness in interviewing has had its compensations; it enabled the men to see the lay-off in a truer perspective than would have been feasible immediately after its occurrence. Further, any social survey concerned with labour mobility inevitably reaches back over a span—usually a considerably greater span—of years,[2] which is not generally held to detract from the value of such studies. In the present instance, if the fieldwork had been carried out at a date sufficiently close to mid-1956 for the immediate effects of the discharges to be observed at close range, the adjustment of the sample in the labour market could not have been satisfactorily portrayed for, as we shall see, this more permanent impact of the redundancy took some considerable time to work itself out. In brief, no one date is ideal for all purposes; financial difficulties, for example, may appear with the onset of unemployment, or they may crystallize several months later, when, say, savings have been exhausted. Thus though from some points of view it would have been preferable to have interviewed the sample nearer the happenings of 1956, the loss of accuracy this may have entailed as regards some of the items is, it is here believed, balanced by the fact that the presentation of a partial and exaggerated picture has been avoided, while the long-run effects of the redundancy in the matter of job adjustment have emerged. The latter would almost certainly have been misrepresented, had the fieldwork been conducted at a substantially earlier date.

Two other potential sources of worry to surveyors are the question of sampling in the first place and that of non-response in the second. Neither constitutes a real problem in this instance. As for sampling frames, there is the qualification previously mentioned regarding those whose redundancy notices were withdrawn more or less immediately; there is also the point that men over 65 who were

[1] The writer commenced duties in the autumn of 1957.

[2] In her study of employment changes in Battersea and Dagenham e.g. Mrs Jefferys *inter alia* set out to obtain a complete record of every job held by her sample between June 1945 and the time of interview in 1951 (Jefferys, *op. cit.*, pp. 49 and 52). See also G. Thomas, *Labour Mobility in Great Britain, 1945–1949* (Social Survey, No. 134 (1951) mimeographed).

induced to retire, etc., have had to be excluded from the interviewing programme. However, neither category is believed to be numerically large, and the two biases to some extent cancel each other, since the former represents those who cannot have encountered any difficulties over the lay-off, while the latter is likely to contain at any rate some where it made a significant difference.

As regards non-response, in so far as the refusal rate is concerned, this was of course negligible, and we may here perhaps digress to summarize the main factors to which this would appear to be attributable. First, the subject of the survey was one of wide general interest, of special concern to those in the sample, and one about the 'historical' nature of which one could, clearly, not be certain. Secondly, the fact that the project was carried out under university auspices was an undoubted advantage. Thirdly, in the initial letter sent out, care was taken to reassure respondents on a number of points—in particular, how they themselves had come to be selected; this was a matter on which some uneasiness had been expressed at the trial interview stage. Again, that a small payment was offered to those who preferred to be seen at the University is likely to have made a difference in a few cases. Finally, the determination to keep refusals to a minimum and, above all, the interviewers' skill in implementing this policy, may also be included in the reckoning.

The main question mark, then, in the sphere of non-response concerns the 'gone-aways', and in a study of redundancy this category must be considered a potentially greater source of bias than in surveys where mobility is a more neutral element. Unfortunately, despite the detective powers of interviewers, the information that could be gleaned about the hard core of 'gone-aways' was uneven. What did, however, emerge is that non-contact was by no means invariably a matter of men having left the area as a result of redundancy—a hypothesis anyhow suggested by the extent of moving unconnected therewith in the case of those who were traced. Thus the 'gone-aways' shown on page 32—and the percentage in this category is slightly smaller for the 1 in 10 sample—include two who returned to Ireland, respectively because of a father's illness and inheriting a house there; two who had deserted their wives, one of whom obtained a job a week after lay-off; one who had switched to London apparently to avoid call-up; another who had betaken himself there only in 1958; one who had left to get married; and one who disappeared to escape from that very event. In some instances, the men were said to have moved some considerable time after the dismissal; in others, they had apparently done so before the lay-off without informing their employer; in yet others there was just no knowledge of them and the most extensive inquiries yielded no clue.

While it would appear that some of the 'gone-aways' simply belonged to the 'mobile fringe' without their mobility necessarily having any link with the redundancy, in other cases one cannot be certain as to whether the latter was a factor, since sufficient details were not obtained. Thus several respondents were stated or believed to have returned to Ireland, one to Scotland, one had joined relatives in Yorkshire, and one had gone to retire in Cornwall. One had emigrated to Australia apparently late in 1956; a Canadian returned to his native land in July of that year, though he had booked his passage before his discharge owing to dissatisfaction over short-time. Two other Commonwealth citizens were likewise reported to have returned home. We may add that only in a minority of instances were actual addresses secured, so that an approach by mail questionnaire was not considered worth while.

As compared with the 447 men interviewed, the main characteristics of the 'gone-aways' are that they comprise a much larger proportion of unskilled and, further, that they include a higher percentage of both Irishmen and coloured, the latter and the unskilled frequently overlapping. However, as we shall see in the next chapter, these three categories account for only small proportions of the 447 respondents; while these groups are therefore under-represented among those interviewed, the numbers are sufficiently small for their exclusion not materially to affect the results for the sample as a whole. Also, the missing Irish and coloured probably cancel each other to a limited degree since, as we shall find, the Irish did rather better and the coloured a great deal worse than the general average as regards unemployment after dismissal. Finally, while the evaluation of the bias introduced by non-response must of necessity be tentative, since 'gone-aways' and all other non-contacts combined amount to only 11 per cent of the original 1 in 10 sample, it would seem to be reasonable not to be unduly perturbed about the matter.

The main reservations which the writer has about the validity of her findings really arise from reservations she has about survey techniques as such, and though this is not the place for a full-length discussion, a brief comment may be appropriate. For in the course of this investigation, she has been made rather uncomfortably aware of some of the pitfalls and shortcomings of survey procedures, and it seems to her that one of the principal reasons why these limitations are not more universally apparent is the widespread resort to pre-coded questionnaires. When replies are recorded in the form chiefly of simple pre-coded scales, the several different angles from which most questions are—and legitimately can be—answered, are to a large extent concealed. As a result, a degree of precision and accuracy may implicitly emerge from the findings, which the data—and factual data no less than those dealing with attitudes and opinions—may not in fact possess. In the present instance, only a bare minimum of pre-coding was incorporated in the interview schedule. Consequently, the variety of ways in which even ostensibly straightforward items were interpreted by a mere 447 individuals—illustrations will follow anon—came to the fore and could, in considerable measure at any rate, be taken into account in the analysis.

While the open-ended technique used for the present inquiry presents its own problems, the conclusion here reached is that it permits of a distinctly more accurate—even though immeasurably more troublesome—analysis of the results than a strictly pre-coded schedule. At the same time, it is by no means perfect itself; working through the body of replies to a questionnaire of the type here employed induces a certain humility. Nothing that has been said, of course, alters the fact that a social survey remains an indispensable tool for the social scientist; for its deficiencies notwithstanding, it is still incomparably superior to the alternatives of generalized prejudice and 'intuitive surmise'.

Given this general *caveat* about the pitfalls of survey procedures—and the milder version of that *caveat* which, it is claimed, is adequate in the case of studies such as the present—there is one further point remaining to be added. This is that in considering the findings of this inquiry, it must be borne in mind that, representative though the sample is believed to be of all except the smaller discharges befalling Birmingham during its peak period of post-war redundancies, these were almost wholly from a single industry.[1] The results of the project are thus those of a motor-car lay-off and, very largely, those of a B.M.C. lay-off: 417 men out of the 447—i.e. 93 per cent of the 1 in 10 sample—were dismissed by that Corporation, 281 or 63 per cent by the Austin Motor Company alone. Nonetheless, the 1956 discharges can perhaps be regarded as a classic example of one type of redundancy that may well recur in the British economy—namely that due to a temporary, but major, contraction of demand occurring against both a general and regional background of full employment. Less dramatic though the effects of such a redundancy are, their study may yet have a contribution to make to a wider problem.

[1] Of the 356 workers involved in 'under 100' (i.e. not sampled) redundancies in the period, 209 were laid off by firms engaged in vehicle, etc. manufacture.

Chapter 2

SOME BACKGROUND DATA ABOUT THE SAMPLE[1]

In the ensuing pages we shall be frequently referring to the *date* of redundancy. For the sake of precision, therefore, of the total of 447 respondents, 398 were discharged on June 29, 1956—'Black Friday' as it was called by some of the men. Of the remaining 49, 15 were laid off earlier during that month—mostly on, and in no case before, June 7th. Thirty-three were dismissed on various dates in July 1956, in one instance the exact date not being known.

AGE, MARITAL STATUS, PLACE OF BIRTH, ETC.

TABLE 5

Age as on Day of Respondent's Redundancy

	No.	%
20 years and under	8	2
21–30 years	142	32
31–40 years	149	33
41–50 years	101	23
51–60 years	37	10
61–65 years	10	
	447	100

As indicated in Table 5, 65 per cent of the sample were between the ages of 21 and 40 at the time of redundancy. Just over 10 per cent were then more than 50 years old, though the total over 45 was 20 per cent. It may be added that the sample is considerably younger than the male labour force in the industry as a whole: of men engaged in the manufacture of motor vehicles, etc. in Great Britain at end-May 1956, 51 per cent were under 40 years,[2] as compared with 67 per cent aged 40 and below in the case of the sample. These figures are merely given as being of some interest; it was not to be

[1] For two interesting articles dealing with the characteristics of the unemployed in the population as a whole, see *Ministry of Labour Gazette*, April 1962, p. 131 and September 1962, p. 347.

[2] Derived from *Ministry of Labour Gazette*, June 1957, p. 196.

expected that the age structure of those laid off—many of them short-service workers—would reflect that of the generality of their colleagues.

TABLE 6

Marital Status and Number of Dependent Single Children at Time of Redundancy

	No.	%	*No.*	%
Single			73	16
Married	*No.*	%		
No children	105	24		
1 child	126	28		
2 children	77	17		
3 or more children	52	12		
No. of children not clear	3	1		
	—	—	363	82
Widowed, divorced or separated			11	2
			447	100

Marital status, etc. at the date of redundancy is set out in Table 6. It is emphasized that only wholly dependent single children are included; single offspring living at home but already at work, as well as all married children, have been omitted. As for the 73 single men, 50 or 68½ per cent stated that they had no dependants at the time of the lay-off. Twelve had then one partly dependent, 10 one wholly dependent,[1] and 1 two wholly dependent, relatives.

As compared with Table 6, about two dozen persons had changed their marital status by the date of interview, the majority being single men who had acquired spouses since mid-1956. At the time of interview, therefore, the sample consisted of 54 single respondents, 378 married, and 15 widowed, divorced or separated. We may add that in a handful of cases the classification is based on household responsibilities rather than on legal status: a few foreign-born single men i.e., who reported 'wives', have been recorded as married.

Place of residence at the time of lay-off is shown in Table 7. 'Birmingham', for this purpose, is co-terminous with the County Borough but, in addition, includes those parts of Rednal and Rubery situated outside the County Borough boundaries. This in the administrative sense untidy definition was decided on in view of the siting of the largest of the six firms in the sample: Longbridge being

[1] Or 2 partly dependent.

TABLE 7

Place of Residence at Time of Redundancy

	No.	%
Birmingham	299	67
Up to 8 miles from Birmingham*	35	8
Over 8–15 miles from Birmingham	84	19
Over 15 miles from Birmingham	6	1
Not clear	23	5
	447	100

* But excluding Birmingham.

close to the city frontiers and within a few minutes' bus ride from Rubery and Rednal, it was regarded as more sensible to treat the whole of these two areas as 'Birmingham'. The location of the Longbridge works so near the latter's boundaries is, incidentally, also partly responsible for the relatively high proportion drawn from 'over 8 miles from Birmingham', many of the men concerned coming from such towns as Bromsgrove, with excellent direct road connections to Longbridge. It was at the last-named that nine-tenths of the 90 respondents residing at 'over 8 miles' were in fact engaged.

As might be expected, comparatively more young men lived at some distance from Birmingham, though the differences are not pronounced. Thus of the 150 respondents in the sample aged 30 years and under, 22 per cent were residing beyond 8 miles from the city; in the case of the over-fifties, the proportion was 17 per cent.

TABLE 8

Place of Birth

	No.	%
Birmingham	228	51
Midlands,* other than Birmingham	118	26
England, other than Midlands*	31	7
Wales and Scotland	16	4
N. Ireland and Eire	35	8
India and Pakistan	4	
West Indies	10	4
Other abroad	5	
	447	100

* 'Midlands' comprises the combined areas of the Ministry of Labour's (pre-1962) Midland and North Midland Regions.

As indicated in Table 8, just over one half of those interviewed were born in Birmingham, the whole of the Midlands accounting for 77 per cent. Apart from the Irish element, the numbers from overseas are very small; however, it will be recalled that in both instances non-response was higher than for the rest of the sample.

As regards place of education, the pattern follows closely that of place of birth, though 246 respondents were either wholly or partly educated in Birmingham—as against the 228 born there.

Of the 447 men, 341 or 76 per cent left school at age 14, 50 or 11 per cent at age 15, and 29 or just over 6 per cent at 16 or over. Twenty-five individuals ceased their education before reaching 14, while two—born abroad—had not had any schooling. As to type of institution attended, 406 respondents or 91 per cent of the sample went to an elementary or secondary modern school, 16 men had been to a grammar school, though one half of these had left at 15 years or under. One of the grammar school boys had also attended a technical school, and there were another 14 men who had received their education at some variety of technical institution. The remaining 9 were brought up abroad or went to miscellaneous establishments in this country.

All respondents were asked whether they had attended night school and/or day continuation classes,[1] a sizeable minority replying in the affirmative. To be precise, 159 men or 36 per cent had attended—prior to the redundancy—either night school, day-continuation classes or both, the majority having been to night school. Two-thirds of the 159 had followed courses of a year's duration and upwards, and the remainder for various lesser periods; in some instances, such instruction formed part of apprenticeship training. Generally speaking, classes were mostly of a vocational or semi-vocational nature—a considerable number having been concerned with sheet metal work or some aspect of engineering. Other subjects studied included painting and decorating, woodwork, coachbuilding, carpentry, mechanics, welding and plumbing, but courses were also taken in English, mathematics, book-keeping, physical training, art and so on.

SKILL, APPRENTICESHIP AND TRAINING

The bulk of the labour force in the motor industry consists of semi-skilled workers, which is clearly reflected in Table 9. Moreover, the level of skill implicit in such status is relatively modest; as a number of men put it, 'there is nothing to it'. At the same time, the term may cover a rather wide range—say, packers at the lower end and finishers, trimmers and engine assemblers at the upper.

[1] Q. 6 of schedule.

TABLE 9

Skill Grading at Firm from which Made Redundant (RJ)*

	No.	%
Skilled	62	14
Semi-skilled	361	81
Unskilled	24	5
	447	100

* As 'firm from which made redundant' is extremely awkward to use in tables and its constant repetition rather tiresome in the text, recourse will henceforth be had—as in the printed questionnaire—to the symbol 'RJ' to stand for either the firm or the job from which redundancy took place. Similarly, the abbreviation 'R' will be employed at times to stand for redundancy—to avoid concoctions such as 'first post-redundancy job'. It is hoped that the lesser of two evils has been chosen.

The figures in Table 9 are as per information received from the firm; they are not based on a questionnaire reply. Each man was, however, asked how the occupation held at the time of redundancy was rated by RJ as regards skill,[1] and it is of interest that 376 out of the 447 (84 per cent) knew their correct grading. Eleven underrated and 50 overrated themselves, the great majority of the latter saying that their job ranked as skilled, though in fact classed semi-skilled.[2]

The extent of overrating can be considered as modest, in view of the prestige attached to being skilled and the natural tendency, therefore, to believe that one is in that category. Also, a number of the 'overraters' belonged to what are in effect commonly recognized as skilled occupations such as sheet metal workers or finishers. These and several others are graded differently even as between the constituent companies of the B.M.C., partly no doubt because processes are broken down to a different degree in the various plants. The sample thus includes both skilled sheet metal workers, finishers and trimmers and semi-skilled sheet metal workers, finishers and trimmers, the latter presumably not being called upon to exercise the full range of duties associated with their craft. As these occupations are likewise regarded as skilled by the trade unions concerned, it is hardly surprising that some of the men assumed that the firm must so class them.

The number who had served an apprenticeship, and the relation of this to skill grading at RJ, is detailed in Table 10.

[1] Q. 10 (*e*) of schedule.
[2] Nine were not sure; one answer was not clear.

TABLE 10

Whether Served Apprenticeship, Related to Pre-R Skill Grading at RJ*

	Skilled		*Semi- and unskilled*		*Total*	
	No.	*%*	*No.*	*%*	No.	%
Served and completed apprenticeship:						
Engineering and allied trades	20		20		40	
Other	1		9		10	
	21	34	29	8	50	11
Started, but did not complete, apprenticeship	8	13	40	10	48	11
Did not serve apprenticeship	33	53	311	81	344	77
Serving apprenticeship at time of interview	—	—	1	—	1	—
Not clear	—	—	4	1	4	1
	62	100	385	100	447	100

* Skill = as per data from RJ.

As will be seen, 50 respondents only had served a full apprenticeship, 40 of these in engineering and allied trades. Of the remaining 10, 4 had served theirs in various building occupations, 3 as butchers, and one each in boot and shoe repairing, cinema projection work and upholstery. Forty-eight persons started but did not complete their course, this group comprising both those who made this clear and those who, judging by the period of years put in, had to be allocated to this category.[1] Another 17 men had undergone what some of them described as 'a sort of an apprenticeship', including as gentleman's page boy, grocer and farmer; these have been treated as 'noes'. Details aside, one of the main points of interest of Table 10 lies in the tenuous connection between skilled status and the serving of an apprenticeship: only 21, or roughly one-third of the 62 respondents graded as skilled by RJ, were fully-apprenticed men.

All respondents were asked whether they had received a formal training at RJ for the job or jobs performed there and, if so, the length of this.[2] The replies indicated that the overwhelming majority —397 men or 88 per cent of the sample—had been given either no,

[1] Expert advice was obtained in all doubtful cases, allowance being made for the fact that in non-engineering trades apprenticeship arrangements are somewhat looser than in engineering.

[2] Q. 10 (g) of schedule.

or not more than a fortnight's, instruction.[1] Of the remainder, 19 reported a training of over two weeks but not more than three months; two had attended courses of six and nine months, respectively; three had served their (or part of their) apprenticeship at RJ, while a further three had started but not completed their apprenticeship there. Eleven were in various 'trainee' occupations, such as that of trainee trimmer.[2]

The small extent to which training was received is not surprising, in view of the low skill content of many of the processes concerned. Further, men may already have had a 'trade' on recruitment to RJ; not to have been given formal instruction by the latter is not, of course, tantamount to being untrained. Thus, as we saw, there are those who had served a full apprenticeship; and there are those who embarked on the latter, frequently 'stuck' it for several years, and who can be presumed to have derived at any rate some know-how therefrom. Next, there are those who attended night school, etc., and who in many instances took courses of a vocational character. Again, 35 men had received a training of one year and upwards in the Forces, while some 120 had there participated in various courses of lesser duration.[3] These were, understandably, a mixed bag including training as pilot, paratrooper and cook, but they also covered carpentry, sheet metal work, fitting and so on—potentially of definite relevance to civil life. Some men had also had the benefit of on-the-job instruction during their previous industrial career, while a handful had been to Government training centres. However, in the absence of more complete data in respect of each respondent, owing to the fact that what constitutes 'training' is one on which an identity of definition can hardly be expected, and having regard to the further fact that worthwhile experience over a number of years may render one as expert as his fellow with a more formal course behind him, it was considered to be impracticable to divide the sample into 'trained' and 'untrained' with a view to measuring the impact of this on their post-redundancy fate.

LENGTH OF SERVICE AT DATE OF DISMISSAL

Table 11 gives details of length of service with the firm from which redundancy took place as at the date of the latter.[4] Some respondents

[1] 336 of the 397 men were straight 'noes'.

[2] Twelve answers were not clear.

[3] Q. 7 of schedule.

[4] The figures in this instance are based on information supplied both by the managements and men (Q. 10 (*u*) and (*f*) of schedule). They are subject to a margin of error because of certain differences of definition as between the firms, and because of the memory factor in the case of the men.

TABLE 11

Length of Service at RJ up to Time of Redundancy

	No.	%
6 months and under	28	6
Over 6 months–2 years	181	41
Over 2–6 years	152	34
Over 6–10 years	46	10
Over 10 years	36	8
Not clear	4	1
	447	100

had several spells at RJ prior to the lay-off, and in these cases the combined total has been included. Time spent in the Forces has, however, not been counted, even where this came in the midst of an otherwise unbroken period of employment.[1] We may here perhaps digress to state that 70 per cent of the 447 men had been in the Forces—for purposes of either national or regular service or both—29 per cent having so spent up to three years, 32 per cent over three but not more than seven years, while 9 per cent of the sample had been in the Forces in excess of seven years.

Length of service varied of course with the men's age, though not perhaps as significantly as might have been supposed. Thus of the 30-and-under age group, 57 per cent had not more than two years' service at the time of dismissal, but for the over-fifties the corresponding proportion was still 30 per cent. At the other end of the scale, those with upwards of ten years at RJ at the date of discharge accounted for 2 per cent of those 30 and below, 5 per cent of the 31–40 year group, 15 per cent of the men aged 41–50, and 23 per cent of the over-fifties.

As regards skill grading, the notion that labour turnover decreases with increasing skill is only partly true in this instance. Thus while of the 24 respondents in the sample classed unskilled by RJ, 88 per cent had been with the firm for 2 years or less, the corresponding proportion for those rated skilled was still 53 per cent—as against 43 per cent for the semi-skilled. Similarly, merely 13 per cent of the skilled had more than six, and only 3 per cent over ten, years to their credit—as compared with percentages of 20 and 9 in the case of the semi-skilled.[2]

[1] Service with one of the firm's war-time subsidiaries has, however, been included.

[2] The proportion of those with not more than six months' service was, however, slightly higher for the semi- than for the skilled—i.e. 4 per cent as against not quite 2 per cent. Forty-six per cent of the unskilled were in this category.

Length of service varied drastically according to firm, some RJs contributing nil to the over-six-years category; in other cases the latter constituted a significant minority of those laid off. Similarly, while in one instance the overwhelming majority of those discharged were men with not above two years' service, in others less than one-third were of this *genre.* These divergences *inter alia* reflect the different criteria according to which redundancy lists were compiled by the several companies.

REASONS FOR JOINING RJ

There are some questions which are of absorbing interest even though the answers may hold no particular surprises, one such being 'What made you join RJ in the first place?'[1] The frequency with which different reasons were advanced—many men gave more than one—are set out in Table 12.

TABLE 12

Reasons for Joining RJ

	No.	*As % of* 447
'Pay' reasons	197	44
Because good prospects or conditions at RJ, because a good firm, etc.	48	11
Interested in work there or other 'work' reasons	43	10
Because RJ near/convenient	59	13
Because friends or relatives there/got him in/ recommended RJ	72	16
Dissatisfaction with previous job*	65	15
Needed work/was unemployed, etc.	109	24
Miscellaneous reasons	23	5

* Other than over pay, etc.

Money was clearly the most important single ground for joining; 'the wages enticed me'—as one put it—was true of a considerable proportion of the sample. There was, however, much variety of circumstance in which this factor operated. Thus one respondent stated that, on leaving the Forces in 1946, RJ's pay for semi-skilled work was as good as anyone's in the Midlands. A second likewise pointed to the firm's financial appeal after four years in the Army; he did not wish to return to his previous job of apprentice draughtsman. A third was a newcomer to the area and 'heard it was the

[1] Q. 12 (*a*) of schedule.

biggest money', while a number of men living outside, but within travelling distance of, Birmingham, observed that they could earn more at RJ than in their immediate vicinity. Others remarked that they were engaged on similar—or on more skilled—tasks at their old firm, but for less remuneration. A few went into the £. s. d. of the matter, one—in his twenties—revealing that he was able to augment his weekly earnings to the tune of £8 by his move to the firm some three years before redundancy.

Some went on to account for their need of 'the big money'. Thus one respondent had a son keen on becoming a farmer, so 'I wanted money to set him up in a small-holding'. A second was anxious to save in order to be able to commence his own business. A third was planning to buy a house and 'the insurance people wouldn't allow me the £1,000 I needed on £9 a week'. One or two commented that they were about to get married; others, that they had a family to provide for. One man joined RJ after 22 years with his previous and only other employer: 'I'd reached the top at . . . and it was only £11.10.0. per week, and I had just had a kiddy and the wife wasn't working . . .'. One respondent, however, ruefully observed that he was foolish enough to leave a skilled job with his former boss to become a semi-skilled worker at RJ; 'listening to other chaps talking . . . tempted me'.

Many men had, of course, a second or subsidiary reason for opting for the firm, although 26 per cent of the sample mentioned pay as their sole motive. Thus some disclosed that they were out of a job or that work in the latter was running low, and that the level of earnings at RJ then led them in that direction. Others had the idea put to them by friends or relatives—with the cash as the chief consideration. One respondent in this group countered 'my missus', adding that 'she certainly put me on a winner'. In another case, the wife was also the operative cause; she was herself employed at RJ, and she amplified her husband's reply to the effect that the real answer was 'me nagging him'. Again, some men cited various other features of the job as co-attractives.

The second item in Table 12 comprises those who countered that RJ was a 'decent' or big firm or one with a high reputation; or that it was a good place to work at, that conditions were favourable, or that it was a large or booming industry. It further includes—somewhat ironically—several saying that they made the move because they wanted a more steady or secure job. It should be added that many in this category likewise brought in the pay—in which case they have also been listed under that rubric. Those who did not no doubt frequently had remuneration in mind when talking about prospects or 'bettering' themselves; however, as these terms could refer to non-monetary factors, only those unambiguously mentioning wages, etc., have been counted under 'pay'.

'Work' reasons—defined narrowly to cover primarily the 'interest', 'skill' and 'experience' aspects—were among those least often adduced for joining RJ. Those specifying this factor include one who had always been interested in the mechanical side of motoring, one who *inter alia* wished to return to his own line of trimmer, two who 'wanted a trade', one who took a fancy to doing sheet metal work, and one who confessed to 'a passion for motor-cycles'. A few pointed out that this was the field in which they had served their apprenticeship; another, that his qualifications from the Forces led him in that particular direction, while yet another had previously gained similar experience overseas. One respondent transferred to RJ in order to broaden his horizon, having spent 17 years in his previous job 'doing the same work all the time'.

Among men opting for RJ because it was near or convenient are both those who happened to find themselves living nearby, and those who had moved into the vicinity for some private/domestic reason, following which their former place of employment proved relatively inaccessible. 'We was living with the mother-in-law at the time, and we moved over this side, so I went up there', as one put it. In some instances, it was a case of being out of a job, and applying at the nearest local factory for another. One respondent explained that, on leaving school, he could not afford the bus fares into town, and therefore turned to RJ; he had some fourteen years' service at the date of redundancy.

As indicated in Table 12, for 16 per cent of the sample a, or the, reason for joining the firm was that friends or relatives worked there, or recommended that he should apply, or actually got him or helped to get him in. Many gave no details as to why RJ had been extolled in this way. Typical replies were 'well, a chap spoke for me'; 'most of the family were there'; 'my next-door neighbour got me the job'; and 'I've a friend who is a gaffer down there—I was out of work at the time, and so he got me a job there'. All levels of kinship were involved. Thus, 'my father had been there 25 years'; 'mother worked there at the time, and she thought she'd get me a job there'; 'my sister was in service with one of the directors and said she could get me a job'—and there was even a grandfather who secured the crucial interview. National ties were also important: 'Well, a chap from home, in Ireland, was working at . . . and when he was home on holidays, he told me I should come over and try there'. This kind of thing no doubt helps to explain some interesting differences in the proportion of various nationals found in different companies.

The 15 per cent shown as having joined because of 'dissatisfaction with previous job' are those who tended to place emphasis on their dislike of the latter rather than on the positive attractions of RJ. Further, they comprise only those who mentioned a reason other than money, nearness, etc., already dealt with. Examples are falling out with the shop steward or disputes with the former firm itself, and unfavourable effects on health—as in the case of a bread roundsman suffering from rheumatism. Several others, including a window cleaner, wanted a change from working 'outside', while a number whose posts entailed constant travelling were anxious for a more settled existence with their families. In thirteen instances, it was a matter of hours or shifts.

Among those who specified their need of a job as the or one of their motives for turning to RJ were those reporting that orders were getting scarce at their previous place of employment, or that they had been made redundant, or that they were out of or at any rate looking for work. One had just left the Forces; a few skilled men were unemployed and sent to RJ by their trade union; another was referred there by a rehabilitation centre and a West Indian by an employment exchange. Two or three other foreign-born men stated that RJ was the first to have offered them a vacancy. The group also includes a self-employed baker who had lost his livelihood, a taxi-driver who found business falling off, as well as a self-employed logs and timber merchant who approached RJ because trade was poor.

One or two brief comments may now be apposite. First, the cash motive for joining RJ is almost certainly understated by the figures in Table 12. Thus, as pointed out, some of those who turned to the firm on account of the prospects, etc., very likely had financial considerations in mind, even though not mentioning them in so many words. Similarly, those who applied because, say, a relative working there commended such a course may also include many where the wages were the chief attraction—on the assumption i.e. that these relatives were themselves frequently lured by 'the big money'. The sample is not probably a-typical in this respect of their ex-colleagues at the several firms. Further, nearly 15 per cent of the 447 respondents gave as their *only* reason that they were at a loose end and looking for a boss. Though some of these made clear that they chanced upon RJ, others purposely turned in that direction, though not stating their ground for doing so. The same is true of others who cited a negative, rather than a positive, motive. Applying to RJ because of being fed up with the building industry, for example, is merely explaining why a new post was being wanted—not why the choice fell where it did. 'Nearness', again, may contain a greater or lesser cash element.

A very rudimentary fact demonstrated by the replies to the question is thus that old-fashioned monetary incentives have not lost their power of appeal. Some men, in fact, had made repeated attempts to secure a niche at RJ though, as we shall see, for many the redundancy took the glitter off the gold. Even before it had made its impact, however, pecuniary considerations did not reign supreme, and the other point that strikes one is the triviality of cause that will often determine where a man will spend years of his working life. Again, even where 'the money' was uppermost, there was a great variety of factors that gave it its pivotal importance: some of the quasi-*Schadenfreude*, therefore, that was encountered by the men when trying to find a new employer after redundancy,[1] must seem a little harsh in the circumstances.

JOB SATISFACTION WITH RJ PRIOR TO REDUNDANCY

As a follow-up to the question as to the reasons for joining the firm, all respondents were asked 'If you had not been made redundant, would you have wanted to remain with RJ?'[2] An overwhelming majority—91 per cent of the 447—answered in the affirmative; i.e. they would have been happy or content to stay on, or at any rate had no intention of leaving. A considerable number—something like one-quarter of all 'ayes'—in fact indicated that they definitely would have wished to remain; a much smaller proportion, relatively, qualified their 'yes' in some way.

Many of those replying in the affirmative added some comment, such as that they would still be there, or that they had planned to hang on until retirement: 'I should have remained there for the rest of my days', as one put it. One or two others, more prosaically, singled out the firm's pension scheme as a special attraction. Some, again, mentioned the money; others referred to the fact that it was a modern factory, that the work appealed to them, that they liked it in general or that it was a good firm to be with. A disabled respondent expressed appreciation of the consideration he had received; one or two explained simply that they were not the 'moving types'. Some made clear that they were anxious to stay on at the time, but had no regrets now, or that they wished to remain in the sense of intending to do so, rather than in that of really liking the job.

Nine per cent of the sample answered the question in the negative or were not sure, some of the latter saying that they would only have wanted to stay on for a limited period. As for the 'noes', half a dozen cited their dislike of night shifts as the ground for their not wishing to remain, other reasons being excessive travelling, the monotony of the job, the lack of prospects, the short-time, the trade

[1] See pp. 58–61 *post*.

[2] Q. 12 (*b*) of schedule.

unions, the 'atmosphere of greed in the place' and 'the place in general'. Twelve men intimated that they were planning to leave the firm or at any rate were actively thinking of doing so, quite apart from the redundancy.

UNEMPLOYMENT PRIOR TO REDUNDANCY

In order to ascertain whether the men affected by the 1956 dismissals had suffered much from unemployment earlier on in their industrial career, the question 'Had you experienced any unemployment prior to redundancy?' was included in the schedule.[1] Seventy per cent replied that they had personally undergone no or practically no previous unemployment,[2] 9 per cent reported occasional spells or odd weeks, while another 9 per cent had been out of work for a few or several months. Only 30 men or 7 per cent had known a great deal or at any rate a considerable amount of unemployment—say, of a year and upwards—or been 'out' off and on for a number of years.[3] Most of those in this group were of course referring to pre-war days, and a few added that they were familiar with the means test or had had a rough time.

The above proportions are broadly what one would expect, bearing in mind the age structure of the sample; at the beginning of the 'thirties only about one-third of respondents were in the labour market and therefore 'at risk'. The figures are not of course a statistically precise record of the men's pre-1956 unemployment, in that the question was deliberately couched in general terms; answers were, accordingly, given both in qualitative and quantitative terms. However, they demonstrate that, when the redundancy came, it could hardly be said that the men were already haunted by the spectre of the dole.

[1] Q. 24.

[2] Sixty-three per cent replied 'none'. Seven per cent mentioned periods of 2 weeks or less, or indicated that it was a case of very little.

[3] The remaining 5 per cent of replies were miscellaneous/not clear.

Chapter 3

UNEMPLOYMENT AND JOB DIFFICULTIES AFTER REDUNDANCY

In this chapter we deal with the situation facing the men in the period following dismissal; we are concerned, in particular, with the difficulties encountered in securing alternative employment. The question of financial hardship is deferred to Chapter 7.

DIFFICULTY IN OBTAINING WORK AFTER, AND UNEMPLOYMENT RESULTING FROM, LAY-OFF

TABLE 13

Whether Experienced Difficulty in Finding Work after Redundancy

	No.	%
Found it difficult	259	58
Found it easy	170	38
Non-committal/miscellaneous/not clear	18	4
	447	100

The figures in Table 13 constitute the men's answers to 'After leaving RJ, did you find it easy or difficult to get a job?'[1] Both the two major groups cover a wide range; between them they span a continuous spectrum from, to quote, 'terrible' to 'dead easy'. While a *precise* grading of the material raises various methodological problems, speaking broadly, nearly three-fifths of the 259 respondents in the first category—i.e. about one-third of the total sample—indicated that things were *very* difficult. The great bulk of the 'easies', however—approximately 30 per cent of the 447 men—found matters easy or very (rather than fairly) easy.

It will be clear that Table 13 presents a subjective evaluation of the

[1] Q. 18 (*a*) of schedule. Material logically part of the reply, but in some instances given under Q. 18 (*b*) or subsequently, has been taken into account.

difficulties met with in the search for work; it describes the position as seen by the men. Thus two individuals with similar experiences may rate these somewhat differently in the light of their past acquaintance with unemployment, their general outlook, or their personality, though since refinements of grading have been avoided, this is unlikely materially to affect the totals in the two categories. In addition, however, the figures inevitably reflect how 'particular' the men were. For example, a number of respondents stated that it was hard because only unsuitable openings—labouring jobs, coalmining or poorly-paid work—were available, some adding in so many words that things would have been less awkward, had they lowered their sights. Such persons are included under 'difficult', as they themselves found it so, the reasons for their troubles being a matter for separate examination. Conversely, a few of those in the 'easy' group added reservations about the posts taken, or intimated that it was so only because they accepted the first offer. Again, those who ascribed their smooth absorption primarily to their good luck were counted as 'easy', as were any 'easies' who went on to remark that all their colleagues had a rough passage. At the same time, with this type of question it cannot be ruled out that here and there men may unwittingly draw on the fate of their workmates in formulating their reply.

Before delving further into these matters, let us look at the unemployment actually ensuing from the dismissals of mid-1956. This—or more accurately the time elapsed between leaving RJ and starting the next job—is set out in Table 14.

TABLE 14

Time Elapsed between Leaving RJ and Commencing Next Job

	No.	%
3 days or under	98	
Over 3 days–1 week	93	54
Over 1–2 weeks	53	
Over 2 weeks–1 month	70	16
Over 1–2 months	52	12
Over 2–3 months	43	
Over 3–6 months	22	15
Over 6 months	3	
Miscellaneous (did not look for work at all, or unemployment after R wholly/mainly due to sickness)	9	3
Not clear	4	
	447	100

The figures in Table 14 represent the answers to 'How long after leaving RJ did you actually start your next job?'[1] Next came 'Did you spend any of this time having a rest, taking a holiday, etc., during which you did not try for a job?' and, where yes, there was the follow-up 'How long was that?' Initially, the intention was to deduct such holidays from the period of *gross* unemployment—to wit, the data given in reply to the first question and summarized in Table 14—in order to arrive at a measure of 'genuine', i.e. involuntary or net unemployment.

However, this plan was abandoned, and the figures in Table 14 include in some cases one, two—and occasionally more—weeks' holiday, rest or periods during which the search for work was only intermittently pursued. The reason for the change of procedure was, quite simply, that the distinction between voluntary and involuntary unemployment was, in practice, found to be rather more nebulous than had been anticipated. On the one hand, there were those who had booked their holiday—and who were determined to have it. Then there were those who felt that it was hopeless touring round factories in the holiday season; many works were closed and they therefore decided—semi-voluntarily, as it were—that they might as well go away. Others stated that they registered at an employment exchange but 'didn't bother much for a week or so'; some did, and some did not, describe such non-bothering as a rest.

Again, one or two respondents were under the impression that they could not accept work immediately, in view of the pay-in-lieu received from RJ. One man 'hung around for a bit' because he was not sure whether the redundancy was official. Two had a rest while awaiting, respectively, confirmation of a provisional offer of employment and the results of a medical examination. One similarly confessed to a holiday, though he was at the same time looking for accommodation from which to launch a shoe-repairing business. An ex-shop steward explained that he had a ten-day break, but in the main was spending this 'sorting things out'.

These examples demonstrate that, while some men clearly did have a holiday, in other cases this was rather a mixed bag, comprising elements of both voluntary and involuntary unemployment. Further, some respondents replied to the 'holiday' question with a simple 'yes', without specifying whether theirs was also a 'rest plus', while where the answer was 'no', there is no guarantee that the men did not also sneak an occasional respite from the rigours of the chase. For these various reasons it was felt that *net* unemployment—if indeed there is such an animal—could, in the present instance at any rate, not be satisfactorily isolated for the sample as a whole.

[1] Q. 25 (*y*) of schedule.

We may, however, point out that the majority of those who were asked the 'holiday' question[1] answered in the negative, a considerable number taking pains to stress that they were continuously on the look-out. Some explained that they had cancelled their booking; others, that they could not afford to go away that year, either because the money was required for more urgent purposes, or because they had not saved sufficient owing to prolonged short-time working during the first half of 1956. It might also be added that where a respondent made no effort whatever at finding a new boss—like one who, at the time, 'went crazy over dog-racing'—he has been assigned to 'miscellaneous' in Table 14. This man, incidentally, did not commence his next job until ten weeks after discharge, during seven of which he received unemployment benefit; on a purely formal definition of the term, therefore, one could have treated him as unemployed. There were several others who drew benefit during their 'holiday'.

The unemployment shown in Table 14 is that experienced *directly* following the lay-off. It does not cover periods out of work after the first post-R job although, where the latter was of very brief duration, such unemployment must almost certainly rank as an effect of the redundancy. Thus one respondent was taken on as a floor layer in a building firm immediately upon discharge, but abandoned it after three days on account of his stomach ulcers. Thereupon he was at large for 10½ weeks. However, of those who had a very short first post-R job—lasting, say, not more than two weeks[2] —this was the only case where such serious trouble ensued. The question of unemployment during the men's subsequent industrial history will be reviewed in Chapter 5.

As far as the immediate post-R situation is concerned, the outstanding feature of Table 14 is that the dismissals of mid-1956 resulted in only brief spells out of work for a substantial majority of the sample. Thus 98 men or 22 per cent obtained a new post within three days of discharge, while 43 per cent did so within one week. In a sense, the time taken to secure a fresh opening is surprisingly short—in the light, for example, of the degree of difficulty reported, summarized in Table 13. We saw there that 58 per cent of the 447 respondents considered it to have been hard to get a job after lay-off; we see now that for only 27 per cent did the operation extend over more than one month. The answer is readily found if we correlate the replies to the 'difficulty' question with the actual length

[1] Where a new job was commenced within 6 days of lay-off, the question was not put.

[2] The number of respondents with a first post-R job of 2 weeks or under was 25. The topic is dealt with more fully in Chapter 5.

of unemployment: of the 244 men commencing work within a fortnight of discharge, 34 per cent nevertheless felt that things had been difficult, while of those 'out' for more than a fortnight but not beyond one month, 76 per cent did so.[1] These figures are not necessarily incongruous, as can perhaps be pinpointed by the fate of a skilled machine toolfitter, according to whom getting fixed up was 'terrible'. This man went after a very large number of jobs; during one week he covered 200 miles in the car, yielding one solitary offer. He was unemployed for three weeks.

This case—by no means an isolated one—illustrates two points of difference between the unemployment of the 'thirties and that of the post-war period, which have struck the writer in browsing through the questionnaires. The first is the only semi-frivolous one that at any rate some of the latter-day unemployed have the satisfaction of an own car-door to slam, after being shown the door by would-be employers: it might make that experience less humiliating. The second is that a man can now, without being guilty of exaggeration, declare that it was very difficult to obtain work, even though his time on the dole was a mere three weeks.

REASONS FOR DIFFICULTIES IN FINDING WORK AFTER REDUNDANCY

We may now look more closely at the causes of difficulty when seeking a new post following dismissal. For this purpose we shall draw on the reasons spontaneously advanced by the men in trying to account for the situation, on their replies to certain specific questions put to them on the subject, as well as on the results of cross-tabulating some of the relevant variables.

(*a*) '*No Jobs*'

The question 'After leaving RJ, did you find it easy or difficult to get a job?' led, in the case of those countering 'difficult', to the follow-up 'What, do you think, made it difficult?'[2] The largest single reason put forward by the 259 men who, as we saw in Table 13, reported trouble was that there were so many unemployed searching for work, so many laid off all at once, or that there was a general recession and no jobs about. One hundred and seventy-three respondents, or 67 per cent of the 259, mentioned this factor in one form or another, approximately 80 men offering no other explanation.

Some stressed the supply aspect of the situation by pointing to the

[1] Of the 120 men unemployed for over 1 month, all except 3 reported difficulty.
[2] Q. 18 (*b*) of schedule.

total unemployed; some the demand aspect, by referring to the shortage of vacancies; others cited both facets of what is of course largely the same thing. In addition, there were several variations on the theme. Thus a number primarily emphasized that there were no openings in the car or engineering industry, or that all the motor accessory firms were stricken, or that all the small concerns had gone down with the great, though others remarked that it was only the small factories that wanted anyone at the time. Two men added that the surplus of labour was aggravated by the presence of foreign workers, while one put part of the blame on the number of women competing for employment.

Eleven respondents explained that all vacancies were filled when they embarked on their quest, in six cases this being due to leaving RJ at some date after the bulk of their colleagues. The remaining five were late in the field on miscellaneous grounds, such as sickness at the time of lay-off. Another eleven men were of the opinion that the dismissals occurring shortly before the industrial holidays was wholly or partly responsible for the dearth of openings, and as already indicated, several others decided that it was pointless looking during this period: 'They wasn't taking any on', as it was put. On the whole, it is safe to say that the coincidence of the discharges with the holiday season was a factor of considerable importance—and more so than the few specifically giving this as a 'reason' would suggest.

A variation on the theme was that there were no suitable vacancies, or only labouring ones, or 'nothing in my line' or 'nothing in my trade'. Again, some remarked that there were no openings in the area in which they lived, either at that particular juncture or that, in general, it was one of few opportunities. We shall return to these topics presently; here we may point out that in so far as the men themselves tried to account for their problems, the majority of the 173 advancing 'no jobs' did not qualify either in a 'nothing in this area' or in a 'nothing in my line' direction.

(*b*) *Reluctance to Employ ex-RJ Workers*

The second most important reason spontaneously put forward by the men was the reluctance of would-be employers to take on ex-employees of the motor industry or, more usually, ex-employees of RJ. Eighty-six respondents, or 33 per cent of the 259 'difficults', mentioned this anti-RJ prejudice.[1] Twenty-nine men (11 per cent)

[1] It should be noted that these figures (like several others in this chapter) are confined to the 259 men who 'found it difficult' to secure work after redundancy. This does not imply that all other respondents were necessarily wholly unaffected by the cause of difficulty in question.

gave it as the sole cause of trouble—or 47 (18 per cent) if the 'no jobs' factor is ignored.

In a nutshell, the main ground—as conveyed to respondents—for employers' disinclination to engage them was their conviction that the men would return to RJ when things picked up, lured by the higher wages available there. A second and related misgiving was that the men were spoilt and bound to be dissatisfied with the much lower remuneration which other firms were able to offer. A number of respondents pointed out that they were never asked whether they were prepared to accept these inferior standards; it was assumed that they were not. A further reason for 'anti-RJness', though reported in relatively few cases only, was that the ex-employees of RJ were looked upon as potential agitators and strike-prone trouble-makers. This, as some observed, may have been aggravated by the strikes over the redundancy itself, which occurred just when some of those affected were trying to secure alternative employment.

A breakdown by firm (RJ) of the 86 respondents citing anti-RJness brings to light that the latter was meted out in rather different measure to men from the several companies. As regards skill grading on the other hand—taking that immediately prior to discharge as our criterion—the composition of the group is not very dissimilar from that of the sample as a whole, the main difference being that the semi-skilled are somewhat over-represented among the 86, with the unskilled correspondingly under-represented.

Employers' reactions on the subject were described in graphic terms; a few examples will be illuminating. Typical are 'they just thought we'd come off the luxury trade, and they wouldn't look at you'; 'if you mentioned . . ., it sounded as if you had the plague'; and 'as soon as they heard where you'd come from, they said "not another bloody £15-a-week man"—and you'd had it'. Some men explained that they were simply not given an interview; others, that frequently they were as good as taken on, but when the fatal name was revealed, the interview thereupon terminated. One respondent, who had concentrated his searches on some of the smaller towns in the vicinity of where he lived, related that a number of firms locally seemed to boycott RJ-men, while various vacancies at the employment exchange were advertised as 'Ex- . . . workers need not apply'. Another similarly observed that the exchanges were up against employers' unwillingness to entertain the likes of him.

A respondent graded as skilled prior to dismissal who—like the preceding cases—reported anti-RJness as the sole problem, was automatically informed that 'we couldn't pay that money'; he was unemployed for five months despite the most extensive inquiries. A second found firms reluctant to countenance ex-RJ workers amongst other things 'as they are not regarded as reliable'. A really unfortunate victim of anti-RJness was a partly disabled man in his middle thirties who, in the event, was at large for four months. He stated that there was actually a fair amount of work about, but even his father—in an industrial post of some influence—could not help. This respondent greatly exerted himself in an endeavour to get settled, trying all over the Midlands and beyond; he went both round factories and building sites, and after a while also applied for labouring vacancies. On several occasions he was nearly fixed up; then prospective employers would discover his antecedents and reject him: 'If you told a pack of lies, you could get a job. But if you told the truth and said you came from . . ., you didn't stand a chance; they thought you were idle and incompetent. And if you told them you were a member of the . . . (union), they thought you were a trouble-maker'.

A skilled man remarked that, although employers wanted tool-makers at the time, they were not prepared to fill their needs from amongst those originating from RJ. Another respondent suspected something of a conspiracy on the part of entrepreneurs—may be, as he put it, 'to show who is boss'. A third thought that there possibly was an agreement between RJ and other managements in the matter. One man, however, made the point that one could not really reproach the firms, while a second, with the scales neatly balanced, commented 'I don't blame them—nor the workers going back because of the money'.

The foregoing is of course exclusively based on the experiences of the sample; the would-be employers of 1956 have not been interviewed. But as respondents were not asked whether or not they had difficulties on the score of anti-RJness—as they were regarding certain other potential causes—the large number spontaneously mentioning this factor would seem to be clear evidence that there was such a prejudice. The latter term is used mainly for want of a better; it is not meant to suggest that the firms' misgivings were groundless. For as a substantial proportion did return to RJ—we deal with this in Chapter 6—would-be employers' suspicions cannot be adjudged unreasonable. Nevertheless, the assumption that money was the chief consideration weighing with the redundant men was unfounded; as we shall see later, it is at best a half-truth. Hence it is unfortunate that so many had to put up with anti-RJness irrespective of whether they had decided to break with the motor industry. The 86 respondents concerned include several with prolonged periods of unemployment who did not in fact rejoin RJ, and where managements' frigidity was—even if not the sole factor—at any rate an important one delaying their absorption in the labour market.

While one cannot chide employers for their lack of enthusiasm in filling permanent vacancies with what might well turn out to be temporary labour, individual bargains with the men—under which the latter would have committed themselves to a minimum period of service—would no doubt have been welcomed by many of them, while at the same time enabling firms to choose their workers on merit without undue qualms about their subsequent defection.

(*c*) *Lack of Skill, Training or Experience*

Of the 259 men in the sample who reported difficulty in securing work after redundancy, only 30—12 per cent—cited their lack of skill, training or experience, or their not having another trade, as the or more usually one of the causes responsible. We might, however, point out that some of those talking of a shortage of the right type of opening without elaborating this further—as indeed others contenting themselves with some version of 'no jobs'—may well have had in mind that there was a lack of the kind of semi-skilled work they had been accustomed to. Also, some respondents subsequently referred—*en passant*, as it were—to only skilled men having been in demand, but in terms that could not be regarded as a 'reason'.

Comments made by the group include 'I'd no training or apprenticeship', 'the fact that I'd got no trade', or 'well, they wanted skilled blokes, and I've no skill'. One man, not yet 18, wanted to get into 'some kind of a trade for when I grow older'; in a sense, therefore, his problem was—he unsuccessfully tried for garage work—his anxiety to acquire expertise rather than his lack thereof. Another, in his early twenties, expressed regret at not having availed himself of an earlier opportunity to serve an apprenticeship. One respondent—though not so rated by RJ—stated that he was classed as a labourer; several in fact ascribed the trouble to their being unskilled, even though treated as 'semi' by RJ. As one put it, 'semi-skilled men in the motor trade haven't got enough experience', though in the opinion of a second the difficulty lay simply in the quantity of such workers at large at the one juncture.

One respondent observed that he merely had his skill at driving, but otherwise nothing to back his applications; another—in his early twenties—that in order to obtain employment, it was necessary to switch to different work altogether, but his meagre experience militated against this. A third mentioned that in the building industry—where he had previously spent about nineteen years—'they queried whether you were a tradesman'. Several comments were to the effect that the firms had the pick of the skilled or experienced men, so that it was hard for the semi-skilled to get a hearing.

Two particularly interesting cases concern men who had very great difficulty in getting placed, though holding skilled jobs prior to discharge. One, in his late forties and who did not commence work until about twenty weeks after dismissal, disclosed that some firms rejected him because he was unable to read drawings; the employment exchange likewise referred him to vacancies beyond his capacity. The second, a sheet metal worker in his late fifties, was unemployed for four months; on several occasions he was informed that he was not experienced enough. These examples illustrate perhaps that skilled status at one company is not necessarily a marketable commodity, and that in any event it may be insufficient to outweigh a handicap such as age.

Some of the men certainly must have felt at the time that they were falling between two stools, since unskilled occupations were beneath their dignity while skilled ones were beyond their reach. One respondent gave expression to this when he stated that 'all the jobs that were available were for either labourers or skilled men', while several others pointed out that the employment exchange had nothing for the semi-skilled. Again, some of the younger men felt at a disadvantage in that, on the one hand, they had not yet gained much know-how but, on the other, had outgrown what one might call the 'willing juvenile' stage.

The 30 respondents citing their lack of skill as a source of worry after redundancy comprise—on the basis of the classification in force at RJ—3 unskilled, 25 semi-skilled and the 2 skilled already quoted. This means that of the 24 men in the sample graded unskilled prior to lay-off, 21 either had no real headaches or else did not regard their lack of qualifications as responsible. More generally, it is surprising that inadequate expertise should have been mentioned by so few as a drawback. A question on the subject was not of course specifically put, but this is likewise true of the anti-RJ reason, so that it is legitimate to compare the 86 respondents spontaneously adducing the latter as a cause of difficulty with the 30 pinning the blame on 'skill'.

A possible explanation is that it cannot be ignored that it is less detrimental to self-esteem to attribute one's troubles to a factor beyond one's control than to one which, though in part equally so, does at the same time reflect on one's own lack of accomplishments. More important perhaps, as would-be employers made no bones about their enthusiasm for ex-RJ workers, refusal of a job on this score may have been more overt than a refusal on lack-of-skill grounds, where the inquirer may have been disposed of by some more neutral formula. Also, in so far as men used agencies such as the employment exchange, trade unions or newspaper adverts, they would not, mostly, follow up vacancies that stipulated qualifications which they did not possess. As they could not know in advance which firms would cold-shoulder ex-RJ personnel, they were not here in the same position similarly to forestall a rebuff.

An alternative explanation is that skill was not in fact as important at the time as it is generally expected to be in such contingencies and there is, indeed, evidence to that effect. First, let us take the total sample and see how those discharged from skilled, semi-skilled and unskilled work, respectively, sized up the job situation facing them after redundancy.

TABLE 15

Relation of Skill at RJ to whether Experienced Difficulty in Finding Work after Redundancy*

	Skilled		*Semi-skilled*		*Un-skilled*		*Total*	
	No.	%	No.	%	No.	%	No.	%
Found it difficult	33	53	210	58	16	67	259	58
Found it easy	26	42	137	38	7	29	170	38
Non-committal/miscellaneous/ not clear	3	5	14	4	1	4	18	4
	62	100	361	100	24	100	447	100

* i.e. answer to Q. 18 (*a*) of schedule. Skill = as per data received from RJ.

The figures in Table 15 show that, asked whether it had been easy or hard to find work after leaving RJ, the proportion reporting trouble rose with decreasing skill. At the same time, it is noteworthy that over one half of those laid off from skilled occupations stated that things were difficult, and it is relevant to add that a higher proportion of the latter than of the semi-skilled described matters as *very* difficult. The skilled also contain a slightly bigger percentage emphasizing that the problem was to get a *suitable* rather than *a* job.

If, instead of skill grading at RJ, we take those who had served a full apprenticeship as our yardstick, the difference between the skilled and the rest of the sample is more pronounced. Thus of the 50 men who—as we saw in Chapter 2—had completed an apprenticeship, 46 per cent reported difficulty in securing employment, as compared with just over 59 per cent of the remaining 397 respondents. This may be contrasted with the proportions of 53 per cent (skilled) and 59 per cent (rest of sample), if we use the classification at RJ. Even so, however, it is significant that not more of the 'apprentices' should have found the process of absorption actually easy.

The relation between skill at RJ and unemployment after lay-off is set out in Table 16.

TABLE 16

Relation of Skill at RJ to Unemployment after Redundancy*

	Skilled		*Semi-skilled*		*Un-skilled*		*Total*	
	No.	%	No.	%	No.	%	No.	%
Unemployment								
2 weeks and under	30	49	206	57	8	33	244	54
Over 2 weeks–1 month	10	16	56	16	4	17	70	16
Over 1–2 months	7	11	39	11	6	25	52	12
Over 2 months	12	19	51	14	5	21	68	15
Miscellaneous/not clear	3	5	9	2	1	4	13	3
	62	100	361	100	24	100	447	100

* i.e. time elapsed between leaving RJ and commencing next job. Skill = as per data received from RJ.

As will be seen from Table 16, those with the highest proportion back in a job within a fortnight of the dismissals were the semi-skilled, not the skilled. This is a somewhat surprising result in the light of the men's own appraisal of the situation, reflected in the figures in Table 15, but one which lends support to the hypothesis that skill was not of overriding importance at the time. The semi-skilled are also the category with the smallest percentage out of work for more than two months, which explains why fewer of them than of the skilled summed up matters as *very* difficult. We may add that if we take those unemployed for upwards of three months, the skilled actually did worse than both the semi- and the unskilled, the proportions 'out' for this length being 10, 5 and 4 per cent respectively.[1]

If, again, we take apprenticeship rather than the classification at RJ as the hallmark of skilled status, the picture is more favourable to the skilled. Thus of the 50 respondents who had completed an apprenticeship, 60 per cent were back at work within a fortnight of discharge—as compared with 54 per cent for the rest of the sample, and by contrast with the 49 per cent shown against 'skilled' in

[1] The total number of unskilled is of course very small. The 4 per cent unemployed for over three months i.e. = one respondent.

Table 16. Similarly, only 10 per cent of the fully apprenticed were at large for over two months—as against 16 per cent of the remaining 397 men, and as compared with the 19 per cent of those skilled at RJ.

The main point emerging from the foregoing—and the figures in Table 16 must be given greater weight than those in Table 15, being the more objective of the two—is that the skilled did not do better than they did. And that the unskilled have a worse record than the other two groups needs to be taken with a grain of salt, both because of the very small numbers, and because the 24 men in question include seven of the thirteen coloured respondents in the sample. These, as we shall see later, had special handicaps at the time. To come back to the skilled, the fact that they did not—as might have been expected—have a distinct advantage over their colleagues is in part at any rate due to the intrusion of the age factor, with which we deal below. Meanwhile, however, we can say that, in so far as the 1956 redundancy is concerned, 'skill' was not the golden key that opened all doors irrespective of other considerations.

(*d*) *Age*

TABLE 17

Age as a Cause of Difficulty after Redundancy

(Based on 259 respondents who found it 'difficult' to secure work)

	No.	%
Age cited spontaneously* as reason for difficulties	23	9
Age not cited spontaneously, but stated in reply to specific question that it affected his prospects	26	10
Age not cited spontaneously, and stated in reply to specific question that it had not affected his prospects	199	77
Not sure/not clear	11	4
	259	100

* i.e. before Q. 21 (*c*) was put.

We now turn to the subject of age as a complicating factor following dismissal. As indicated in Table 17, of the 259 men who had trouble in securing alternative employment, only 23 spontaneously mentioned their years as wholly or partly responsible when asked, in general terms, 'What, do you think, made it difficult?'[1] This 9 per cent is again directly comparable with the 33 per cent citing 'anti-RJness' and the 12 per cent giving lack of skill. In this instance, however, respondents were—at a subsequent stage of the interview—expressly asked whether their age had affected their prospects in

[1] i.e. Q. 18 (*b*) of schedule.

any way when looking for work after redundancy,[1] and a further 10 per cent of the 259 men replied in the affirmative when the specific question was put. Seventy-seven per cent of the 259 'difficults' on the other hand did not, knowingly, suffer for being too old: they did not refer to the topic *impromptu* and, when queried, confirmed that it had not prejudiced their prospects.

Of the 49 respondents who did find themselves at a disadvantage, seven were actually young men in their 'teens or twenties at the date of discharge. Two of these had difficulties solely owing to impending national service; one gave this as a subsidiary reason. The remaining four made comments primarily to the effect that more amenable or lower-paid juveniles were being sought. While these seven respondents are, in one sense, in a distinct category, nevertheless the particular age-point reached was a stumbling-block after lay-off. The remaining 42 men comprise three aged 31–40, twenty between 41 and 50, and nineteen who had passed the 50 mark.

Generally speaking, the group includes a number encountering real hardship after redundancy, though age both was, and was felt to be, a much more serious handicap in some cases than in others. There was, for example, the respondent born in 1895 and unemployed for three months, who found it 'very hard indeed' to secure a job—entirely because of his years. Another, born in 1906, had similar experiences, being likewise 'out' for three months. A third, in his late fifties at the time and again considering this fact the sole cause of trouble, managed to obtain work after three weeks, going out every morning in search of it; 'horrible' is how he summed up the state of affairs. Another explained that at 53 he was desperate to get fixed up; he felt that no one wanted him, adding that 'I lowered myself right down to get a job'.

A respondent born in 1899 was at large for ten weeks, everyone telling him he was too old. This man remarked with some bitterness that he was fit and a good worker, 'and it was hard to be called too old'. Unlike some of the elderly, he made numerous inquiries both in Birmingham and outside; in his own words, 'I walked all over the place for nine darned weeks'. This respondent also found his RJ antecedents a big obstacle, and confessed that 'what with being 58 and a . . . man, it nearly drove me mad'. Quite a number in fact suffered from a combination of old age and anti-RJness, though in some instances disablement or lack of skill were additional complications. A few also reported that their age prevented their being reinstated by RJ.[2]

One man commented that there was so much superannuation

[1] Q. 21 (*c*).

[2] To be dealt with more fully in Chapter 6.

these days that firms would not engage anyone over 40. A second, born in 1912, was refused a post for analogous considerations. A third, 56 at the time and with 16 years' service at RJ to his credit, pointed to the valuable pension rights lost: had he continued with the firm until 65, his future would have been assured; instead, his entitlement was forfeited and to take out an insurance policy himself was wholly beyond him. He thought there should be some scheme whereby a sound worker would be provided for when approaching retirement; as it was, if one had been a good tradesman in a particular industry but had had several bosses, there was no chance of a pension. This respondent was unemployed for ten weeks; he could not remember how many applications he made because of their number. He approached nearly all his old employers, but his age was invariably against him. 'I was always told that "we will let you know" '.

In the experience of one, the first thing managements asked was one's age; he was 63 when dismissed, and in one instance was informed that 'young chaps wouldn't work with you'. A second, aged 46 only, was also rejected; 'even at 36 you were too old', he added. A third similarly found that 35 was the crucial watershed; 'employers look at you and tell you point blank that they are not engaging anyone over 35'. A man in his early thirties reported that in one respect his age bothered even him; he made inquiries at the fire station and with the police but, being over 31, was not accepted. By contrast, a respondent discharged two weeks before his 65th birthday—and forced by the redundancy into semi-retirement after a prolonged spell of unemployment—thought that one was all right until 60. It will be seen, therefore, that 'too old' was an elastic concept, though no doubt this is in conformity with employers' very different practices in the matter.

Of those of the 259 men who answered the question in the negative, one or two observed that their age did not prejudice them on that particular occasion; others, that they never got that far, being shown the door before such items were raised. One, born in 1915, remarked that his looks belied his years; a second, just under 50, that he always described himself as ten years younger. Of the few who were not sure whether they were adversely affected, one similarly confessed that he always 'knocked a few years off'.

The 'age' question was not only addressed to the 259 men reporting difficulty in securing work following redundancy, but also to the 'easies', etc., provided they made more than one attempt to obtain employment. Over half of the 188 respondents concerned actually made not more than one application;[1] of those who did make more,

[1] This topic is dealt with more fully in Chapter 4.

only a tiny handful answered the age-question in the affirmative. However, as we shall see, the number of jobs gone after was itself materially influenced by 'antiquity'. It is quite possible, therefore, that older respondents, for whom it was merely *fairly* easy to get fixed up, would have been settled more speedily but for the inhibiting effect of their years on the steps taken to that end. We may add that of those who on the whole considered it straightforward to find a new niche, one or two commented that their age advanced their prospects at the time—like one, born in 1935, who became a salesman four days after discharge. He felt that he had reached just the right point for the sales world—in which he was still employed at the date of interview.

We may now leave on one side whether age was a *tangible* obstacle after redundancy, and look at the relation between it and unemployment for the sample as a whole.

TABLE 18

Relation between Unemployment after, and Age at Time of, Redundancy

	Age				
	-30	31–40	41–50	51 & +	*Total*
*Unemployment**	%	%	%	%	%
2 weeks and under	59	64	42	36	54
Over 2 weeks–1 month	18	11	20	17	16
Over 1–2 months	13	10	14	6	12
Over 2 months	9	13	21	30	15
Miscellaneous/not clear	1	2	3	11	3
	100	100	100	100	100
No. in category	150	149	101	47	447

* i.e. time elapsed between leaving RJ and commencing next job.

As indicated by Table 18, unemployment clearly increased with years: while the proportion settled in a new post within one month of lay-off was more than three-quarters in the case of those aged 30 and below, it was only 53 per cent for the over-fifties. Similarly, of the latter, the proportion 'out' for upwards of two months was 30 per cent—as against 9 per cent for the thirty-and-unders, and as compared with 15 per cent for the sample as a whole. Again, the proportion without job in excess of three months was 3 per cent for those 30 years or younger, 4 per cent for those aged 31–40, 8 per cent for the 41–50 year-olds, but 13 per cent for the over-fifties. Nevertheless, it is plain that age was not an invariable handicap:

17 of the 47 respondents in the sample aged over 50, or 36 per cent, commenced employment within a fortnight of discharge, these 17 including 10 men who started within a week of the latter after no more than one attempt to obtain work. Another interesting point emerging from the table is that the 31–40 group—rather than their juniors—were the category with the highest proportion absorbed within two weeks of redundancy.[1]

Here we may revert to the fact noted earlier that the skilled were not more successful in the matter of job-finding; as briefly mentioned, this seems to be in part attributable to the age composition of the three skill groups. Thus of those graded semi-skilled by RJ—who had the shortest amounts of unemployment—only 29 per cent were over 40 years at the time of dismissal; of the skilled and unskilled, on the other hand, the corresponding proportions were 48 and 54 per cent. Similarly, not quite 9 per cent of the semi-skilled had passed the 50 mark—as compared with nearly 15 per cent of the skilled and 29 per cent of the unskilled. Owing to the predominance of the semi-skilled in the sample, the numbers do not permit of any breakdowns with the age factor held constant; there is little doubt, however, that the skilled would have put up a better performance, had their ages more closely resembled those of their semi-skilled colleagues. This is indeed borne out by the fact that the 50 men who had completed an apprenticeship—and who were absorbed more quickly than those classed skilled at RJ—were significantly younger than the latter. Their age structure is much more akin to that of the semi-skilled, the chief difference being that the apprentices include an exceptionally high proportion—46 per cent—aged 30 and below and only 24 per cent in the 31–40 group, as compared with 35 and 36 per cent in these two categories in the case of the semi-skilled. However, the main point is that the 'apprentices', even though not—like those rated skilled by RJ—having an unfavourable age composition relative to the rest of the sample, and though their status as skilled is hardly in question, nevertheless did not, as we saw earlier, have more of an advantage in the labour market following the lay-off. Hence taking the evidence from this and the preceding section together, the conclusion is that while skill was doubtless of value, and while old age was by no means an insuperable handicap, as a broad generalization it was youth rather than skill which was a boon after redundancy.

(*e*) *Low Wages*

Table 19 overleaf is concerned with the topic of inadequate wages as a source of trouble after dismissal. This 'reason' is again one which

[1] This point is further discussed in Chapter 7: see p. 183 *post*.

some advanced *impromptu* in reply to the general question 'What, do you think, made it difficult?' In addition, at a later stage of the interview, respondents were asked 'When looking for work after R, did you turn down—or not follow up—jobs because (the) pay (was) too low?'[1]

TABLE 19

Low Pay as a Cause of Difficulty after Redundancy

(Based on 259 respondents who found it 'difficult' to secure work)

	No.	%
Low pay cited spontaneously* as reason for difficulties	29	11
Low pay not cited spontaneously, but stated in reply to specific question that turned down jobs on that account	75	29
Low pay not cited spontaneously, nor turned down any jobs on that account	151	58
Not clear	4	2
	259	100

* i.e. before Q. 21 (*a*) was put.

As will be seen, only 29 individuals spontaneously pointed to inferior pay standards, and the great majority of these regarded them as a, rather than the, problem *à propos* of procuring work following lay-off. The number is almost the same as, equally without prompt, adduced their lack of skill, and here again does not cover those merely speaking of the dearth of 'decent' or suitable jobs, who may or may not have referred to the cash aspect. However, in this case this is a negligible qualification in view of the specific question subsequently put on the topic. As shown, a further 29 per cent disclosed, when directly asked, that they had not taken up employment opportunities because of the remuneration offered.

It will be clear from the wording of the question that respondents were not required to state how many jobs were turned down, though many volunteered these particulars. Thus of the total of 104 men who either gave poor pay as a cause of difficulty or who had not entertained possible openings on that account, 33 added that they had rejected one job on that score. Eighteen had refused a few, while only 14 said that they had spurned several or numerous posts—among them one who, on financial grounds, did not pursue about a quarter of the 321 vacancies he tried for after redundancy. The remaining 39 respondents did not specify a number.

[1] Q. 21 (*a*) of schedule.

The question was whether men had either turned down or not followed up vacancies for 'fiscal' reasons. The 'not followed up' was included so as to obtain a more adequate picture of the role played by cash considerations at the time: clearly, if a whole host of low-paid jobs were not applied for in the first place, the opportunity to reject them would be correspondingly limited. Yet it must be admitted that to account for openings not followed up for a given motive is an awkward exercise; such non-action may be quasi-automatic, so that one could hardly expect anyone to keep a precise mental register of the matter. Though the question did elicit some of the desired comment, it is likely that the number not *following up* posts on monetary grounds is understated by Table 19. There is actually some evidence to that effect in that a handful of men, who initially answered in the negative, revealed subsequently that the employment exchange had offered them vacancies, which they considered unsuitable because of the wages attached to them.

If, to be on the safe side, we take the figures in Table 19 as primarily covering jobs *turned down* for financial reasons, it remains significant that 58 per cent of the group did not reject any employment opportunities for pecuniary motives. A good many made the point that they never had the chance to refuse work, or that they were prepared to take anything, or actually accepted the first offer. Coupled with the fact that of the remainder a considerable number had rejected either one or at most a few jobs on grounds of cash, one might perhaps comment that the men were not inordinately fussy.

This view is confirmed by the data given as to what was regarded as 'too low' in this context: of the 104 respondents who cited prevailing pay levels as a source of difficulty or who had rejected work on that score, 40 volunteered details. Thirty-one of these had refused posts offering up to but not exceeding £8 a week, the highest wage spurned by the remainder being £10–£11. The crux of the matter, however, lies in the standards of the jobs which the men actually took after redundancy—to be dealt with in Chapter 5. We shall there see that, both in absolute terms and by comparison with pre-R incomes, the level of post-R earnings was such that the label 'spoilt' is not warranted.

An interesting point is that among those who refused employment for pecuniary reasons were several who—by contrast with many of their colleagues—maintained that work was to be had at the time, except that the remuneration was unsatisfactory. Thus in the opinion of one 'there were stacks of jobs going . . . you could get a job anywhere at about £6 a week'. A second could have returned to his old trade of electrical engineering, but did not think the wages were good enough. A third—born in 1918, skilled at RJ, and unemployed for two months—stated that posts were about 'but at starvation wages; no self-respecting man would take them'. His retort to the pay question was 'yes, definitely; I know what I'm worth'. Yet another, who went fruit-picking while looking for more permanent employment, commented that 'you go to work for yourself, not for the benefit of an employer, unless you're a hypocrite'. One respondent, who had cold-shouldered two openings on financial grounds, then struck lucky; he landed a post by accepting it at £1 less than the previous caller. Another, however, confessed to slipping up in the matter, turning his back on a £9.10.0.-a-week vacancy, only to take one subsequently at £8.10.0.

Of those who rejected posts for reasons of cash, several referred to them as being mere labouring jobs. Thus one remarked that, not being skilled, 'it was only labouring I was offered'. A second posed the rhetorical question 'if you think you are capable of more than sweeping up a floor, you hesitate, don't you?' A third, by contrast, felt there was nothing wrong with the available vacancies apart from the financial aspect. One man accounted for the situation by observing that the larger concerns were not then engaging anyone; the posts were with the smaller firms, which could not afford the same wages. A second, however, thought that 'they dropped the prices on jobs, knowing lots were out of work', while a third likewise stated that one reason for his problems was that employers 'offered very poor money, because they knew we were desperate'.

Some of the men explained that posts were rejected because the remuneration was insufficient in the light of the various other conditions of employment. For example, one declined permanent nights at £10 a week; another, a job down the mines because it would have meant his moving north for a weekly income of £9; a third, driving a six-ton lorry 5½ days a week at £8. Again, several respondents stressed that one could not keep a family on £6, £7 or £8, or that it was pointless taking work that would involve getting into debt.

We may add that here again the specific question of whether respondents turned down openings because the remuneration was poor was not only addressed to the 259 men who found it difficult to get placed after discharge, but also to those 'easies', etc., who made more than one attempt to that end. Twenty-four of these answered in the affirmative, so that the total having 'low pay' trouble or rejecting vacancies on that score is 128 respondents or 29 per cent of the sample. As it can be assumed that those who made only one application for work cannot, at any rate, have turned down any posts on financial grounds, this means that about 70 per cent[1] of the 447 men did not

[1] One per cent of replies were not clear.

refuse an offer of employment after redundancy by virtue of the inadequacy of the reward attaching to it.

(*f*) *Closed Shop Difficulties*

Another 'reasons' question put was whether respondents encountered any difficulty because of closed-shop agreements.[1] Of the 259 men, only 6 answered that they had; one was non-committal, the rest replying in the negative. None of the six spontaneously drew attention to the matter and, with one exception, mentioned one instance only of trouble. Of the remainder of the sample ('easies', etc.) who were asked the question, merely one experienced 'closed shop' complications.

Some of the 'noes' were emphatic, countering 'none whatsoever' or similar. A few remarked that, as union members, they were immune, or that if one went into an open or 'black' shop, the pay was below par. One respondent disclosed that it was a case of certain managements rejecting him because he was a trade unionist rather than one of closed shops, while another was offered a post after confirmation with RJ that he had not caused any disturbances there. A third cited what was normally a 'union firm', refusing T.U. men in 1956. On the other hand, some stated that they did not try 'union places' at the time, one observing that there was no point in inquiring at a union shop independently, since requests for labour were directly transmitted to the relevant union H.Q. Others commented that the subject was never mentioned, one adding that most concerns did not bother and that 'it's only in the motor trade that they're particular'.

(*g*) *The Coloured*

The salient figures bearing on the relation between place of birth and length of unemployment are set out in Table 20 (page 74).

The most prominent feature of the table is the poor performance of the 'other abroad' category, primarily due to the fact that its 19 members comprise 13 coloured men.[2] With one exception, all these had a very tough time securing a post following dismissal, the exception being one respondent recalled to RJ two weeks after the lay-off—the only one of the coloured to be fixed up within a fortnight of the latter. Ten of the 13 were out of work for more than one month—including 5 for over two, and 2 for upwards of three, months.

Only a minority of the 13 respondents specifically adduced colour prejudice as a reason for their difficulties, and even these did not

[1] Q. 21 (*b*) of schedule.

[2] The number shown in Table 8 as born in India, Pakistan and the West Indies is 14: one of these was not coloured.

TABLE 20

Length of Unemployment after Redundancy* of Respondents Born in Different Areas/Countries

	Unemployment		
	1 month and under	*Over 2 months*	*Total in group*
Place of birth	%	%	No.
Birmingham	71	14	228
Midlands, other than Birmingham	70	17	118
England, other than Midlands	78	13	31
Wales and Scotland	87	13	16
N. Ireland and Eire	77	6	35
Other abroad	26	42	19
Total sample	70	15	447

* i.e. time elapsed between leaving RJ and commencing next job.

attribute all their troubles to this. A Pakistani, for instance, stated that though a few concerns would not take on coloured men, this did not seriously affect his prospects. A few, however, considered themselves to be at a distinct disadvantage—in some cases, this emerged only at subsequent stages of the interview. Thus one reported that he did not apply to firms 'on the off-chance'—as many of the redundant did at the time—because employers were 'partial'. A sanitary inspector in his country of origin was sore that his qualifications were not regarded as adequate when he tried for a local authority vacancy in that field. A third commented that 'a lot of us have a trade and good education—I feel we are not treated right', the gist of his complaint being that coloured workers were not given a chance to prove themselves at the more skilled type of occupation. We may add that at one interview—conducted in the presence of some eight or ten compatriots—there were many expressions of resentment at the existence of a colour bar in Birmingham factories; a further grievance was that this frequently operated on a selective basis—i.e. was reserved for Indians and Pakistanis, while the West Indians were spared.

The employment exchanges also came in for some hard words. Thus one respondent, when asked whether he thought that the exchange could have done more to help redundant workers, replied that 'several times I have been there and they have jobs, but they give them to white man, not send out coloured men'. A second similarly remarked that neither on that nor on previous occasions had he received any assistance from that source, which was 'as bad as anybody else', officials being 'prejudiced against our colour'. He added 'I see them send out white fellows and we sitting; don't know if firms said "no want coloured" or no'. A third likewise considered that, after allowing for the exchanges having to comply with employers' wishes in the matter of both 'skin' and qualifications, they did not display the same interest in their coloured as in their other clients. Two men hinted at the trade unions also being less helpful to them.

One respondent, who left Birmingham in order to secure employment, reported 'colour' difficulties in finding accommodation, 7 of the 13 men in all looking for work in areas beyond daily travelling distance from the city.[1] A second was unable to accept a post in Nottingham, because he could not borrow sufficient money for his immediate subsistence, though 4 of the 13 actually left Birmingham for purposes of their first post-R job. As we shall see later, the coloured were much the most mobile sector of the sample. On the whole, then, there is little doubt that the small band in this group was at a special disadvantage at the time of redundancy, though the numbers are of course too small to warrant any sweeping conclusions. The hardship experienced was also aggravated in a few instances by the burden of dependants to be maintained—either in England or country of origin.[2] Thus a West Indian, with a wife, five children and two relatives all wholly dependent on him, was still in debt at the date of interview from money borrowed after his dismissal.

It remains to be pointed out that 7 of the 13 coloured respondents were classed as unskilled by RJ, the rest being semi-skilled; however, while this may have been a contributory factor, it would appear that lack of skill was not the primary obstacle.[3] Nor can the men's age be held responsible, only 3 of the 13—a smaller proportion than of the sample as a whole—being over 40 years at the time. We may add that most of the 13 were very recent arrivals, 8 having landed on these shores during the 18 months preceding lay-off. A mere 2 had come to England before 1954, and a few had special language handicaps. The fact, therefore, that colour was expressly mentioned by a minority only is not necessarily significant. Two West Indians, for example, unemployed for six to seven weeks and who both went after more than a hundred jobs, could not in any way account for the situation.[4]

1 All the 13 coloured men were living in Birmingham at the time of redundancy. 'Beyond daily travelling distance' here means more than 25 miles from place of residence. This topic is being dealt with in general in the next chapter.

2 Four of the 13 coloured men (31 per cent) had 3 or more dependent children, as compared with 12 per cent in the case of the sample as a whole. Some were also maintaining other relatives.

3 Of the 5 coloured men unemployed for more than two months, 3 were graded semi-skilled (RJ).

4 In all, of the 259 men finding it difficult to obtain work after lay-off, 3 could not give any reason to account for this.

Apart from the topics dealt with, various miscellaneous grounds for difficulty in securing work after redundancy were advanced. Some of these were of a more personal nature. Thus two men found themselves at a disadvantage, amongst other things because of their height (too short); one confessed that he had lost confidence in himself since the war. In about a dozen cases health, disablement or temporary sickness were cited as either a complication or as a main worry at the time.

Chapter 4

THE MECHANICS OF JOB-FINDING

In this chapter we are more specifically concerned with the steps taken to obtain work following the discharges—with what might perhaps be called the mechanics of job-finding. The subjects to be covered include the number of openings followed up, the areas in which the search for these was made and related topics affecting mobility, the methods tried and the agencies by which posts were actually secured—with a special section on the men's experience of employment exchanges.

NUMBER OF JOBS GONE AFTER

TABLE 21

Number of Jobs Gone After Following Redundancy

	No.	%
Went after 0 or 1 job	106	24
Went after 2–20 jobs	194	43
Went after 21–40 jobs	55	12
Went after more than 40 jobs	65	15
Miscellaneous/not clear	27	6
	447	100

Table 21 sets out the replies to 'Can you remember about how many jobs you went after?',[1] the main purpose of the question being to get some idea how hard respondents had tried to find work. It was realized that too high a degree of accuracy could not be expected—both because this is a matter of which an exact mental record is not necessarily kept even at the time, as also because this type of question is particularly susceptible to lapses of memory. A further point is that 'number of jobs gone after' is not altogether precise in meaning, just as it is none too elegant in phrase, and allowance must be made for differences in interpretation—for

[1] Q. 19 (*b*) of schedule.

example, as regards writing or telephoning firms. Even in the case of on-the-spot applications, there is evidence to suggest that these were under-reported by some of the men—where, for instance, a respondent was rebuffed forthwith rather than rejected as the result of an interview. On the whole, it is fairly certain that the total of jobs tried for—in the sense of all types of solicited and unsolicited inquiries—is understated by the data in Table 21.

Despite these qualifications, however, the figures are of interest. Thus there is little doubt that 106 respondents, or almost one-quarter of the sample, made—or needed to make—merely one attempt to procure employment following dismissal. Conversely, the 15 per cent pursuing more than forty would-be openings can be taken as having gone to some considerable trouble to acquire a new boss. A breakdown of the data also brings out some revealing trends, which there is no reason to discount.

As regards age, 34 per cent of the over-fifties in the sample made only one direct application to obtain work—as compared with percentages of from 21 to 24 for the three younger age-groups. Similarly, the proportion chasing after more than twenty jobs was one-quarter for men 30 years and under, nearly 32 per cent for both the 31–40 and 41–50 categories, but merely 8½ per cent for the over-fifties.[1] It will be seen, therefore, that the over-fifties made fewer direct attempts to get fixed up—only 4 per cent applied for upwards of forty posts—although they suffered longer periods of post-redundancy unemployment than their juniors. By contrast, it was the 41–50 group which tried hardest to find a new niche, 19 per cent making more than forty inquiries, though the difference between it and the 31–40 year-olds was small.

Table 22 deals with the relation between the number of jobs tried for and the period out of work. The first three lines show the expected trend: with increasing unemployment, the proportion making one attempt only shrank—with a corresponding rise of those embarking on numerous inquiries. What must at first seem surprising is that in the case of those at large in excess of two and three months, the proportion going after over forty jobs—and, similarly, after more than twenty—*fell*. However, this appears to be due to those unemployed for upwards of two months containing a relatively high

[1] It is pointed out that the comparability of the figures may be affected by the fact that while the proportion of 'miscellaneous/not clears' ranged from 3 to 5 per cent for the three younger age-groups, 10 of the 47 over-fifties (21 per cent) were in this category. The miscellaneous/not clears include those who did not look for work at all, those answering the question in vague verbal terms, as well as a number where the answer was plainly inconsistent with earlier descriptions of the efforts made to secure work. Among the last-named were several of the elderly.

TABLE 22

Number of Jobs Gone After by Respondents with Varying Lengths of Unemployment after Redundancy*

	No. of Jobs gone after					
	0–1	2–20	21–40	*Over* 40	*Total*†	*No. in category*
Unemployment‡	%	%	%	%	%	
2 weeks and under	38	50	7	5	100	244
Over 2 weeks–1 month	10	46	20	20	100	70
Over 1–2 months	2	31	21	40	100	52
Over 2–3 months	—	37	19	28	100	43
Over 3 months	8	28	16	20	100	25

* The table covers all 447 respondents, except the 13 whose length of unemployment was not clear.

† The missing percentages, which in this instance are unusually large, are accounted for by item 'no. of jobs gone after = miscellaneous/not clear'. It should be noted that this varied widely for individual unemployment categories—from less than ½ per cent (first line of table) to 28 per cent (last line).

‡ i.e. time elapsed between leaving RJ and commencing next job.

number of elderly men; as we have just seen, these tended to exert themselves less than their more youthful colleagues.

A breakdown of the figures by skill—taking that operative at RJ prior to redundancy—reveals that just over 27 per cent of the skilled, 23½ per cent of the semi-skilled and about 17 per cent of the unskilled found a new post as the result of merely one application. At the other end of the scale, 16 per cent of the skilled, about 14 per cent of the semi-skilled and 12½ per cent of the unskilled tried for over forty jobs. The skilled thus contain the largest proportion fixed up with no or little trouble to themselves but, at the same time, also had the highest percentage pursuing more than forty openings. We may add that of the 50 respondents who had completed an apprenticeship, 28 per cent were in the '0–1 job' category as compared with 23 per cent of the rest of the sample, though the difference in the proportion making above forty inquiries was only fractional as between apprentices and non-apprentices.

A few illustrations may be in place from among the 106 respondents who succeeded at the first attempt to find employment after discharge. As might be expected, the great majority (89 per cent) considered it to have been easy to secure work—and hence did not qualify for attention in our last chapter—though it is not the case that all of the 106 simply 'walked' into a new job.[1] To start off with

[1] In terms of Table 13 (Chapter 3), 3 of the 106 men actually found it difficult to obtain work, 9 were in the non-committal, etc. category, while the remaining 94 (89 per cent) found things easy.

one who did, there was the man who went out the same night, applying at one firm; he was still employed there at the date of interview. A second, born in 1899, put his fate into the hands of the employment exchange, which duly got him settled after about a fortnight. A third, who initially 'was so disgusted that I didn't want to work again', then successfully followed up a newspaper advert. Another thought that the reason for his getting the first post tried for was that everyone else had spurned it. Yet another hopped on the recruiting van stationed outside RJ, inviting men to join a concern of bus and lorry builders at some distance from Birmingham. One respondent pointed out that he was one of the fortunate ones in that he was re-engaged by a former employer. There were several others in this group who rejoined an old boss—a subject to which we return later.

One man's single call was at a dairy, where he was duly enrolled as a milk roundsman; two were fixed up in coalmining through the employment exchange. Another rang up a firm and was taken on as safety engineer; yet another telephoned a coach proprietor and was asked to commence the same day. Two or three respondents already had a haven of refuge. In the words of one, 'when the rumour went around before redundancy, I got myself a job before the axe fell'.

Skill or having 'another trade' did the trick in some instances. For example, a sheet metal worker, who had spent his entire previous working life as such and who had served a full apprenticeship, was placed in the same field by his trade union. A respondent—semi-skilled at RJ who had, however, likewise completed an apprenticeship—received, from the employment exchange, a list of companies requiring skilled labour, and picked an inspection job with a concern of electrical manufacturers. A man who had previously spent some eleven years in the building industry returned to the fold as a carpenter, while two went back to painting and decorating—all 'first time lucky'.

The 65 individuals shown in Table 21 as having pursued more than forty openings include some making clear that they had tried for a large number, but who used expressions such as 'stacks of them', 'a terrible lot' or 'dozens and dozens'.[1] These, of course, are the men whose quest for work was fraught with trouble, and they have already been dealt with in Chapter 3. We shall not, therefore, here give any further illustrations beyond stating that the record total

[1] The other categories in Table 21 likewise include a few 'verbal equivalents'; for example, 'several' was treated as 2–20. This procedure was only adopted if it appeared reasonable in the light of other replies; where the 'verbal equivalent' was too vague, it was assigned to 'not clear'. The great majority of the sample answered the question in *numerical* terms.

of jobs gone after, reported in numerical terms, was 321—by one unemployed for nearly three months.

Generally speaking, the number of posts applied for diverged widely—from nil in the case of those offered a vacancy without any exertions on their part, to over 300. While these variations obviously depended on the need to make inquiries—i.e. the degree of difficulty encountered in securing a new niche—this was not the only factor. For one thing, how 'particular' the men were entered into the picture, some trying merely for *a*, others for *the*, job. Clearly also, the zeal devoted to the whole operation differed—one respondent, for example, managed to compress about a hundred calls into four days—though it was not solely a question of zeal either. Thus much may have depended on the method used for purposes of finding employment: the man relying on the employment exchange or his trade union would only follow up openings if such were notified to him, while unproductive trips to the latter would not be reflected in the figures. On the other hand, those chancing their luck by visiting prospective employers direct, would be entitled to count all such journeys. Similarly, taking action on a newspaper advert may or may not have been preceded by an intensive scrutiny of the relevant column for several previous nights, while the trouble involved in 'going after jobs' also varied according to whether a would-be boss was telephoned, written to or contacted in person, though we can take it that the totals in Table 21 by and large represent personal applications. As far as these latter are concerned, finally, the effort entailed was also a function of the area in which respondents lived, that in which they searched, as well as of the mode of transport used or available. It is to this aspect of the business of job-finding that we next turn our attention.

AREA IN WHICH SEARCH FOR WORK WAS MADE

We shall now examine various matters of geography and mobility, beginning with the locality in which the men endeavoured to obtain employment. All respondents—except the 106 who only made one application—were asked in what areas (towns) they had looked for work after lay-off, plus a number of specific follow-up questions.[1] Their replies disclosed that 346 or 77 per cent of the 1 in 10 sample had searched for a job in Birmingham, 227 or 51 per cent in the Midlands outside the latter, while 38 individuals (8½ per cent) had ventured beyond the Midlands. Of those who tried in Birmingham,

[1] See Q. 20 of schedule. In the ensuing figures the 106 respondents making only one application are included on the basis of the area in which they *accepted* work.

199—nearly 45 per cent of the 447 men—had looked there exclusively. Conversely, 91 respondents, or one-fifth of the sample, had confined their inquiries to 'Midlands outside Birmingham', i.e. cold-shouldering the city on the one hand and more distant parts on the other. Only two men had looked exclusively beyond the Midlands.[1]

To give a few illustrations before going more closely into the figures, there was the respondent, born in 1930 and single at the time, who together with three friends travelled all over the country by car, journeying to such cities as Bristol, Corby and Gloucester. Another of the bachelors looked in Cheshire and Birmingham, and also registered at an employment exchange some 8 miles from the latter 'where it was quiet'. A third found it impossible to get fixed up locally, and ended up in London where his union had referred him. One man, on the Monday following 'Black Friday', simply got on his bicycle to Wolverhampton and struck lucky; the firm moreover—one of public road works contractors—set him on in Birmingham where he lived. By contrast, another respondent left home 'nights on end' hunting in various towns; apart from extensive inquiries throughout the Midlands, he had answered newspaper adverts as far away as Middlesbrough, Newcastle and Blackburn. He applied for more than 200 jobs, but was unemployed over five months notwithstanding his 'mobility'.

TABLE 23

Whether Looked for Work in Birmingham after Redundancy by Place of Residence at Time of R*

	Looked in B'ham		*Did not*		
	Exclusively	*Other*	*look in B'ham*	*Total*	*No. in category*
Place of residence at time of R	%	%	%	%	
Birmingham	57	36	6	100†	299
Up to 8 miles from B'ham (but excluding B'ham)	29	37	34	100	35
Over 8–15 miles from B'ham	4	27	69	100	84
Over 15 miles from B'ham	—	—	100	100	6

* The table covers all 447 respondents, except the 23 whose place of residence (at R) was not clear.

† The missing 1 per cent = 4 men where 'area where looked . . .' was not clear.

Table 23 shows the extent to which respondents living in, and at various distances from, Birmingham concentrated their search for work on the latter: the figures demonstrate that place of residence

[1] Four replies were not clear.

made a significant difference as to where the men tried their hand. It is also of interest that, although RJ was in all cases situated in the city, 97 of the 447 men, or nearly 22 per cent of the sample, did not attempt to obtain a job there following discharge.

Among reasons for ignoring Birmingham as a potential source of fresh employment was the belief—expressed by some Brummies, though more so by non-Brummies—that it was not worth while doing so, as too many others would be looking there. Some of those living outside the city explained that it was too far away, which may be explicable in terms of the siting of the Longbridge plant, which might well have been regarded as accessible even if 'Birmingham' was not. At the same time, what is considered too far is doubtless rather elastic, depending on the balance of advantages and disadvantages of the particular occupation. As for the large numbers confining their inquiries to Birmingham, these did so from such variegated motives as having no money for fares, age, or simply—and frequently—because there was no need to try further afield.

It might here be pointed out—and these remarks apply *mutatis mutandis* to all subsequent figures involving the 'area' factor—that where respondents stated that they had looked in Birmingham, their word was invariably taken for it, though it can hardly be expected that they defined its identity in exactly the way adopted in these pages.[1] That definition, it will be recalled, is co-terminous with the County Borough, plus those parts of Rednal and Rubery lying outside the C.B. boundaries. 'Midlands', in turn, corresponds throughout to the combined area covered (until end-March 1962) by the Midland and North Midland Regions of the Ministry of Labour.

Another detail about which a word is necessary, as it is of more than technical import, is what is meant by 'looking for work'. The latter is not a precise concept, and hence again is subject to certain differences of interpretation on the part of the men. This factor aside, 'looking for work' has been taken to cover both physically making inquiries in a district, and accepting a post there without doing so. For example, some respondents were offered or told of an opening, but did not consider that they had 'looked' for it; however, the locality of the first job held after redundancy has in all instances been reckoned as one in which men 'looked'.[2] Similarly, those who had written to firms in some area have been treated as having 'looked' there, though such epistolary activities may not always have been

[1] For example, men may have referred to Smethwick as 'Birmingham', etc.

[2] In the case of the 106 men who were not asked where they had searched, because they only made one attempt to obtain work, 'area looked in' is, accordingly, identical with location of first post-R job.

reported in full. We may add that a few men stated that they had registered at employment exchanges in other towns or had made inquiries about emigration. These, again, have been counted as having 'looked' in the regions concerned, though those merely contemplating such action were not deemed to have done so.

TABLE 24

Farthest Area (Distance from Birmingham) in which Looked for Work

(Respondents living in Birmingham at time of R)

Farthest area	No.	%
Birmingham only	170	57
Up to 8 miles from Birmingham	13	4
Over 8–15 miles from Birmingham	39	13
Over 15–25 miles from Birmingham	38	13
Over 25 miles from Birmingham, but in Midlands	7	2
Beyond Midlands	27	9
Miscellaneous/not clear	5	2
	299	100

The purpose of Table 24 is to give some idea as to the actual range of the men's geographical mobility—i.e. how far out they went in their quest for a new job—and in order to hold the variable 'place of residence' constant, the figures have been compiled for those 299 respondents only who were living in Birmingham at the time of lay-off. As will be clear, the table is not concerned with the total of areas toured; one 'peep' outside the Midlands qualifies for 'beyond Midlands'.

As might have been expected, there was a tendency for the elderly to stick to Birmingham to a greater extent than their more youthful ex-mates. Thus of the 299 respondents covered by Table 24, 35 were aged 51 and plus. Of these, 77 per cent searched exclusively in Birmingham, as compared with proportions of from 52 to 56 per cent for the three younger age-groups. Similarly, while 14 per cent of those 30 years and under looked beyond 25 miles from their home town, only 3 per cent of the over-fifties did so.

As regards skill, taking that in force at RJ and basing ourselves on the same 299 respondents, the proportion confining their searches to Birmingham was 44 per cent in the case of the skilled, 59 per cent of the semi-skilled, and 58 per cent of the unskilled. While the skilled were thus more mobile than the semi-skilled, the difference is mainly accounted for by the larger proportion of the former prepared to put up with a longer journey to work. The percentage looking beyond 25 miles from their home—what may be regarded as beyond daily travelling distance—was broadly similar for the two categories, i.e. not quite 12 per cent for the skilled and almost 10 per cent for the semi-skilled.[1] It was nearly 32 per cent for the unskilled, but this 32 per cent merely comprises six men, for four of whom the fact that they were coloured is likely to have been the crux of the matter.

TABLE 25

Relation between Farthest Area (Distance from Birmingham) in which Looked for Work and Unemployment after Redundancy

(Respondents living in Birmingham at time of R)*

	Farthest area in which looked				
	B'ham only	*Up to 25 miles from B'ham*	*Over 25 miles from B'ham*	*Total*	*No. in category*
Unemployment†	%	%	%	%	
2 weeks and under	67	28	4	100‡	159
Over 2 weeks–1 month	53	30	17	100	53
Over 1–2 months	43	28	29	100	35
Over 2 months	37	47	16	100	43

* i.e. 299 men, but 9 whose unemployment was not clear have been omitted.
† i.e. time elapsed between leaving RJ and commencing next job.
‡ The missing 1 per cent = 2 respondents where 'farthest area . . .' was not clear.

Table 25 shows the relation between length of unemployment following dismissal and 'farthest area looked'; the data are again limited to those living in Birmingham at the time of lay-off. As will be noted, the percentage confining their inquiries to Birmingham was 67 in the case of respondents fixed up within a fortnight, but fell to 37 for those without work for over two months. However, the latter was not the group with the highest proportion trekking beyond 25 miles from the city, although this otherwise increased with unemployment. This would appear to be due to the fact that those at large in excess of two months contained a relatively high number of over-fifties who, as we saw previously, were inclined to be less mobile than the younger men.

LOOKING FOR WORK IN AREAS BEYOND DAILY TRAVELLING DISTANCE

For reasons explained, Tables 24 and 25 were restricted to those living in Birmingham at the date of discharge. Although the 299

[1] The difference in the proportion of skilled and semi-skilled seeking work beyond 25 miles from their place of residence was somewhat greater for the total sample: see *post*.

men in question constitute two-thirds of the sample, they are not altogether representative of the latter. For instance, the proportion unemployed for upwards of two months after lay-off was 14 per cent in the case of the 299, 17 per cent in that of the 35 men residing outside but within 8 miles of Birmingham, and 20 per cent if we take those then living over 8 miles from the city. It may therefore be appropriate to supplement the foregoing with a few figures for the small band seeking a post in areas beyond daily reach, and to do so by including all those in this category in the sample.

We define as 'looking beyond daily travelling distance' anyone hazarding more than 25 miles from his home town. This is in many ways an arbitrary definition, since what is within reach depends on such factors as the location of the home, the frequency and speed of transport services and/or the mode of travel available. It is also a function of individual habits, attitudes and so on, which in turn are liable to vary according to the conditions of employment of the particular job. The 25-mile limit did, however, seem reasonable in the present instance, since despite the undoubted attractive power of RJ, only 6 individuals in the sample were living at over 15 miles from Birmingham at the time of redundancy, none of whom resided more than 25 miles away.

In all, there were 46 respondents among the 447—the 38 looking beyond the Midlands and 8 others—who extended their inquiries beyond 25 miles from their home town. What were the characteristics of these men who, in broad terms, were the only ones in the sample to make efforts at job-finding in a locality beyond daily reach?

Not surprisingly, 39 per cent of the 46 were single, although the latter constituted only 16 per cent of all respondents at the date of lay-off. Seven of the 46 were coloured, and one other was born abroad; in addition, one-fifth originated from N. Ireland or Eire. *In toto*, therefore, the 46 include 37 per cent stemming from outside Great Britain, though merely 12 per cent of the 1 in 10 sample were in this category.

Seventy-four per cent of the 46 men were forty years or below, and only 2 per cent above fifty—as against proportions of 67 and 10 per cent for the sample as a whole. Again, 13 per cent of those classed skilled by RJ were among the 46, but only 9 per cent of those then semi-skilled. Of the 50 respondents who had completed an apprenticeship, 7 looked for work beyond 25 miles from their home.

A mere 20 per cent of the 46 respondents were fixed up with a new job within a fortnight of dismissal, as compared with 54 per cent of all 447 respondents. Similarly, 28 per cent of the 46 were unemployed in excess of two months, although only 15 per cent of the sample as a whole were in this predicament. As for the number of openings tried for, just over 43 per cent of the 46 went after more than twenty jobs; the corresponding percentage for the total sample, as we saw, was 27.

Among the 46 men were at least 7 more or less actively considering emigration after the redundancy. One was planning to enlist in the Kenya Police, though it fell through. A second—a married respondent in his middle thirties, who *inter alia* wrote several letters a night after such jobs as the Malayan Police—revealed that he would have journeyed 'anywhere in the world' or, alternatively, would have hooked up his caravan and set off for any promising vacancy in the U.K. Most of the rest had instituted inquiries about going to Australia or Canada; in one instance, it was merely a last-minute tip from an earlier migrant which led to a change of mind. We may add that a further seven or so respondents were considering emigration as a possibility, but had not pursued it to the form-filling stage, while one or two others commented that they would have emigrated, had they been younger, etc.

HOUSING

As previously stated, 199 respondents or almost 45 per cent of the sample confined their endeavours to secure work to Birmingham. The remainder—though with the further exception of those making one attempt only at job-finding—were asked whether there were any posts they could not accept because of the lack of nearby housing.[1] A mere five men answered in the affirmative.

These five comprise one—then round the forty mark—who was unemployed for three months after lay-off, despite the most extensive efforts to get placed. He had *inter alia* formerly been in the mines for 3½ and in the Forces for 13 years, and would have returned to coalmining in Nottingham but for his inability to obtain a house there. A second, out of work for only four days, had applied to a firm at Luton: 'I should have started there, but they couldn't find us any housing'. Another was thwarted by the lack of accommodation in the London area, while a fourth turned down an opening in Corby, as it would have involved staying in digs. The last of the group was one living in Birmingham, who remarked that he could not accept a vacancy in Wolverhampton because there was no accommodation; this is of interest since many others took posts at a similar or greater distance, travelling to and fro each day.

Of those replying in the negative, some simply repeated that they were prepared to take anything at the time but that there were no openings, while two observed that the subject did not affect them as single men. Others, however, made clear that in exploring

[1] Q. 20 (*a*) E of schedule.

prospects in other towns, they had no intention of leaving home, and that the question did not arise because they only looked in the vicinity of the latter. Thus one respondent, who actually considered emigrating, explained that, in so far as his inquiries in the neighbourhood of Birmingham were concerned, he never pondered the housing problem as he was planning to travel daily.

That so few should have been frustrated by the lack of housing is not of course surprising; as we saw, only 46 respondents made inquiries beyond 25 miles from their place of abode so that, in one sense, housing problems had little chance to be awkward. At the same time, it is not the case that the housing factor was of no consequence except in the handful of instances cited. Thus several other men enlarged on the topic, in particular when asked at a subsequent stage of the interview whether they had considered leaving their home town, and whether they would contemplate such action in any similar future contingency. We come back to the first of these items presently. Here we may remark that the number who cannot accept a job because of lack of accommodation is in any event liable to be much below that of those whose mobility is affected by the matter. The time has probably passed when people search for employment in distant areas, on which they then actually embark when accommodation can be found. The order of priority is now different and less clear-cut, while the mere knowledge that housing is likely to be a headache will have a potent restraining influence on mobility in the first place. We might add that several of those who did take a job away from home made adverse comments about the nature and/or cost of the accommodation they secured.

CONSIDERING A MOVE

The decision to quit familiar surroundings either permanently or temporarily is of course a difficult one, and over and above those searching for work in areas involving this step, there were others who had considered doing so when dismissed in mid-1956. Thus, as we saw in Table 24, 11 per cent of the 299 respondents living in Birmingham at the time of redundancy looked for a boss either beyond the Midlands or at any rate in districts more than 25 miles from their home. A further 18 per cent of the same group—or 29 per cent (88 men) in all—had *considered* leaving the city.

A *caveat* should here be sounded, as 'to consider' something can, clearly, mean different things; the 88 respondents residing in Birmingham[1] who considered leaving it after discharge are not, accord-

[1] The relevant question (Q. 54 of schedule) was put to all respondents, but the figures are again being confined to the 299 men living in Birmingham at the date of redundancy.

ingly, a homogeneous group. Thus they comprise those who actually took a job away from home;[1] those who looked in such areas but, in the event, did not leave; those who considered the matter but, for one reason or another, left it at that—like several mentioning towns they 'had thought of going to' but which they did not get round to visiting; and, finally, those who considered the subject in the sense that they were prepared to contemplate a move, should this be necessary.

In many cases that need did not of course occur, and as far as the last-mentioned category is concerned, in particular, it must be regarded as partly accidental whether men enlarged on their hypothetical readiness to bid farewell to Birmingham in circumstances which had not in fact arisen. Accordingly, although the figures are of some interest, it would be wrong to infer from them either that two-thirds of the 299 respondents[2] were wholly opposed to departing from the city, just as it would be inaccurate to treat the 29 per cent who did consider moving as *actively* contemplating that step—let alone as being ready to implement it. It may, however, be worth adding that of those of the 299 who were unemployed for over two months after discharge, 53 per cent had not given any thought to seeking their fortunes outside Birmingham.

Another complication, which is of some methodological interest, is that in a number of cases replies may have depended on whether respondents were reporting the end-product of the 'considering' process or some earlier phase thereof. For instance, several men answered the question in the affirmative—i.e. they *had* considered leaving their home town—but went on to explain that their wives had been against it. Others replied in the negative for precisely the same reason. While this may *inter alia* reflect the differential 'say' which the respective good ladies had in the households concerned—or the strength or immediacy of uxorial opposition—such differences could also simply be due to the fact that the men were referring to a different stage of the argument.

Although, therefore, too much should not be read into these particular data, some of the comments offered may be illuminating. Thus several of those who had not considered moving were quite definite about it; others disclosed that it had not occurred to them, though the most common observation was that there was no need to contemplate so drastic a step. Another point frequently made was that the men and/or their families liked the area, were born and brought up in it, or had at any rate lived there for many years.

[1] The actual location of first post-R jobs is reserved for Chapter 5.

[2] The proportion of 'noes' i.e. was 66 per cent, 5 per cent being not sure/not clear.

Thus a single respondent, who experienced great difficulty in finding a job, was asked by the employment exchange if he would accept work outside Birmingham, but 'I was born and bred here, and there was a lot of foreigners here, and I didn't see why I should leave the town and get work elsewhere'.[1] With perfect logic, he confined his inquiries strictly to Birmingham.

Apart from reluctant spouses, some men cited relatives whom they did not wish to abandon. A few felt they were too old or had had enough of travelling—like one who had only recently returned from five years in the Forces. A second answered in the negative, because his son was apprenticed at RJ. A third, with more than 15 years' service with the latter, thought he would get his job back fairly soon, and this belief may well have weighed with a number of others. Another opinion frequently expressed was that Birmingham was the best place for work, and that if there were no vacancies there, there were unlikely to be any elsewhere—a view with which, when all is said, it is hard to quarrel.

Among those replying in the affirmative was one who countered 'I considered it, but that was as far as it got'; however, he was 'out' for merely four days. A second, unemployed for ten weeks, stated that he would have gone anywhere, had he found a willing employer, while a third remarked that he did not mind where he lived, so long as he had a good job. A respondent who had searched in Birmingham, Wolverhampton and Coventry, and who was at large for three months, said that during the latter stage, if something 'reasonable' had been offered away from home, he would have taken it. Another, without work for four months, similarly would have moved if he had secured an opening in another area; however, he could not find one, although himself making intensive inquiries all over the Midlands and beyond.

One respondent considered rejoining the Navy, having spent some seven years in the Forces previously. A second would have migrated to Scotland to teach schoolboys how to do sheet metal work, but did not have the money to move house. Others who had given thought to the matter disclosed that they were put off by the housing problem. One particular variation on the theme—indicating that the men concerned were thinking purely in terms of a temporary departure—was that a change of abode was decided against, as they could not afford to keep two homes going.

METHODS TRIED IN ORDER TO FIND WORK

We now turn to a brief review of the methods used by respondents with a view to securing work after redundancy, leading on to a more

[1] The reference to foreigners was not typical.

detailed examination of the agencies by which the first post following that event was actually secured. Taking the sample as a whole, 73 per cent registered at an employment exchange after discharge, while 17 per cent—or one-fifth of those who were then T.U. members—applied to their union for details of vacancies. At least 59 per cent either looked at or followed up newspaper advertisements, while about two-fifths stated that they had followed up factory gate notices.[1] Approximately one half of the sample asked relatives or friends to tell them of openings, while about seven in every ten men applied to firms on the 'off-chance'—i.e. without there being an advert or gate notice inviting such application. These figures emerge from a specific question on each of these topics;[2] other steps taken were, for example, turning to a former employer, of which more anon. As previously mentioned also, one or two men already had a job lined up when the axe fell—forewarned by rumours, persistent short-time working or their own intuition.

It should be pointed out that those who were *offered* posts or otherwise helped without any action on their part—for instance, who were given a job by an acquaintance aware of their dilemma, or who got placed through a relative spontaneously having a word with an obliging foreman—are not included among the above figures, as they did not in fact resort to the method concerned. Further, each 'action' has only been counted once: the man who approached a friend, who subsequently told him of a vacancy about which he then inquired on the off-chance, has been taken as having asked a friend, but not also as having made an 'off-chance' application. At the same time, it may well be that in so far as the various questions on the subject were answered with a simple 'yes', some duplication has crept in.

It will be clear that most of the men tried more than one method; quite a few in fact employed five or six, though others—such as many of those who got fixed up at the first attempt—also had recourse to only one[3] agency. While the number of methods used by different individuals is not being summarized—*inter alia*, because they are not really comparable—it is evident that the great majority were not content to rely on one agency only. Thus of the 325 respondents who registered at an employment exchange, all except 21 also took other steps with a view to finding employment.

We devote the last section of this chapter to the men's experience of employment exchanges; a few remarks may here therefore be apposite about some of the other agencies. As regards press adverts, the question 'Did you follow up newspaper adverts?' was by some answered in the negative because they interpreted it strictly; i.e. they

[1] But see *post*. [2] Q. 22 (*a*) and Q. 19 (*c*), A.–E. of schedule. [3] Or nil.

made plain that though they followed the adverts, there was nothing to follow up. Others replied in the affirmative on the strength, simply, of having perused the relevant column. In order to get over this difficulty, the 59 per cent quoted earlier have been defined so as to represent all those who either followed up newspaper adverts, or who at any rate scanned the papers with a view to doing so; it may well be, however, that the 'scanners-only' are under-represented among the 59 per cent.[1]

Still *à propos* of press adverts, several men indicated that they looked at these daily, one saying that he was broke buying copies. Others observed that they did not see any suitable ones, while a common complaint was that, when one reached the firms concerned, the vacancies were already filled. One respondent attributed this to employers inserting adverts for a few consecutive nights, getting suited after the first, but with no cancellation of the remainder. A second thought that it was useless trying to obtain semi-skilled work by this means, while a number felt, more generally, that if a vacancy was advertised, it was no good. 'More cut-price, like', as one put it, while another went so far as to opine that 'newspaper jobs are jobs that the labour exchange would not insult a bloke by sending them to'. One man reported that the letters he wrote in response to press adverts were not acknowledged, although he enclosed stamped addressed envelopes.

While two-fifths of the sample stated, in reply to the specific question, that they had followed up factory gate notices, it is doubtful whether, except in a small number of cases, this was an independent method of obtaining employment. Thus of the 181 men concerned, all except 8 had also approached firms on the 'off-chance', and the impression gained is that gate notices were mainly an adjunct to 'on spec.' applications. In the words of one respondent, 'I was touring round and I happened to see the notice board "men wanted", so in I went'. Or as another explained, 'I just ignored any notices, and went straight in everywhere and asked . . .'. Others remarked that no notices were up at the time—or none except 'no vacancies'.

Applying to employers on the 'off-chance'—the most favoured method if we leave aside the employment exchange, which is in rather a special category—includes doing so on foot, by bicycle, public transport or 'just rode round and pulled up at the factories'. One man rang up firms, guided by the trade directory; a second opted for the telephone because it was cheaper. One respondent, however, felt that the whole technique of unsolicited applications was bad; he had tried it in the past and come to regret it bitterly.

[1] i.e. because they answered the question in the strict sense, without elaborating on the subject.

Comments about requesting the T.U. for details of vacancies ranged from 'I used to go up there every day' to 'I didn't even know where the office was'. Some men ignored this source because they thought the unions would be flooded with applicants; others confirmed that they could not help at the time. One man did not seek out his T.U. because he did not like the way he was made redundant; two others respectively confessed to disillusionment and disgust and therefore by-passed theirs. We deal with this and related trade union topics more fully in Chapter 8.

Queried as to whether they had approached relatives or friends to tell them of jobs, replies again ranged from 'no, don't work with relatives' and 'yes, casually' to 'yes, I asked everybody'. One respondent revealed that his father and five brothers were in the car industry at the time, all except two brothers being made redundant. A few others likewise remarked that most of their friends were in the same boat. One man explained that 'we used to talk at the Labour, and tell one another if we heard of anything', a second felt that this kind of informal help was not as readily forthcoming as formerly, while a third made clear that he preferred 'not to get obligations'. Several respondents stressed that aid was forthcoming *spontaneously*—like one who countered that 'my father-in-law did it voluntarily', or a second who stated firmly that he did not ask anyone, though actually obtaining his first job through one of his juniors at RJ informing him of a vacancy. As previously pointed out, these cases are not included among the 50-odd per cent who themselves turned to this source for succour.

AGENCY BY MEANS OF WHICH WORK WAS OBTAINED AFTER REDUNDANCY

In Table 26 overleaf are set out the agencies through which work was actually secured following dismissal. The first column of the table relates to 'first interim' jobs; the second to *all* posts held directly after discharge—i.e. irrespective of whether they proved 'interim' only or not.[1] The figures in the last column refer to 'present' posts—i.e. those held on the day of interview—in so far as their occupants had not returned to RJ.

The 'knew foreman/boss', etc. category comprises all those who secured work through knowing someone in authority to offer it to them—in contradistinction to the 'relative/friend' rubric, which

[1] 'Interim jobs'—which form the subject matter of the next chapter—are those held after redundancy but no longer occupied by the date of interview. The 'first post-R job', therefore, is either the first interim job or, in the case of those who had no 'interim' employment, the present job.

TABLE 26

Method of Obtaining Work after Redundancy

	First interim jobs		*All first post-R jobs*		*Present jobs (not back at RJ)*	
	No.	%	No.	%	No.	%
Through employment exchange	50	15	66	15	25	12
Through trade union	5	2	12	3	13	6
Through newspaper advert	43	13	55	12	22	10
Knew foreman/boss. Or applied to/was offered job by a former employer*	34	11	54	12	40	19
Through relative/friend/'connection'	64	20	86	19	47	22
Applied on own initiative/'off-chance'	114	35	141	32	56	26
Miscellaneous	6	2	25	5	10	4
Not clear	7	2	8	2	2	1
	323	100	447	100	215	100

* Other than RJ.

covers those obtaining employment through knowing a useful third party. The 'knew foreman/boss' entry therefore includes some where the foreman or boss was, say, a relative. Very largely, however, this group is composed of those who either applied to, or were offered a post by, a former employer.

Obtaining work 'through relative/friend', etc., covers a fascinating miscellany, including being helped by 'one of the fellows at the football club', a friend in the Labour Party, a policeman outside RJ's gates, a girl friend intervening with her boss, and writing to a firm with whom the wife dealt through the shop. It also comprises widely varying degrees of help, ranging from a brother-in-law actually getting a man the job, a friend 'speaking' for him, a neighbour telling him of a particular opening, to a former workmate merely suggesting that he should apply 'at his place'. Where, however, a respondent stated in very general terms that he had heard that firm X were setting people on, this has been classed as 'applied on own initiative'. This last-named group, therefore, consists of all those who had no specific outside aid in securing employment.[1]

[1] The small handful of men who, in the course of their searches, saw a notice outside firms' premises inviting applications, or who took advantage of the recruiting vans which a few companies had stationed outside RJ, have, however, been included under 'own initiative/off-chance'. They are a marginal category, but akin to those others who picked up information—say, in pubs or newspapers—about the recruitment position in different firms.

The 'miscellaneous' item is made up of a few setting up on their own account or joining H.M. Forces and, as regards the first two columns of Table 26, those whose first job after dismissal was at RJ.[1] These, that is, are not included under 'knew boss', etc., RJ being a rather special boss to have been acquainted with in the circumstances. In addition, the group comprises some genuinely 'miscellaneous' cases, such as an ex-T.B. patient sent to Remploy by his doctor, a West Indian who got fixed up through the good offices of a municipal welfare officer, and a third who, in his own words, was 'down in the mouth', wrote a letter to a newspaper and was offered work by a sympathetic reader.

It will be seen from Table 26 that the most important single method of securing work was the time-honoured one of simply trying one's luck oneself. Nearly one-third of all first post-R jobs were obtained in this way. At the same time, there is an interesting difference here between the temporary (first interim) and the more permanent (present) jobs, 35 per cent of the former being accounted for by 'own initiative' as against 26 per cent of the latter. This is partly explained by the greater preponderance, among present posts, of the 'knew or returned to former boss' element. Apart from these two groups, there seem to be no striking differences in the methods leading to the more temporary and the more permanent appointments, respectively.

In looking at Table 26, a few further points might be kept in mind. First, item 'own initiative/off-chance' may include some where outside help was received, but where this was not made clear. On the other hand, this category has been given a special and limited definition for purposes of classification, in that some of the other methods also involve calls on personal initiative. This is not to refer to the obvious fact that all job-hunting does so; the term would become meaningless if used in this wide sense. But even leaving aside the initiative required in, say, actually securing the vacancy notified by an employment exchange, in so far as friends merely suggested possible openings, or to the extent that former employers were fairly impersonal entities who had to be approached afresh—as it were, cap in hand—the borderline between these other agencies and 'own initiative' becomes blurred. Less rigidly defined, therefore, the latter played a larger part than is indicated by Table 26 so that, on balance, the leading position of the own initiative/'off-chance' method need not be queried.

In the foregoing examples there is a genuine mixture of two methods; a related point is that some of the agencies may in them-

[1] Subject to one exception: i.e. one respondent got back to RJ via his trade union and is listed accordingly.

selves fulfil more than one role vis-à-vis the job-seeker. Thus the foreman who offered work on a building site may also have been a relative; the trade union official who acted as intermediary may have been a friend. Though for purposes of the table the categories were made mutually exclusive, in real life they are not necessarily so. Accordingly, some of the entries show the contribution to job-absorption only in the special sense in which these agencies have been defined. However, this is a minor qualification, and in any case does not apply to the more formal means of placement such as the employment exchange, the trade union and newspaper adverts. Thus where a man obtained his post via an exchange and this *happened* to be with a former employer, he has been listed as 'through employment exchange'.

The relation between place of residence and agency through which first post-R jobs[1] were secured is detailed in Table 27. The figures are of considerable interest, but will perhaps speak for themselves.

TABLE 27

Method through which First Post-R Job Obtained by Place of Residence at Time of Redundancy*

	Place of Residence		
	B'ham	*Up to 8 miles from B'ham†*	*Over 8 miles from B'ham*
Agency/method	%	%	%
Employment exchange	18	—	12
Trade union	3	3	3
Newspaper advert	14	11	8
Knew foreman/boss. Or applied to/was offered job by a former employer‡	11	17	16
Relative/friend/'connection'	18	23	17
Applied on own initiative/'off-chance'	28	37	39
Miscellaneous/not clear	8	9	5
	100	100	100
No. in category	299	35	90

* The table covers all 447 respondents, except the 23 whose place of residence (at R) was not clear.

† But excluding Birmingham. ‡ Other than RJ.

A breakdown of 'method through which' by place of birth reveals that of the 19 men stemming from India, Pakistan, West Indies or other abroad, none secured their first post-R boss via an employment

[1] All the following analyses relate to first post-R jobs only; totals are as for second column of Table 26.

exchange, and that less than 6 per cent of the Irish did so. For the 228 born in Birmingham, on the other hand, the proportion was nearly 17 per cent, while for the small band (16) of Welsh- and Scotsmen, it was as much as one-quarter.[1] Nearly 6 per cent of the Irish obtained their first placing through their trade union, although merely 3 per cent of the total sample did so. However, only about 8½ per cent of the Irish successfully followed up a newspaper advert, the corresponding proportion being 12 per cent for both the Brummies and Midlanders, 19 per cent for 'England, other than Midlands' and—somewhat surprisingly—21 per cent for the coloured/abroad group. As for the 'knew foreman/boss', etc. method, 10½ per cent of the Brummies got their first post in this way, 15 per cent of those born in the Midlands outside Birmingham, and about 19 per cent of others originating in Great Britain; however, only 5 per cent of the coloured/abroad and not quite 6 per cent of the Irish were in this rubric. The extent to which relatives, friends and 'connections' came to the rescue was between 19 and 21 per cent, except that only just under 10 per cent of 'England, other than Midlands' but nearly 26 per cent of the Irish were fixed up by this means. Finally, the percentage applying on the 'off-chance' ranged from 29 for those born in Birmingham and 31 for the Midlanders to 40 for the Irish and 42 for the coloured/abroad group.

TABLE 28

Method through which First Post-R Job Obtained by Age at Time of Redundancy

	Age				
	-30	31–40	41–50	51 & +	*Total*
Agency/method	%	%	%	%	%
Employment exchange	15	17	8	21	15
Trade union	3	1	3	4	3
Newspaper advert	12	13	12	13	12
Knew foreman/boss. Or applied to/was offered job by a former employer*	13	10	14	13	12
Relative/friend/'connection'	19	22	17	17	19
Applied on own initiative/'off-chance'	32	30	39	19	32
Miscellaneous/not clear	6	7	7	13	7
	100	100	100	100	100
No. in category	150	149	101	47	447

* Other than RJ.

[1] For those born in 'Midlands, other than Birmingham' the proportion was 14 per cent; for 'England, other than Midlands', 16 per cent.

Table 28 is concerned with the relation between age at date of dismissal and the agency through which first post-R jobs were procured. Perhaps the two items of greatest interest are the different proportions of the four categories respectively finding a vacancy through the employment exchange and 'off-chance' inquiries. It is also noteworthy that the chief point of contrast is between the over-fifties and their immediate juniors. We may add that the relatively large number of 41–50 year-olds obtaining work through 'off-chance' applications and the comparatively small percentage of over-fifties doing so is in line with the totals going after numerous jobs in the case of these two age-groups.[1]

TABLE 29

Method through which First Post-R Job Obtained by Skill at RJ

	Skilled	*Semi-skilled*	*Un-skilled*	*Total*
Agency/method	%	%	%	%
Employment exchange	11	16	13	15
Trade union	11	1	4	3
Newspaper advert	16	12	—	12
Knew foreman/boss. Or applied to/was offered job by a former employer*	11	13	4	12
Relative/friend/'connection'	20	19	21	19
Applied on own initiative/'off-chance'	28	32	42	32
Miscellaneous/not clear	3	7	16	7
	100	100	100	100
No. in category	62	361	24	447

* Other than RJ.

One of the main features of Table 29 is the relatively high proportion of skilled men placed in their first post-R niche by their trade union, *inter alia* reflecting the different extent to which these services are provided by the various unions. Another interesting fact is that none of the unskilled were fixed up as a result of following up a newspaper advert, while only one of the 24 respondents is in the 'knew foreman/boss', etc. rubric. However, the incidence of relatives and friends was fairly evenly spread, though the importance of 'off-chance' applications increased with decreasing skill.

As for the 50 respondents who had served a full apprenticeship, merely 8 per cent landed their first post after dismissal through the

[1] *Cf.* p. 78 *ante*.

employment exchange—as compared with nearly 16 per cent of the rest of the sample. Only two of the 50 men were placed via their trade union. The most striking difference between the 'apprentices' and the rest of their colleagues, however, was in the proportions securing employment through newspaper adverts: 28 per cent of the former acquired their first post-R job in this way, as against only just over 10 per cent of the remaining 397 respondents. In the case of the 50 men, press adverts tie with 'off-chance' applications for pride of place.

TABLE 30

Method through which First Post-R Job Obtained and Unemployment after Redundancy*

	Unemployment†				
	2 weeks and under	*Over 2 weeks–2 months*	*Over 2 months*	*Total*	*No. in category*
Agency/method	%	%	%	%	
Employment exchange	48	30	20	100‡	66
Trade union	33	8	50	100‡	12
Newspaper advert	51	29	18	100‡	55
Knew foreman/boss. Or applied to/was offered job by a former employer§	80	17	2	100‡	54
Relative/friend/'connection'	57	33	10	100	86
Applied on own initiative/'off-chance'	57	27	14	100‖	141

* The table covers all 447 respondents, except the 33 where method of obtaining first post-R job was miscellaneous/not clear.

† i.e. time elapsed between leaving RJ and commencing next job.

‡ The missing per cent = 1 respondent where unemployment after R was not clear.

§ Other than RJ.

‖ The missing 2 per cent = 3 respondents where unemployment after R was not clear.

Table 30 shows the length of unemployment after discharge of respondents fixed up through the various methods/agencies. These particular figures should be interpreted with considerable caution, as the causal connection between unemployment and 'method' is by no means a straightforward one. As was pointed out earlier, the majority of respondents tried more than one agency. Men may, for example, have set out to find a job off their own bat, but then, being unsuccessful, have turned to the employment exchange, so that it would be misleading to saddle the latter with the time taken to get settled. Similarly, the poor showing of those helped by their trade union should not be taken to reflect on the efficiency of the latter's employment services; it may well be due to some of those placed by these means—and the numbers are very small—holding out for an opening in a particular craft or industry, even though posts in these were then at a discount. What can, however, be clearly deduced from the table is that those who had an old boss to return to or knew an obliging foreman, etc., were at a distinct advantage in getting speedily absorbed after redundancy.

The question of the relative 'success' of the various job-finding agencies is of course an intriguing one, though it is extremely difficult to devise a satisfactory measure—i.e. one with all other variables held constant. If, for instance, we look at the matter taking as criterion the proportion of 'permanent' posts secured—posts, that is, still held at the time of interview some two or so years after the lay-off—some interesting differences are revealed. Thus while 28 per cent of all first post-R jobs proved 'permanent' in the sense just defined, the proportion was 58 per cent in the case of those obtained through trade unions, 37 per cent for the 'knew foreman/boss' group, and 26 per cent for those procured with the aid of relatives or friends. As regards placings via the employment exchange, 24 per cent were 'permanent'; for newspaper adverts the proportion was 22 per cent, while of those who, after dismissal, found their first niche through their own initiative/'off-chance', only 19 per cent had made no change by the date of interview. It must be emphasized, however, that the reasons for leaving first post-R bosses were, as we shall see, many and variegated; the foregoing data are therefore suggestive rather than conclusive.

THE EMPLOYMENT EXCHANGE

In view of the special position of the employment exchange in the context of job-finding, we devote this additional section to it, although we have of course already made numerous references to the subject in the preceding pages. Perhaps the two most important figures cited so far are that 73 per cent of the total sample registered at an exchange after redundancy, and that 15 per cent of all first post-R jobs were, in the final upshot, secured by this means.

The first question that arises is why 26 per cent of the sample—118 men—did not register at an exchange following dismissal.[1] Asked to account for this,[2] 82 of the 118 respondents answered to

[1] The number who registered at an employment exchange after redundancy i.e. was 325 (73 per cent), and the total who did not register was 118 (26 per cent). In the case of the remaining 4 men (1 per cent), the position was not clear.

[2] Q. 22 (*e*) of schedule.

the effect that it was not necessary, that they were not 'out' long, that they managed to obtain their own job or felt confident of doing so. Another ten explained that they had gone to the exchange, but did not register for reasons such as 'too much of a queue', 'I couldn't get near the damn place', and 'I queued but became disheartened, so I never got to the counter'. One respondent arrived on the spot at 9 a.m. 'and was still there at 12.30—still outside', while 'people who came out told me they couldn't do anything for them'. Two others, being informed directly that there were no vacancies, did not sign on. One man stated that he was not 'allowed' to register—he was given to understand he would not qualify for at least a week, while a second had gone up merely to ascertain whether he was permitted to search on his own. It is possible that others were likewise confused as to their rights and duties *à propos* of exchanges—in particular, their entitlement to register for employment and the quite separate matter of their eligibility for unemployment benefit.

Another 16 of the 118 non-registrants indicated that they did not think it was worth registering, preferred to make their own arrangements, or did not approve of the type of post available. Examples are 'I thought I could get a job off my own bat—I'd rather do that'; 'well, it's done through the union, and in any case I knew it wouldn't be much good'; and 'I don't like getting a job through the labour exchange—I don't think they ever get anything worth while', adding 'jobs registered there are what nobody else wants'. One respondent observed *inter alia* that 'the money they give you isn't enough to live on', though a second intimated that he would have registered, had he been at large longer. A third, who described himself as 'not a great lover of them', confessed later that his real motive for not reporting was that people were being placed out of town: 'I knew I hadn't a chance as a single man of not being sent out of Birmingham'. Another stated more generally 'I didn't want to have to take a job maybe I didn't like'. We may add that the remaining ten men did not sign on on miscellaneous grounds such as sickness, or not being interested in finding work immediately.

The foregoing is merely an approximate grouping of the men's replies—in particular, since the various motives for not registering at times tended to merge into one another. Also, some of those not reporting because they were not out of work long enough made adverse comments about exchanges subsequently, indicating that in any case they had little faith in them. Again, answers such as 'there was no need to register' contain an element of ex-*post* reasoning, in that the brevity of unemployment could not always have been foreseen when the decision not to sign on was made. Nevertheless, it is pertinent to look at the relation between time 'out' and not registering.

TABLE 31

Whether Registered at Employment Exchange after Redundancy by Length of Unemployment after R*

	Whether registered				
	Yes	*No*	*Not clear*	*Total*	*No. in category*
Unemployment†	%	%	%	%	
2 weeks and under	54	45	1	100	244
Over 2 weeks–1 month	93	6	1	100	70
Over 1–2 months	96	4	—	100	52
Over 2 months	100	—	—	100	68

* The table covers all 447 respondents, except the 13 whose length of unemployment was not clear.

† i.e. time elapsed between leaving RJ and commencing next job.

As shown by Table 31, the overwhelming majority of those not placed within a fortnight of dismissal signed on. Or putting it another way, of the 118 respondents who did not register, 110 were settled in a new post within two weeks of lay-off. All the same, as just intimated, the speed of absorption is not the entire explanation for over one-quarter of the sample not registering at an exchange after redundancy, especially since—as we saw in Chapter 3—considerable numbers of those with short unemployment experienced difficulty in securing work.

Let us now turn to the 325 respondents who did register 'at the Labour' after the discharges, with a view to throwing light on the fact that only 66 of these—one-fifth—actually obtained their first job in this way. All 325 men were asked 'Was the Exchange of help to you in your search for work?',[1] and their replies are summarized below.

TABLE 32

Whether Employment Exchange Was of Help in Search for Work

(All respondents who registered at an Employment Exchange after R)

	No.	%
Obtained first post-R job via exchange	66	20
Exchange helped or was/tried to be helpful	34	10
Exchange did not help	184	57
Yes and no/non-committal/miscellaneous	38	12
Not clear	3	1
	325	100

[1] Q. 22 (*b*) of schedule.

The figures in Table 32 are startling, for they reveal that well over one half of those registering at an exchange considered that they had not had any help from the latter in their quest for work. This proportion would seem to be particularly damning, since—as indicated—receiving help includes being the object merely of 'helpfulness'; in one sense, it could be argued that only the 66 men who actually secured their first boss through an exchange had concrete assistance in the matter. At the same time, this suggests that different individuals may have interpreted the question slightly differently, some taking the line 'no job, *ergo* no help', while others answered in terms of the efforts made by the exchange rather than on the basis solely of the end-product of these endeavours. However, since the latter themselves were frequently reported as deficient, too much cannot be made of this point.

In so far as the 66 men who obtained their first post-R job via the exchange are concerned, the enthusiasm with which they responded to the question varied. Thus there was 'yes definitely, they were more than helpful'. At the other extreme, there were half a dozen answering to the effect that the exchange came to the rescue eventually, while another handful went so far as to reply in the negative. These comprise one who—at the end of a nine-week hunt—merely saw a notice outside an exchange and 'went in and inquired and they gave me the ticket, like'. A second feeling he had not been succoured was one living in Birmingham at the date of dismissal, who finally got placed via an exchange out of town. Among other replies from the 66 was 'yes, they found me the job at . . ., but there was a big difference in pay between what the labour exchange said and what I actually drew', while a second revealed that though he did not really want the post in question, 'it was that or nothing'. One respondent, however, who had served an engineering apprenticeship, was handed a list of firms and was able to choose the one that appealed to him, while another—told by officials that he would have to accept the next vacancy—did so and found it to be the ideal one for him.

Taking the 34 men who felt that the exchange had aided them even though not actually procuring them their new niche, replies included 'yes, what jobs there were, we were told about' and 'yes, they put me on the disability list—I think it was a big help in my case'. A respondent approaching retirement age expressed appreciation *inter alia* of the efforts made to find him light work; a second was advised of other exchanges at which to inquire, and as a stranger to the area this was useful to him. A third had a selection of posts offered in the building trade, while a fourth commented that 'they put me on the right lines—they were very helpful in the commercial department'. One respondent was informed of a vacancy in Scotland, which he would have accepted but for the cost of the move, while another was sent 'to a decent few, but I hadn't got the experience they wanted'. Yet another was apprised of various openings, though others got there before him, while one stated that the exchange volunteered to help 'but they had no jobs to send us after'. Here, therefore, the 'ayes' are getting dangerously close to the 'noes', while the last few illustrations also suggest that such factors as the courtesy of officials and the men's general opinion of exchanges may, in certain instances, have affected their reply.

Turning now to the 184 respondents saying that the exchange had not helped, comments ranged from 'well no, not really' to 'they were hopeless' and 'no, a dead loss'. Many contented themselves with a simple 'no', many others answered in terms such as 'they couldn't do anything for anybody', though a sizeable number also countered 'none at all' or gave vent to some outspoken criticism. Among the more neutral type of reply was 'no, they hadn't got nothing in'; 'no, they told me to look myself first'; and 'they kept telling everybody "we've got next to nothing—find your own" '. One respondent disclosed that 'they just refer you back to your union'; rather ironically, others made clear that they had been recommended by their T.U. to try the employment exchange.

Among the not so neutral answers were, first, a number concentrating on the frustration experienced, like one who could not get near for three days as 'it was complete chaos'. A second, unemployed for five weeks, had called at the exchange every other day, but it was always 'nothing doing—it was standing in a queue for 1½–2 hours, then nothing'. A third observed 'they provide you with one, you go there, probably waste half a day, and find it's unsuitable'. We may add that among subsequent suggestions as to how some of the confusion could have been prevented was that the exchanges should have set up temporary booths and had more interviewers: 'We actually stood outside from 9 a.m. to 3 p.m.; by employing extra men, they could have given us that time for looking round . . .', as one put it. Others were that there should have been separate queues for the various grades of skill so as to avoid having to line up twice over, and that each person should have been accorded a proper and more personal interview.

Others among the 184 respondents commented more specifically on the reception they were given: 'They had a couldn't-care-less attitude' and 'they weren't very nice, and other chaps told me the same' are examples. A third remarked that the line adopted by officials seemed to be 'you're in the motor trade, you've had a good job, and now you can afford to be out for a bit'. Again, 'they gave everyone the impression that they didn't worry whether you got a job or not; they were quite willing to just pay you your Labour pay and then take no further notice of you'.

Yet others had a different complaint. Thus a respondent, who thought 'it was a waste of time going', mentioned that during the first week he had presented himself to the exchange two or three times—in vain; during his second week of unemployment he was given a few jobs, but they had already been filled when he applied for them. In all, at least 21 respondents were referred to posts which were no longer available—and the total may well be larger, since a question was not expressly put on the topic. We may add that one man tried to account for the situation by suggesting that firms notified vacancies to several exchanges, but only informed the one from which the successful applicant originated when they had been suited. Others, however, placed a less charitable interpretation on their fruitless journeys, regarding them as a device on the part of harassed officials for getting rid of importunate callers.

In all—and not counting those referred to no longer existing posts—fully 113 respondents, or nearly 35 per cent of those who registered at an exchange, simply found that the latter 'had nothing to offer' them.[1] Here it needs to be pointed out that the distinction between declaring that the exchange had no vacancies and reporting that it had unsuitable ones only—we deal with these presently—is somewhat blurred. For example, asked whether the exchange offered any jobs which they thought unsuitable,[2] several men stated that they had been advised of openings in the mines or as policemen, and on the strength of this replied in the affirmative. Others had mentioned the mines, etc. *en passant* earlier on during the interview; for them, however, this type of work was so much out of the question, that they considered that officials 'had nothing to offer'. Much may also have depended on the pressure on the particular exchange to which a respondent resorted. At the time, presumably all had vacancies for miners and certain other unpopular occupations; whether these were specifically brought to the notice of the men or whether it was left to the relevant poster to advertise itself must be regarded as partly accidental. Be that as it may, it is significant that more than one-third of those registering at an employment exchange after redundancy should have found that the latter had nothing—or nothing that was felt to be in any way suitable—to offer them.

Leaving aside those who were not referred to any, or only to 'dead', posts, there was another group who were notified of unsuitable ones: in all, 95 of the 325 respondents were advised of such openings,[3] though being in this category does not preclude also having been recommended some suitable ones. Asked why the jobs

[1] Q. 22 (*c*) of schedule. [2] Ibid. [3] Ibid.

in question were unsuitable,[1] in 49 cases this was because the wages were too low, in 47 because the work was unsuitable, in 21 because they involved too much daily travelling, and in 19 because they would have meant moving to another district. Others were considered as unsatisfactory on miscellaneous grounds such as entailing night shifts.

It will be realized that the above are frequencies, some of the 95 men rating a particular job as uncongenial under several heads, while others disapproved of a series of posts on one score only. As indicated, poor wages and 'work' factors were much the most common causes of complaint; further, the figures for 'too much daily travelling' and 'moving to another district' contain some duplication, in that a number of mining jobs would have involved one or the other of these alternatives and were described as not meeting the bill under both. Also, those reporting that they had been told of openings unsuitable on work grounds cover not only those adjudging these to be beneath their dignity or not in their line/trade,[2] but a few who commented that the vacancy concerned was too skilled or otherwise beyond them. Here, however, the line between the respondent classing the job as unsuitable and having himself been found as such by his would-be employer is a delicate one, and the extent to which such posts were included in the reckoning was probably not uniform.

The feeling that employment exchanges only have inferior vacancies to dispose of—both as regards type of work and remuneration—was certainly very widespread. In the opinion of one, 'the exchanges have not advanced with the times; they wait for management to send in for cheap labour, and they are prepared to handle these poor jobs'. Or to quote a second, echoed by many of his colleagues, 'if a job comes into the Labour, you can bet it's no good'. A third remarked that the exchanges only offered labouring jobs; further, that if one once accepted such a one and attempted to obtain a better one later, reclassification was refused—he had 'learnt that the hard way'. Again, a skilled respondent painted a contrast between securing employment through one's union with doing so via an exchange. If one applied to the former, one could rely on being placed in one's own trade and at T.U. rates; the unions got the first choice of any vacancies because the firms notified them before contacting the exchanges. In this man's view, the majority of car companies did not bother with the exchanges at all; they preferred dealing with the unions, because in that way they were making sure of the right man.

[1] Q. 22 (*d*) of schedule.

[2] Or, in isolated cases, unsuitable on health grounds.

Other comments in this context were that the exchanges did not know much about the posts to which they despatched their clients: they were not aware of the remuneration nor of the exact nature of the duties involved. One respondent saw notices at the exchange for a particular calling in which he had previously been engaged; however, the clerk would not send him to the factory 'because he had no proof of my being a . . .'. Others maintained that exchange officials did not appreciate the similarity between related types of work if of dissimilar nomenclature, and referred one rigidly to openings in one's stated occupation only. At the same time, there was the rather different complaint that they 'would offer you a list of jobs which you couldn't do because they were skilled and not in your trade', while in the opinion of one 'they didn't really consider what you were suitable for—they just offered jobs which, if you didn't like, you could lump it, and come back to them again'.

By way of putting the foregoing into perspective, it should be pointed out, first, that considerable numbers of those who received no help from the exchange in their search for work exonerated the latter subsequently.[1] In other words, they expressed the view that the exchanges did the best they could in the circumstances, bearing in mind the mass of men laid off simultaneously, the lack of vacancies in general or for the semi-skilled in particular, the absence of warning, and so on. To this one might add that in so far as the queues and the confusion are concerned, the blame cannot primarily be laid at the doors of the Ministry of Labour, for even at the highest level the latter had—as regards the bulk of the dismissals—only four days' notice, while the exchanges themselves had even less than this. The overcrowding was also greatly aggravated by the concentration of a large part of the redundant men into one Birmingham exchange. With a more reasonable period of notice, the latter might have been better equipped to cope with the onslaught.

Secondly, the 184 respondents who had no assistance from the employment exchange were of course out of work for varying spells: 74 of the 184, or two-fifths, in fact secured a new post within a fortnight of discharge. At the same time, the proportion stating that they were not succoured differed very little with length of unemployment, being between 55 and 58 per cent for those at large for two months or under, and actually slightly higher—i.e. 60 per cent—in the case of those without job for over two months.

A further important consideration is that the calls made on the exchange for help were by no means uniform; though the degree to which the latter was requested cannot be precisely deduced either from the fact that men registered or from their period of unemployment,

[1] i.e. in reply to Q. 23 of schedule.

that it varied is not in doubt. Thus a skilled sheet metal worker disclosed that he did not ask for aid as his union looked after that, a second made clear that he was not interested in finding a boss at once, while a third—'out' for only two days—commented later that he 'never gave 'em a chance'. Again, not all men registered immediately after redundancy, either because of the moneys received on leaving RJ or because, say, they were about to go on holiday. Others did not apply for work because they felt, as indicated, that the exchanges did not have the right type of post; others again, having been told initially to search on their own or discouraged by their experiences when registering, thereafter reduced the attention devoted to the exchange. Both the reputation which the latter enjoyed in the minds of the men as a result of earlier encounters or otherwise, and the lack of help it was able to provide when the men first signed on, affected the extent to which such help was sought subsequently.

Despite these and other factors, one cannot feel altogether confident that, even with more adequate notice, a sizeable proportion of the sample would have been positively aided by the exchanges in their endeavours. Thus there is the disturbing fact that in the case of more than one-third of those registering, there were no vacancies to which to refer them, while the total who were advised of either no, 'dead' or unsuitable openings only—but not, that is, of any potentially suitable ones—was almost certainly substantially larger. That considerable numbers were informed that they had a better chance of obtaining a job on their own must also rank as something in the nature of an indictment. Yet all the men had to, and did, find work. The vacancies i.e. were there, but those that were both acceptable and suitable[1] had evidently not been channelled through the exchanges. A relevant point here is that the Notification of Vacancies Orders had been revoked with effect from May 7, 1956.[2] Following this, the jobs notified to exchanges were—though doubtless also owing to the changed economic climate—significantly reduced. Nevertheless, as we saw in Chapter 1, the Midland Region remained one of full employment throughout 1956: why, in such a period, firms do not feel inclined voluntarily to intimate details of their requirements to the only national network of employment agency in existence is the obvious question which arises, though one which is beyond the scope of this inquiry to probe.

[1] As we saw in the Introduction (Table 3), the number of vacancies for adult men in the Midland Region on the books of the Ministry of Labour actually exceeded the wholly unemployed until December 1956. However, many of the vacancies were for skilled men, while most of those made redundant were semi-skilled.

[2] Notification of Vacancies (Revocation) Order, 1956 (S.I. 1956 No. 649).

As far as the men themselves are concerned, it is clear that more would have signed on, if the suddenness and scale of the 1956 operation had not prevented the Ministry of Labour from sending in teams of clerks to register them on RJ's premises—as is the policy of the Ministry in such contingencies. Further, almost certainly more respondents would have reported to an exchange, if they had worked off their notice in the usual manner; technically, the men were not unemployed during the first week following the lay-off. In other words, many no doubt postponed registration in the knowledge that they would not immediately qualify for benefit; the additional holiday money received and the modest size of the unemployment benefit itself worked in the same direction. All this, however, does not alter the fact that these men felt no incentive to register for purposes of finding a job.

Generally speaking, the question of the worker's faith in the employment exchange is obscured by the latter's performing the two functions of employment agency—intended as its primary one—and the paying out of unemployment benefit. The last-named is meant to be an ancillary service merely, performed on behalf of the Ministry of Pensions and National Insurance, but it remains an interesting speculation how many of the 447 respondents would have registered if the exchange were solely a job-finding agency. It can, however, be said that the statement of the Ministry of Labour—that 'it seems that over the years the acceptance of the Employment Exchange as being merely a "dole paying bureau" has disappeared'[1]—is not borne out by the present investigation.

In all probability, were it not for their very 'dole-paying' activities, many more in the present sample would have ignored the exchanges following dismissal, though as it was, the men did not simply by-pass this source for purposes of securing an opening. Thus a considerable number, when asked earlier during the interview how they had actually set about finding work, mentioned spontaneously that they had trekked 'to the Labour', and it is clear that many who wanted help from that direction could not be given it after the redundancy of 1956. Nor can this—exceptions apart—be attributed to sights having been set too high; as we shall see in Chapter 5, the first post held after discharge was in many instances a great 'come-down'. All in all, then, one cannot really quarrel with the respondent who observed that the exchanges 'were not ready for the situation—they just had neither the jobs nor the organization'. And while the last-named would no doubt have been improved with more ample notice of the impending lay-off on the part of the managements concerned, it is

[1] *Annual Report of the Ministry of Labour and National Service for 1956*, Cmnd. 242 (H.M.S.O. 1957), p. 134.

difficult to feel convinced that matters would have been very different in the crucial sphere of jobs. If the *raison d'être* of a national system of employment exchanges is its potential efficiency in bringing together those offering and those seeking work, then the fact that only 15 per cent of the sample, or 20 per cent of those registering at exchanges, obtained employment by this means seems rather less than adequate.

Chapter 5

INTERIM EMPLOYMENT

In this chapter we are concerned with the 'interim job' period—primarily, that is, the number, duration and nature of the posts held in the interval between redundancy and the more or less permanent employment secured by the time of interview.

NUMBER OF INTERIM JOBS

TABLE 33

Number of Interim Jobs Held before Joining Present Employer

	No.	%
None	124	28
1 interim job	203	46
2 interim jobs	81	18
3 interim jobs	28	6
4 or more interim jobs	9	2
Miscellaneous/not clear*	2	—
	447	100

* Includes 1 'not clear' and 1 who retired at end-1956, having had one job since dismissal. The interim jobs of those *unemployed* on day of interview have, however, been counted, as unemployment is unlikely to have affected the number of these posts.

The definition of 'interim job' is, quite simply, any post occupied since dismissal other than the present, and other than purely casual employment. By 'present job' we mean that held on the date of interview some 2 to 2½ years after discharge; as we shall see subsequently, these present jobs can lay some claim to representing the final adjustment of the sample to the events of 1956. A few remarks may, however, be apposite regarding the distinction between interim and casual employment—though the problem cases were a small, if awkward, minority.

In brief, the principle adopted has been to treat all work accepted after lay-off as 'interim', unless it was of a kind—say, window-cleaning at week-ends or odd building repairs—that did not provide its recipient with something at least approaching a living wage. In each doubtful case the decision was made in the light of factors such as the number of hours per week devoted to the job, the time of day during which it was performed, whether it was for one or for a collection of employers, the duration of the post, and weekly income. Thus a farm job lasting one month at £1 a week was classed as casual, but one for a like period at £6 weekly as interim. We may add that the part-time assignments which a few men had prior to, and continued after, redundancy—we deal with these in Chapter 7—have not been reckoned as 'interim'.

An important point in this context is that men anyhow tended to view their first post-R job differently, some accepting anything rather than be unemployed, while others were determined—and able—to hold out for something that was potentially, at any rate, a new permanent niche. It is for this reason that the £6-a-week farm job, for example, was classed as interim: though definitely taken on as a stop-gap only, it is in several respects in the same category as the labouring vacancies accepted by others until a more suitable one would come along. It follows that where there were no other grounds for doing so, work was not regarded as casual solely because it was relinquished within a short period. Thus one man abandoned his job as cement works labourer after a few hours because it was too hard; another, after three days, took leave of his master butcher because he could not get on with him and was generally dissatisfied. These posts were embarked upon as would-be regular employment, and though they proved otherwise, this did not render them 'casual'.

The relation between number of interim jobs and unemployment after redundancy is shown in Table 34.

TABLE 34

Number of Interim Jobs of Respondents with Varying Lengths of Unemployment after Redundancy*

	No. of Interim Jobs					
	None	*One*	*Two*	*Three +*	*Total*	*No. in category*
Unemployment†	%	%	%	%	%	
2 weeks and under	25	48	19	8	100	244
Over 2 weeks–1 month	24	42	23	11	100	70
Over 1–2 months	21	46	25	8	100	52
Over 2–3 months	33	51	7	7	100‡	43
Over 3 months	56	28	12	4	100	25

* The table covers all 447 respondents, except the 13 whose length of unemployment was not clear.

† i.e. time elapsed between leaving RJ and commencing next job.

‡ The missing 2 per cent = 1 respondent where number of interim jobs was not clear.

As indicated, of the 314 persons fixed up within a month of discharge, about one-quarter were still in the same post when interviewed—i.e. they had no 'interim boss'. However, 28 per cent of these 314 men had had at least two jobs in the interval. By contrast, those with relatively long spells out of work had made fewer changes: of the 68 respondents at large for more than two months, 41 per cent had no interim post, while the corresponding proportion for those 'out' in excess of three months is, as shown, 56 per cent. This is not due to those unemployed for this length having no opportunity, as it were, to switch. As we saw in Chapter 3, only three individuals in the sample were without work for over 6 months, so that there was plenty of time for the overwhelming majority to change firms by the date of interview. To some extent, therefore, those with longer periods of unemployment after dismissal had some compensation in the greater stability of the opening they then secured, though the main key to the preceding figures is provided, here again, by the age factor.

TABLE 35

Number of Interim Jobs of Respondents in Different Age Groups

	*Age**				
	-30	31–40	41–50	51 *and*+	*Total*
Number of Interim Jobs	%	%	%	%	%
None	19	25	36	47	28
One	46	49	44	34	46
Two	20	19	15	17	18
Three or more	15	6	5	—	8
Miscellaneous/not clear	—	1	—	2	—
	100	100	100	100	100
No. in category	150	149	101	47	447

* As on day of respondent's redundancy.

As will be seen from Table 35, there was a definite link between youthfulness and job-changing: only 19 per cent of those 30 years and below were still with their first post-R firm when interviewed; for those aged above 50, on the other hand, the proportion was 47 per cent, while of the 10 over-sixties in the sample, 8 had no interim employer. Similarly, though 15 per cent of the 30-and-unders had three or more interim bosses, none of the over-fifties could boast that distinction. Clearly, a wide variety of factors had a bearing on the total of interim jobs held; the initiative for their termination came sometimes from the side of management, though frequently from that of the men. On the whole, however, Table 35 contains no particular surprises.

As for skill—using that in force at RJ prior to discharge—the proportion having no and one interim post, respectively, was practically identical for the skilled and the semi-skilled. However, since the former were older, on the average, than the latter, it would appear that, age for age, the skilled were less ready to remain in their first and second post-R jobs. As regards frequent changes, only 3 per cent of the skilled had three or more interim employers, as compared with 9 per cent of the semi-skilled; as rapid labour turnover is not normally associated with skilled status, no doubt skill and age were here pulling in the same direction. This is indeed borne out by the record of the 50 respondents who had completed an apprenticeship. As mentioned earlier, this group had a much younger average age than those graded skilled by RJ, 46 per cent being 30 years and under at the time of redundancy. What is significant, however, is that a mere 18 per cent stayed with their first post-R boss—i.e. about the same proportion as of *all* those aged 30 years and below. Similarly, despite their greater youth, only 4 per cent of the 'apprentices' had three or more interim jobs—as against 9 per cent for the rest of the sample.

Turning to the unskilled, these were actually the most stable of the three categories, 46 per cent making no move from their first post as compared with 27 per cent of both the skilled and semi-skilled, while the proportion with two or more interim jobs was likewise smaller than for the other two groups. However, as previously pointed out, the unskilled had the highest average age of the three, and they also contain a much larger proportion of coloured respondents. The effect of 'unskill' on job-changing is here therefore blurred by these two factors.

DURATION OF INTERIM JOBS

Table 36 sets out the duration of interim jobs, with the exception of the fourth and any subsequent ones. As will be seen, 13 per cent of those with interim employment remained in their first post for not more than three weeks. Thirty-seven per cent had quit within three months, though almost as big a proportion stayed put—whether of choice or necessity—for upwards of half a year. If we relate these figures to the sample as a whole—i.e. including those who, when interviewed, were still with the firm they had joined after lay-off—the proportion abandoning their first boss within three weeks was only 9 per cent, while those leaving within three months was 27 per cent. On the same basis, 54 per cent of the sample stuck to their first employer for over 6 months and 32 per cent in excess of a year.

TABLE 36

Duration of Interim Jobs

(All respondents with 1 or more interim jobs)

	First interim job		*Second interim job*		*Third interim job*		*Total*	
	No.	*%*	*No.*	*%*	*No.*	*%*	*No.*	*%*
1 week or under	14	13	4	4	1	8	19	10
Over 1–3 weeks	27		1		2		30	
Over 3 weeks–3 months	79	24	36	31	15	40	130	27
Over 3–6 months	82	25	39	33	7	19	128	27
Over 6–12 months	97	30	24	20	7	19	128	27
Over 12 months	19	6	11	9	1	3	31	6
Miscellaneous/not clear	5	2	3	3	4	11	12	3
	323	100	118	100	37	100	478	100

TABLE 37

Duration of First Interim Job of Respondents with Varying Lengths of Unemployment after Redundancy

(All respondents with 1 or more interim jobs)*

	Time in First Interim Job					
	3 weeks and under	*Over 3 weeks–3 months*	*Over 3 –6 months*	*Over 6 months*	*Total*	*No. in category*
Unemployment†	%	%	%	%	%	
2 weeks and under	15	19	26	40	100	182
Over 2 weeks–1 month	13	26	23	34	100‡	53
Over 1–2 months	7	34	32	27	100	41
Over 2 months	5	38	25	32	100	40

* i.e. 323 men, but excluding 7 where length of unemployment after redundancy was not clear.

† i.e. time elapsed between leaving RJ and commencing next job.

‡ The missing 4 per cent = 2 respondents where duration of first interim job was not clear.

Time spent in first interim jobs relative to unemployment after lay-off is detailed in Table 37. What emerges is that finding a niche quickly was not an entirely unmixed blessing; those who did so within a fortnight contain the highest proportion staying put for no more than three weeks, while of the 14 respondents whose first post-R venture lasted seven days or less, all except two had embarked on this within a fortnight of discharge. However, if we treat as one those whose first post was of not above three months' duration, the trend is reversed: the longer the initial unemployment, the bigger the percentage with a first job of three months or under. Similarly, those with the shortest time 'out' contain the largest proportion remaining with their first firm for over half a year. If, here again, we take the sample as a whole, the percentages with brief first post-R jobs are of course smaller than those in Table 37. By definition, the 124 respondents without interim employment were faithful to their first boss for considerable periods. Nonetheless, the figures demonstrate that getting fixed up immediately or very soon after dismissal was not invariably tantamount to a painless transition from RJ. Even if we base ourselves on the total 1 in 10 sample, exactly one-quarter of the 244 men who secured work within a fortnight of redundancy had given or received their notice again within three months of commencing duties.

LOCATION

Having dealt, in Chapter 4, with the areas in which respondents tried to get placed after discharge, we now come to the actual location of these posts. Table 38 sets out the relevant particulars in respect of first, second and third interim jobs, while the last column shows where *all* 447 men found their first foothold following lay-off.

TABLE 38

Location of Interim Jobs and All First Post-R Jobs

	First interim job	*Second interim job*	*Third interim job*	*All first post-R jobs*
	%	%	%	%
Birmingham*	60	59	62	62
Up to 8 miles from Birmingham†	7	8	11	8
Over 8–15 miles from Birmingham	21	20	16	20
Over 15 miles from Birmingham but in Midlands‡	8	9	8	7
Beyond Midlands‡	3	4	3	2
Miscellaneous/not clear	1	—	—	1
	100	100	100	100
No. in category	323	118	37	447

* County Borough of Birmingham, plus those parts of Rednal and Rubery outside the C.B. boundaries.

† But excluding Birmingham.

‡ The definition of 'Midlands' is co-terminous with that of the Ministry of Labour's (pre-1962) Midland and North Midland Regions.

As indicated, 62 per cent of all first post-R jobs were situated in Birmingham, which means that of those who had searched in the city—either exclusively or in conjunction with efforts elsewhere—approximately four-fifths obtained employment there. Of those who had looked—again either exclusively or otherwise—in the Midlands *outside* Birmingham, about two-thirds secured or accepted work there, but of the 38 respondents trying their hand beyond the Midlands, less than three-tenths had their first post in such regions. Speaking very crudely, therefore—i.e. ignoring the question of differential effort, as well as the element of choice which enabled at any rate some of the men to pick as between openings in different localities—Birmingham was the best place in which to have sought a haven. Some support for this is also to be found in the fact that of the 279 respondents whose first post-R job was in Birmingham—and of whom 199 had confined their inquiries to the city—58 per cent were placed within a fortnight of discharge; the corresponding proportion for the rest of the sample was only 49 per cent.

TABLE 39

Location of First Post-R Job by Place of Residence at Time of Redundancy*

	Place of Residence		
	Birmingham	*Up to 8 miles from B'ham†*	*Over 8 miles from B'ham*
Location of first post-R job	%	%	%
Birmingham	80	52	8
Up to 8 miles from Birmingham†	3	34	13
Over 8–15 miles from Birmingham	8	11	61
Over 15 miles from Birmingham but in Midlands	5	—	15
Beyond Midlands	3	—	1
Miscellaneous/not clear	1	3	2
	100	100	100
No. in category	299	35	90

* The table covers all 447 respondents, except the 23 whose place of residence (at R) was not clear. The definition of Birmingham and Midlands is as for Table 38.

† But excluding Birmingham.

Table 39 deals with the location of the first post after redundancy relative to that of the men's home; it confirms that the latter made a significant difference to the whereabouts of the former. Though, common sense apart, this was to be expected in the light of the figures on place of residence and the region in which inquiries were conducted in the first place,[1] quite a number of respondents—in fact, approximately 38 per cent—searched in more than one area,[2] but no doubt opted for the job nearest their home whenever they were in the position to do so. Thus of the 299 individuals living in Birmingham at the time of dismissal, 170 had tried for work there exclusively while 22 did not look there at all: of the remaining 107 men who had a go both in Birmingham and outside, 68 secured their first post-R niche in the city.

As pointed out in Chapter 4, 46 of the 447 respondents pursued their quest in localities more than 25 miles from their place of residence—what we have described as beyond daily travelling distance. Of these 46, only 15 had their first job in such areas, 4 of the 15 being coloured. Twenty of the 46, by contrast, landed with a Birmingham employer.

The 15 who left home in order to take up their first post include 11 who went beyond the Midlands, and 4 others respectively joining firms in Corby, Stoke, Nottingham and Chesterfield. Among the 11 venturing outside the Midlands were two placed with a Gloucester concern by the local employment exchange, and one engaged by the representative of a well-known Dagenham company, who had come to Birmingham for recruitment purposes. A Pakistani was told by a friend that he could get him into a Sheffield steel mill; a Jamaican likewise ended up as a labourer in that city. An Irishman was called home as it happened to be the busy season on his father's farm. Another in the group, unable to get suited locally, became a British Railways porter in London, three men in all having a first post-R employer in the metropolis.[3]

INDUSTRY

Table 40 is concerned with the industry in which respondents obtained employment after redundancy, the first three columns again dealing with those who had a first, second and third interim job, while the last shows the industrial fate of the whole sample following dismissal. The grouping adopted is in accordance with the Standard Industrial Classification:[4] while care has been taken to allocate

[1] See Table 23 *ante*.

[2] 'Area' is here used in the special sense of being either 'Birmingham', 'Midlands, outside Birmingham' or 'beyond Midlands'.

[3] The remaining two jobs were in Yarmouth (part-time) and Eire.

[4] Central Statistical Office, *Standard Industrial Classification* (H.M.S.O., 1958).

TABLE 40

Industry Group of Interim Jobs and All First Post-R Jobs

	First interim job	*Second interim job*	*Third interim job*	*All first post-R jobs*
	%	%	%	%
Manufacture of motor vehicles and cycles (including parts and accessories)*	10	15	22	13
Engineering;† metal goods; metal manufacture	37	39	54	35
All other manufacturing industries	10	14	3	11
Mining; agriculture	2	1	3	2
Construction	15	10	5	13
Transport and communications	11	3	3	10
Distribution	6	9	5	6
Miscellaneous‡	7	7	5	9
Not clear	2	2	—	1
	100	100	100	100
No. in category	323	118	37	447

* Consists only of first two Minimum List headings of Order VIII (Vehicles) of the Standard Industrial Classification; manufacture of aircraft and locomotives, e.g., have been classed as engineering. Those engaged by firms making cars plus other engineering products have, however, been allocated to 'vehicles'.

† All branches other than motor vehicles and cycles.

‡ Includes gas, electricity and water; financial, professional and miscellaneous services; public administration (in the S.I.C. sense) and defence.

each item to its appropriate category, perfection is not claimed for the result.[1]

It will be seen that 13 per cent of the sample—60 individuals—managed to find their first niche in the very industry from which

[1] Though reference books such as the *Stock Exchange Year Book* and *Classified Trades Directory* were consulted, it was not considered worth while to research extensively into the precise nature, processes, etc., of employers' activities. A firm of cabinet makers e.g. was classed as 'furniture manufacture'—with a prayer that it was not steel cabinets which were being produced. Other problem cases were frequently settled in the light of the men's occupation. For instance, 'minerals' was treated as 'distribution' and not as 'other manufacturing', since the individual's occupation was that of driver-salesman. An enterprise of heating engineers was assigned to 'engineering', there being no mention of the installation of equipment; a concern of consulting heating engineers, on the other hand, where respondent travelled constantly, was assumed to be primarily installing equipment and therefore, in accordance with S.I.C. rules, classed as 'construction'. These examples are being quoted as illustrative of a problem likely to be met with in many unofficial—and no doubt also some official—inquiries.

they had been laid off,[1] though many of them did so only after varying periods of unemployment. Further, the proportion in vehicles and cycles rose steadily as between first, second and third interims, although the numbers in the last-named category are of course small. It might here be pointed out that those respondents who had RJ as employer in this period are included in the figures. For example, of the 60 first post-R jobs in 'manufacture of motor vehicles and cycles', 16 were at RJ, 15 of the men still being there at the time of interview.

Another interesting feature of Table 40 is that construction and transport between them absorbed 23 per cent of the sample after redundancy, though as the latter receded into the background, these industries lost some of their attraction again. A mere 7 men went into mining and agriculture; of these, 4—or less than 1 per cent of the sample—joined the National Coal Board. We may add that of the 10 per cent—43 respondents—whose first post was in transport and communications, only 9 persons were recruits to British Railways, 19 being engaged by municipal and other public utility transport organizations, 5 by the G.P.O., and 10 by private, etc. concerns. What emerges, therefore, is that the special arrangements announced in Parliament immediately following the dismissals—for the (then) British Transport Commission and the National Coal Board to accelerate their rate of labour intake, so as to help in the placement of the redundant men[2]—were not particularly popular with the latter.

Of the 11 per cent—48 respondents—whose first post was in 'other manufacturing industries', the biggest single contingent, i.e. 17 individuals, had found a niche in food and drink. Of these 17, 13 had joined a well-known Birmingham firm of chocolate makers—the same number as had turned to the National Coal Board and British Railways combined. Among other industries represented under 'other manufacturing' are furniture, bricks and cement, plastics, and paper and printing.

Of the 29 men—6 per cent of the sample—whose first refuge was in distribution, 13 had joined grocery or other food and drink establishments, both wholesale and retail. Others in this group had become employed by firms of timber merchants, coal merchants, selling hardware, books, and so on. The 40 respondents (9 per cent) making up the 'miscellaneous' item in Table 40—we again refer to

[1] Another 9 of the 447 first post-R jobs fell under 'motor repairers, distributors and garages'—included under 'miscellaneous' in Table 40. In the case of accessory firms, allocation as between the first two items of the table is, again, not foolproof.

[2] See p. 23 *ante*.

the last column—include *inter alia* 7 in gas, electricity and water; 4 in the hospital, etc. service; 4 in catering, etc.; and one each in insurance, the police, the fire service and H.M. Forces.

There were some interesting differences in the length of post-R unemployment as between respondents absorbed by the various industry groups. Thus the proportion out of work for over two months was 7 per cent of those whose first job was in construction, 7 per cent likewise of those going into distribution, 11 per cent of the men absorbed in engineering and metals, 16 per cent of those joining transport and communications, 17 per cent in the case of 'all other manufacturing industries', and 33 per cent of respondents whose first niche was in motor vehicles and cycles. Similarly, the percentage back at work within a fortnight of lay-off ranged from 66 for those whose first boss was in distribution, 62 for engineering and metals, 59 for construction, 58 for transport and communications, to 42 for motor vehicles, etc., and not quite 38 per cent for 'other manufacturing'.

The reason for the relatively poor showing of those sticking to motor vehicles and cycles is not surprising. That one-third of this group was unemployed for over two months—the proportion is 15 per cent for the sample as a whole—is, however, to a considerable extent due to the fact that it includes those who actually had RJ as their first post-R employer, some of whom were at large for long spells prior to their return there. It should also be added that being absorbed by a given industry does not of course mean that the individual concerned devoted all his energies to securing work in it. Some men, as we saw, were prepared to accept any kind of opening irrespective of industry and occupation; others were more particular and restricted their searches to defined sectors of the labour market, while yet others tried in their own line first but then progressively became less choosey. Nevertheless, it is unlikely that the variations found are purely accidental: the speed of absorption in the case of those turning to the building industry, for instance, is explicable simply by the discharges occurring at the height of the summer.

TIME PREVIOUSLY WORKED FOR FIRM

Of the 323 first interim jobs, 34 or 10½ per cent were with a firm for which the respondent had already worked before redundancy. In 10 cases the period so spent was not more than twelve months; in 15 instances it was over one but not above four years, while 9 respondents returned to a boss by whom they had previously been engaged for upwards of four years. Of the 118 second interim jobs, only six were with a pre-R employer, while of the 37 third interims, merely one was.[1] The few men who had interim employment at RJ are excluded from these figures.

As far as the whole sample is concerned, 56 of the 447 respondents —12½ per cent—had a first post-R job with a former employer. Twenty-two of these 56 men, or 39 per cent, were still with him at the date of interview although, as we have seen, the proportion of all first post-R jobs proving 'permanent' was only 28 per cent. Not surprisingly also, the proportion of old bosses providing a new permanent home increased with length of previous service. Thus the 56 individuals in question comprise 34 who had spent up to but not above four years with the company prior to lay-off; of these, almost three-quarters had left again by the second half of 1958. But of the 22 respondents who, after dismissal, returned to a pre-R employer of more than four years' standing, 59 per cent were still on his payroll at the time of interview.

OCCUPATION

Table 41 sets out the occupation of the first job held after redundancy, though the 124 respondents who had no interim employment are excluded from the figures in this instance.

TABLE 41

Occupation of First Interim Job*

(All respondents with 1 or more interim jobs)

	No.	%
Workers in metal, engineering and allied trades†	147	46
Other occupations in productive processes	19	6
Construction occupations‡	20	6
Transport occupations‡	30	9
Warehousemen, storekeepers, packers	9	3
Labourers, etc.	50	15
Shop assistants, salesmen, roundsmen§	12	4
Miscellaneous	36	11
	323	100

* At the time of compiling this table, no official standard occupational classification was in use. Accordingly, both Census and Ministry of Labour practice/data were drawn upon, though various modifications have been made.

† Including vehicle building occupations, but excluding labourers.

‡ Other than labourers.

§ The figure includes 1 manager in a firm of butchers.

[1] In addition, one second interim was with the same firm as the first interim job—with a period of 6 months' unemployment in between. One third interim post was likewise with a 'first interim' employer. The position regarding fourth and subsequent interim jobs is not known, but the numbers involved are very small.

As might have been anticipated, the proportion in metal, engineering and allied trades was substantially smaller than before the discharges, when well over four-fifths of the sample were in this category. By contrast, 9 per cent of all first interim jobs were in transport occupations, though only 3 per cent were drivers, etc. prior to dismissal. It may also be noted that while—as indicated in Table 40—15 per cent of all first interims were in construction industrially speaking, only 6 per cent were personally employed in 'construction' occupations.

The 36 men in the miscellaneous group *inter alia* comprise four farm workers/gardeners, three miners or trainee miners, six other trainees, a clerk, a postman, a male nurse in an old people's home, a barman and two self-employed window cleaners. In all, three respondents had a first interim job working on their own account, the third—to whose fate we refer again later—entering the shoe repairing business.

One interesting feature of Table 41 is that just over 15 per cent of all first interim posts were in labouring, etc. occupations—including building and foundry labourers, a few garage hands/assistants, porters, a night watchman and so on. This 15 per cent is not strictly comparable with the 5 per cent of the 1 in 10 sample graded as unskilled by RJ. As previously mentioned, the skill level implicit in semi-skilled status in the car world may be quite low; for example, a bus cleaner—treated as 'labourer, etc.' for purposes of Table 41—may have been on not dissimilar tasks before dismissal, though then rated semi-skilled.[1] Nevertheless, there is little doubt that the 'labourer' element increased after redundancy. If, for instance, we ignore the firms' classification, it is significant that a mere 18 of the 447 respondents, or 4 per cent, described their pre-R occupation as labourer, while of the 323 individuals concerned, 10 per cent so designated their first interim job.

In the case of the 124 men without interim employment—i.e. whose post at the date of interview was that first taken after lay-off—no question was asked as to their occupation directly after discharge, and it cannot be assumed that this was necessarily the same as that in which they were engaged when interviewed. While one or two volunteered the information that they had graduated to their present calling from some form of unskilled work, it is probable that the 124 respondents as a group contain fewer, relatively, who were labourers immediately after dismissal than the 323 men covered by Table 41. As far as the whole sample is concerned, therefore, the proportion

[1] Similarly, one of the firms in the sample employed a category of *semi-skilled* labourer, though for purposes of Table 41 any respondent describing himself as 'labourer' has been automatically so recorded.

landing in labouring occupations as a result of the redundancy is likely to have been less than 15 per cent, though it seems reasonable to suggest that it was still well above the proportion in such occupations at RJ.

As for the 50 individuals themselves whose first interim job was as labourer or similar, 4 had been rated skilled by RJ, 38 as semi-skilled and 8 as unskilled. Taking as our base the total in these three categories with interim employment,[1] this means that 9 per cent of the skilled, 14 per cent of the semi-skilled, and nearly 62 per cent of the unskilled took a labouring etc. post after dismissal.[2] As regards age, 24 per cent of the over-fifties[3] had a first interim job as labourer, etc.; for each of the younger age groups[3] the proportions were smaller, being practically identical at 15 or 14 per cent.

As seen by themselves, the 50 'labourers' found it distinctly harder to secure employment after redundancy than the rest of the sample. Thus 86 per cent stated that they had had trouble, as compared with 58 per cent taking the 447 respondents as a whole, while just over half of the 50 considered things to have been *very* difficult, as against about one-third of the total sample. Conversely, only 12 per cent of the 50 men reported it to have been easy to obtain a vacancy at the time; the corresponding proportion for the whole sample was 38 per cent.

As for actual length of unemployment, 44 per cent of the 50 labourers commenced work within two weeks of lay-off; as we saw earlier, 54 per cent of all 447 respondents did so, though the difference might have been expected to be larger in the light of the replies to the 'difficulty' question, just quoted. What must at first seem even more odd is that only 10 per cent of the labourers were 'out' for more than two months, although 15 per cent of the whole sample were in this position. The explanation may well be that, in recording the difficulty encountered, men took into account the type of post purchased, as it were, with their exertions. A month's search leading to a labouring job merely was possibly regarded as indicative of greater trouble than, say, a longer spell on the dole resulting in a more congenial end-product.

As might have been anticipated, the 50 labouring etc. posts were of shorter duration than the remaining 273 first interims; 10 per cent of the former lasted for not more than one week, as compared with 3 per cent of the latter. Similarly, 46 per cent of the labouring jobs

[1] The number of skilled, semi-skilled and unskilled (skill = as per RJ) with interim employment was 45, 265 and 13, respectively.

[2] As previously pointed out, however, 'unskilled' (RJ) and 'labourer, etc.' (Table 41) are not identical.

[3] With interim employment.

had been terminated or abandoned within three months of their inception, as against not quite 36 per cent of other first interim employment. Twenty-eight per cent of the labourers nevertheless stayed with their boss for over half a year, although 37 per cent of their colleagues did so.

HOURS OF WORK

TABLE 42

Net Average Weekly Hours Worked before, and in First Interim Job after, Redundancy

	At RJ: prior to R		*After R*
	July–Dec. 1955	*Jan.–June* 1956	*First interim job*
	%	%	%
35 hours and under	1	24	1
Over 35–40 hours	4	10	4
Over 40–45 hours	51	42	35
Over 45–50 hours	24	13	27
Over 50–55 hours	12	7	14
Over 55–60 hours	4	} 3	11
Over 60 hours	1		6
Miscellaneous/not clear	3	1	2
	100	100	100
No. in category	417*	447	313†

* The remaining 30 men were not yet at RJ during the second half of 1955.

† Ten respondents, whose first interim job lasted *less* than one week, have been excluded.

The last column of Table 42 shows the hours worked after dismissal by those respondents who had interim employment; so as to place them in perspective, those put in at RJ prior to lay-off are set out alongside. The reason for giving two series of figures for the pre-R period is, quite simply, that those for the six months preceding redundancy are, in isolation, somewhat misleading. As previously mentioned, the mid-1956 sackings in the car industry were sudden primarily in their manner of announcement and implementation; there was a considerable slackening of activity already in the preceding half-year, with inevitable repercussions on working schedules and pay-packets. In view of this, all data relating to shifts, hours and earnings at RJ were obtained both in respect of the half year immediately before the dismissals—broadly speaking, that is, January–June 1956 when the firms were already in difficulties—and for the last six months of 1955, when they still had full order books.

All the percentages in Table 42 relate to net hours, i.e. excluding the lunch-break. They are in each case an *average* for the particular period, as reported by the men; where hours differed for days and nights, they represent a weighted average.[1] It should perhaps be pointed out that the extent of 'averaging' on the part of respondents —i.e. the degree to which minor fluctuations were included in the reckoning—is bound to have varied somewhat. However, this need not be regarded as too serious a matter, since all replies have anyhow been bracketed in ranges—a course which makes some allowance also for the tricks of memory to which hours and earnings data must be regarded as particularly susceptible. We may add that in so far as first interim jobs are concerned, a few men did shorter hours during a brief initial training etc. spell; in these instances, the figure referring to the *post*-breaking-in period has been coded.

As regards the pre-R position, the substantial reduction in hours as between the second half of 1955 and the first six months of 1956 will be clear from Table 42. As for the impact of this phase on individual respondents, 213 or more than half of the 417 men in question[2] worked shorter hours in 1956 than in 1955, 152 or 37 per cent experiencing a drop of upwards of six hours a week, while for 18 per cent the fall in average weekly hours was over ten.[3]

By any standard, however, hours in first interim jobs were very long for a sizeable proportion of those having such employment: for 31 per cent they averaged more than 50 a week, while for 17 per cent they exceeded 55. Although working schedules in the half year leading up to the dismissals were, as just indicated, abnormally low, it is nevertheless illuminating to look at the effect of the redundancy on the length of individuals' hours of duty (Table 43).

The 37 men, whose hours in their first interim post were more than 18 above those in the half year preceding discharge, include 24 where they had risen by over 22 a week. Among these—admittedly extreme—cases was one who became a coach driver immediately after lay-off, doing 85 hours a week; he left after four months on

[1] Table 42 i.e. is based on the replies to Q. 11 (*j*), cols. II and I and to Q. 27 (*j*) of schedule, after due vetting/processing in the light of shifts worked. Where hours were given as a range, the mid-point was coded. In the few cases where gross hours only were given, the assumption was made that net weekly hours were 5 below these.

It is pointed out that, since it would have been impracticable to contact the various 'interim' (and 'present') employers of all 447 respondents, all hours and earnings data in this and the following chapter are based exclusively on information supplied by the men.

[2] i.e. who were at RJ during both periods.

[3] For 174 men hours were the same, and for 16 they were longer in 1956 than in 1955. Fourteen cases were miscellaneous/not clear.

TABLE 43

Net Average Weekly Hours Worked in First Interim Job as compared with those at RJ in 6 Months preceding Redundancy (Jan.–June 1956)

(All respondents with 1 or more interim jobs)*

	No.	%
Hours = same or ±2	76	24
Hours in first interim job above those at RJ (1956):		
By more than 2–6 hours	47	15
By more than 6–10 hours	36	12
By more than 10–14 hours	37	12
By more than 14–18 hours	28	9
By more than 18 hours	37	12
Hours in first interim job below those at RJ (1956):		
By more than 2–6 hours	26	8
By more than 6 hours	14	4
Miscellaneous/not clear	12	4
	313	100

* Except 10 who had a first interim job of less than one week's duration.

account of his working schedule. Another joined a firm of butchers within two days of dismissal—first as trainee manager and then as manager: his average hours increased from 37 to approximately 61 a week, his income, incidentally, falling from £18 to £9 (after training). A third became a labourer in the building industry, putting in about 60 hours; he had earned the same at RJ when on 31. Finally, we may quote the man who was out of work for some five months following discharge, when he obtained an opening as security officer entailing seven day or night shifts a week of over 12 hours each. He quit on this score after eight months, followed by a further three months' unemployment. We may add that others had to exert themselves excessively because their first interim post involved travelling—such as a house-to-house salesman for a retail chain and a pipe fitter/welder for a firm of heating and ventilating engineers.

Hours in second interim jobs were somewhat less arduous. Although in both instances 6 per cent of those concerned worked upwards of 60 hours a week, the proportion putting in more than 50 was only 17 per cent in the case of second, as compared with 31 per cent in that of first, interim posts. Similarly, 54 per cent of the 118 respondents with a second interim employer did not, on the average, do more than 45 hours weekly. As shown by Table 42, only 40 per cent of first interims were in this rubric.

EARNINGS

TABLE 44

Distribution of Gross Average Weekly Earnings before, and in First and Second Interim Job after, Redundancy

	At RJ: prior to R		*After R*	
	July–Dec. 1955	*Jan.–June* 1956	*First interim job*	*Second interim job*
	%	%	%	%
£10 and under	2	11	43	30
Over £10–£13	14	29	32	30
Over £13–£16	38	34	16	21
Over £16–£19	27	16	6	10
Over £19	14	6	1	5
Miscellaneous/not clear	5	4	2	4
	100	100	100	100
No. in category	403*	435†	306‡	115§

* The remaining 44 respondents were not at RJ in the period or were aged under 21.

† The remaining 12 men were aged under 21.

‡ The missing 17 respondents comprise 10 whose first interim job was of less than one week's duration, and 7 who were then aged under 21.

§ The remaining 3 men were aged under 21.

Table 44 gives the distribution of earnings for the sample in the boom conditions of 1955, in the rather different circumstances obtaining during the six months preceding the dismissals, and the incomes accruing in first and second interim jobs—for those who had such employment. As will be seen, earnings fell significantly already before the lay-off, but while this was in consequence of the reduced working schedules dealt with earlier, a further and much more substantial drop in wages—in no way caused by 'hours' considerations—occurred as a result of redundancy. Thus 43 per cent of the 306 men concerned earned, on average, not more than £10 a week in their first interim job; 3 per cent were making not above £7. These figures, further, are *gross*. The proportion taking home £7 or less *net* was 7 per cent of the 306 respondents, while the percentage with a net pay-packet of £10 or below was approximately 57.[1]

The drastic fall in earnings between pre- and post-R, as it affected *individual* respondents, is detailed in Table 45. It will be noted that 36 per cent of the 304 men experienced a drop in their gross weekly

[1] Although both gross and net earnings were obtained in respect of RJ, interim and present jobs, it was subsequently decided to confine the analysis to *gross* earnings. *The above are therefore the only net figures to be quoted.*

TABLE 45

Gross Average Weekly Earnings in First Interim Job as compared with those at RJ in 6 Months preceding Redundancy (Jan.–June 1956)

(All respondents with 1 or more interim jobs)*

	No.	%
Earnings = same or ±£1	52	17
Earnings in first interim job above those at RJ (1956):		
By more than £1–£4	16	5
By more than £4–£7	9 }	3
By more than £7	1 }	
Earnings in first interim job below those at RJ (1956):		
By more than £1–£4	100	33
By more than £4–£7	71	23
By more than £7	38†	13
Miscellaneous/not clear	17	6
	304	100

* Except 10 whose first interim job was of less than one week's duration, and 9 who were aged under 21 in one or both periods.

† Including 8 'by more than £10' below.

income of upwards of £4, while 13 per cent had first interim job earnings of more than £7 a week below those received at RJ in the six months before dismissal. We may also add that, if we count in differences of £1—plus or minus—the *total* whose earnings in their first interim post were below those at RJ (1956) is nearly 77 per cent, while the proportion better off is a mere 14 per cent.

Relating these figures to the period of unemployment following redundancy does not reveal a very consistent pattern, although those longest out of work tended to do somewhat less badly than the rest, as far as reduced interim job wages are concerned—once, that is, such jobs had been secured. Thus of the 304 men covered by Table 45, 40 were at large for over two months; of these, 15 per cent actually managed to improve their earnings by more than £1 above those at RJ—as compared with proportions of from 6 to 8 per cent for those with less unemployment. Similarly, the same 40 respondents contain the smallest percentage with first interim earnings of more than £1 below those prior to discharge. However, it was among those fixed up within a fortnight of dismissal that there were fewest, relatively speaking, suffering a large drop in weekly remuneration—i.e. one above £4.[1]

[1] The proportion was 31 per cent, though it was 42 per cent in the case of those out for 'over 2 weeks–1 month', and nearly 48 per cent for the 'over 1–2 months' category. Of the men unemployed for upwards of two months, 35 per cent had a first interim post entailing an average reduction in their pay, as compared with their final half year at RJ, of more than £4 a week.

As regards the *absolute* level of interim job wages and post-R unemployment, there appears to have been a greater readiness to accept '£10 or under' as unemployment lengthened, though not entirely so. Thus of those without work for not more than a fortnight, 38 per cent had first interim earnings of £10 or below; for those 'out' over two weeks up to a month, the proportion was 47 per cent, while for those unemployed for more than one up to two months, the percentage rose to 55. Of those at large in excess of two months, however, not quite 48 per cent drew £10 and under in their first interim post. We may add that there was no very clear relationship between length of unemployment and a more-than-£13-a-week first interim pay-packet.[1]

Reverting again to the *relative* figures in Table 45, it was men aged 51 and over at the date of redundancy who were least affected by extreme variations in their immediate post-R remuneration. Thus 24 per cent of the over-fifties had wages from their first interim boss which were the same ±£1 as in the six months preceding dismissal; for the three younger age-groups, the proportions were between 14 and 18½ per cent. Similarly, though 24 per cent of those 51 and over suffered an average drop in their weekly income in excess of £4, for the three lower age categories the proportions were between 36 and 38 per cent. If we simply divide the 304 respondents into 40-and-under and over-40, the same trend is in evidence: 10 per cent of the younger men[2] improved their first interim earnings by more than £1 above those accruing to them in the six months leading up to their discharge, as against 4 per cent of their elders. At the same time, 15 per cent of the 40-and-unders faced a drop exceeding £7 a week, though only 6 per cent of the over-forties did so.

As for skill grading, the 304 individuals to whom the figures relate consist of 12 classed unskilled prior to dismissal, 247 semi-skilled and 45 skilled. While the number of unskilled is thus very small, it is of interest that only a quarter of them experienced a loss of income after redundancy exceeding £1, though 65 per cent of the skilled and 71 per cent of the semi-skilled did so. We may add that, as regards these two categories, the proportion worse off to the tune of £4 and upwards was practically identical, but of the 38 individuals whose earnings shrank by over £7 a week, only two were skilled and the remainder semi-skilled.

If we break down the totals in Table 45 by the industry group in which the 304 men secured their first interim employer, it emerges,

[1] The figures in this paragraph are, like the third column of Table 44, based on the 306 respondents who had a first interim job of at least one week's duration, and who were aged over 20 at the time.

[2] Seven per cent of those 21–30 years; 13 per cent of those aged 31–40.

rather ironically, that those who stuck to motor vehicles and cycles contain the highest proportion—13 per cent—who managed to enhance their earnings,[1] as compared with their income in the six months preceding lay-off. However, those entering construction were a close second with not quite 12 per cent, and it was those finding a niche here who likewise had the smallest proportion encountering a more-than-£4 drop in wages—in this instance, with vehicles close behind.[2] If we group the figures in a different way, taking together all those who improved their takings, maintained them or at any rate did not undergo a more-than-£1-a-week average loss, construction again leads with 37 per cent, followed by vehicles with 33 per cent. As against this, only 22 per cent of those joining transport and merely 12 per cent of those absorbed in distribution were in this category.

As we saw earlier, 50 of all those who had a first interim job were engaged in labouring or similar occupations, but 5 of these are not covered by Table 45, as they left their post in less than a week. Of the remaining 45, none increased their first interim earnings by more than £1 above those prior to dismissal, though 10 per cent of the rest of the 304 men did so. Similarly, 42 per cent of the labourers experienced an over-£4-a-week drop in their first interim employment, as compared with 35 per cent of those landing in more exalted occupations.

The preceding breakdowns have been given because of their intrinsic interest. However, when it comes to accounting for the fact that some men's earnings fell substantially after redundancy, while others did so to a much lesser extent, the data in Table 46 (overleaf) are perhaps the most revealing of all. They suggest that one of the main factors at work was, quite simply, the actual cash level of pre-R earnings enjoyed by the men in the half year leading up to the lay-off.

These figures speak for themselves. We may add that of the 59 men in the 'over £16–£19' range, 31 per cent had wages in their first interim job which were more than £7 a week below those in the six months preceding dismissal. Of the 25 respondents who had earned over £19, fully 56 per cent suffered a drop in their gross remuneration of this magnitude.

Before we conclude this section, it may be illuminating to relate

[1] By more than £1 i.e.

[2] The proportion suffering an average drop of income in their first interim job of more than £4 per week i.e. was not quite 26 per cent of those entering construction, 27 per cent in the case of motor vehicles, 35 per cent for engineering, etc., 44 per cent for distribution, and 47 per cent of those absorbed in transport. The overall percentage for the 304 men concerned was 36.

TABLE 46

Drop/Rise of First Interim Job Earnings* Relative to Level of Actual Earnings in 6 Months preceding Redundancy (Jan.–June 1956)

(Respondents with 1 or more interim jobs)†

	Earnings in First Interim Job =					
	Over £1 above RJ	*Same ±£1*	*Over £1–£4 below RJ*	*Over £4 below RJ*	*Total*	*No. in category*
Earnings at RJ (Jan.–June 1956)	%	%	%	%	%	
£10 and under	19	46	31	—	100‡	26
Over £10–£13	19	29	39	12	100§	75
Over £13–£16	6	12	43	38	100§	107
Over £16–£19	2	8	24	63	100‖	59
Over £19	—	—	12	88	100	25

* Gross weekly average.
† The table relates to the same 304 men as Table 45, except that the breakdown for 12 respondents, whose earnings at RJ (1956) were not clear, has been omitted.
‡ The missing 4 per cent = 1 'not clear'.
§ The missing 1 per cent = 1 'not clear'.
‖ The missing 3 per cent = 2 'not clears'.

the data on interim job incomes to those on hours of work dealt with earlier in this chapter. In Table 47, therefore, we give a breakdown of the wages accruing in first interim posts by the hours of duty which had to be put in in order to earn them.

As Table 47 indicates, a sizeable number within each earnings range worked overtime, and except in the case of the £10-and-under

TABLE 47

First Interim Job:
Gross Weekly Earnings by Net Weekly Hours*

(Respondents with 1 or more interim jobs)

	Hours Worked					
	–40	*Over* 40–45	*Over* 45–50	*Over* 50	*Total*	*No. in category*
Earnings	%	%	%	%	%	
£10 and under	8	48	28	13	100†	132
Over £10–£13	1	30	28	41	100	99
Over £13–£16	2	19	33	46	100	48
Over £16	—	10	15	75	100	20

* Weekly average over duration of job in both cases.
† The missing 3 per cent = 4 respondents whose hours in first interim job were not clear.

category, a large proportion did a substantial amount of such overtime. It may also be pointed out that of those doing over 50 hours per week, more than half were actually putting in upwards of 55 hours.[1] And if we contrast those in the same income bracket before and after redundancy, the differences in working schedules are indeed startling. Thus of the large number of respondents drawing £10 and under in their first interim job, 8 per cent only were working 40 hours per week or less; of the small proportion of the (total) sample earning £10 and under in the half year before discharge, on the other hand, 55 per cent were working 40 hours or below. Similarly, while three-quarters of those receiving above £16 in their first interim post put in over 50 hours, of those with this income in their final six months at RJ, only 12 per cent had to exert themselves to that extent.

It will be clear, therefore, that the deterioration in hourly rates of pay as between RJ and first interim jobs was far more dramatic than that in weekly incomes. Of the 100 respondents whose first interim takings were 'over £1–£4' below those at RJ (1956),[2] for instance, 19 were working upwards of 14 hours longer. Likewise, of the 109 men whose interim earnings had shrunk by above £4, 6 per cent were putting in over 14 hours and 29 per cent over 6 hours more.

A few points remain to be added. First, that all the earnings data represent averages;[3] those for the last six months at RJ may, for example, have been higher than those accruing in the final weeks preceding dismissal. Similarly, a small number of respondents—such as some of those joining British Railways—mentioned that, on first commencing duties, they were on a special 'trainee' rate: in these instances, the full wage payable after completion of training has been coded. In other words, the contrast depicted between pre- and post-R is that between two periods—and in the case of interim posts, one of varying length—rather than that between, say, June and August 1956.

More generally, in so far as *net* earnings are concerned, the differences between incomes before and after discharge were of course less pronounced than those emerging from the tables, in view of the men's reduced liability to income tax. On the other hand, a few respondents pointed out that, while on short-time at RJ, they

[1] Of the 306 men covered by Table 47, 97 were working more than 50 hours, including 53 doing over 55 hours. Of these 53, only 11 were earning above £16 per week. (The 'No. in category' column does not add up to 306 because the hours breakdown for 7 men, whose earnings were not clear, etc., has been excluded.)

[2] *Cf.* Table 45 *ante.*

[3] Where earnings differed for days and nights, the figures represent a weighted average.

qualified for unemployment benefit; such payments were not available to supplement the much more meagre first interim standards. What should also be made clear is that any subsidiary forms of income—before or after lay-off—are not reflected in the figures, which are concerned exclusively with the wage-earnings of the redundant men. Finally, the reader is reminded that the 124 respondents who had no interim employment have not been dealt with in this and the preceding section. It is likely that this 28 per cent of the sample, who at any rate remained with their first post-R boss until the time of interview, suffered a rather smaller drop in remuneration than the rest of their 447 colleagues. For all that, the drastic effect of the dismissals on hours and earnings in the immediate post-R period is not in doubt. We shall review the long-term position in the next chapter.

UNEMPLOYMENT AND REDUNDANCY IN THE 'INTERIM' PERIOD

TABLE 48

Unemployment since Redundancy, Other than that Immediately after Redundancy

	No.	%
None*	361	81
Unemployed:		
2 weeks and under†	39	8
Over 2 weeks–1 month†	19	4
Over 1–3 months‡	15	5 (Over 1–3 months and Over 3 months combined)
Over 3 months†	7	
Length of unemployment not clear	3	1
Not clear	3	1
	447	100

* The figure includes one who retired after his first interim job.
† The figure includes one who was unemployed on day of interview.
‡ The figure includes two who were unemployed on day of interview.

The figures in Table 48 represent the combined total of all spells of unemployment following the discharges *other than that immediately thereafter*, dealt with in Chapter 3.[1] Periods off due to sickness and so on have been excluded, but in the case of five respondents out of

[1] i.e. the figures in Table 48 = the combined total of Q. 27 (*y*), 28 (*y*), 29 (*y*) and 30 (*y*) of schedule.

work at the time of interview, total unemployment up to the date of the latter has been counted.

As shown, 83 respondents or 18 per cent of the total sample had some unemployment in the 'interim' period; as a proportion of the 323 men most immediately at risk—i.e. who did not proceed straight to their present job—the 83 represent nearly 26 per cent. Of these 83, 62 individuals (75 per cent) had one spell of unemployment, 16 respondents (19 per cent) had two spells,[1] 4 men had three, while 1 had four spells. Of the 22 persons with interim unemployment in excess of one month, 13 had more than one spell.

Since unemployment immediately after redundancy tended to be higher for the older age groups, it might have been thought that that in the interim period would likewise affect a relatively larger proportion of the elderly. This was not, however, so: of the 83 individuals, only 30 per cent were over 40 years, although the over-forties constitute 33 per cent of the sample as a whole.[2] The explanation for this seems to be that—as we saw earlier—the elderly were inclined to remain with their first post-R boss to a greater extent than their juniors, and those who had no interim job could not, by definition, undergo further unemployment. It might also be added that of the 8 over-fifties who were at large in the interim period, 4 were out of work for more than one month; in the case of the younger age groups with interim spells on the dole, less than a quarter were 'out' for this length.

As regards skill, if we use that operative at RJ, 8 per cent of the 83 men were unskilled, as compared with 5 per cent of the sample as a whole. Conversely, the skilled were slightly under-represented among the 83, contributing only 12 per cent—as against 14 per cent to the sample. As for place of birth, the main point of interest is that of the 13 coloured respondents among the 447 men, 7 witnessed interim unemployment—including one for ten weeks and two for more than three months—over and above that experienced directly after dismissal.

Of the same 83 respondents, 42 were actually made redundant again in the 'interim' period, 36 men once and 6 twice. Among these 6 was one who in mid-1956 went as a brush hand into the building trade, but the contract finished after about seven weeks; his second interim post, likewise in building, was terminated by the firm's bankruptcy. A second respondent laid off consecutively from two building labourer's jobs then became a trainee miner, but had to give this up for domestic reasons. Each of his three interim ventures was followed by some unemployment, adding up *in toto*

[1] Including 1 with *at least* two spells.

[2] Age is as on day of redundancy in both cases.

to about seven weeks; this man had also found things extremely difficult immediately after discharge. A third from among those sacked twice had four interim jobs in all, as well as three spells 'out' aggregating to 10–11 weeks. His troubles seem to have been partly due to his excessive loyalty to the motor industry.

Apart from the 42 men who were both made redundant and unemployed in the interim period, another 15 were declared redundant[1] but suffered no actual unemployment. Taking the sample as a whole, 57 respondents—i.e. 13 per cent—were thus the subject of further redundancy in the interval between that of mid-1956 and the time of interview. Of the 323 individuals who did not proceed straight to their present firm, nearly 18 per cent were in this category. It might here be added that for purposes of these figures some decision had to be made as to what precisely was to rank as 'redundancy', and reasons for leaving posts such as 'the firm closed down', 'they had to cut down on staff', 'the contract finished' or 'the owner went bankrupt' have all been treated as such. But replies to the effect that work was getting slack merely or that short-time was being introduced—with a reference, frequently, to the repercussions of this on earnings—or leaving because of the *fear* of redundancy have not been counted.

Of the 83 respondents with some interim unemployment, eight had to resort to National Assistance as a result. All eight had prolonged periods of interim joblessness, ranging from a total of seven weeks to ten months.[2] Three of the eight were out of work at the time of interview.

This brings us more generally to the 22 men who, as indicated by Table 48, experienced interim unemployment of more than one month; frequently, these had also encountered relatively long periods on the dole *immediately* after lay-off. Thus 10 of the 22, or just over 45 per cent, had been at large for upwards of two months following dismissal from RJ, though the proportion of the total sample in this quandary was only 15 per cent. Among these 22 are some who can be said to have had real trouble as, for instance, a respondent in his middle fifties, out of work for three months in mid-1956 when he was engaged as a local authority gardener. However, he was discharged again at the end of the year—there being no work then except for permanent staff—and was at a loose end for a further eight weeks. A not dissimilar case concerns a man born in 1895, and also unemployed for three months following the 1956 lay-off. He then became a painter and decorator, but left at Christmas because staying on would have involved him in travelling about; he was

[1] Including one on two occasions.

[2] In one case, the length of interim unemployment was not clear.

likewise without a job for eight weeks, and in both instances it was RJ which came to the rescue.

Another respondent—in his early forties when sacked in 1956—succeeded in obtaining an opening as engineering fitter after five weeks. However, within six months he was discharged again, and was out of work for eight weeks before getting settled with his present boss. A second, in his middle twenties, had a total of six interim jobs; four of these were followed by some unemployment, amounting *in toto* to 18 weeks. Perhaps the most tragic case, however, was that of a man in his late fifties—a skilled sheet metal worker with considerable service at RJ to his credit. This respondent remained unplaced for four months after lay-off when his trade union managed to fix him up, but after eleven months the job was made automatic, and he was 'out' for a further half year. His second interim post—though, like the first, in his own trade—was of only five weeks' duration because of a sudden deterioration in his firm's fortunes. The result was another seven months' unemployment so that, by the date of interview, this man had spent well over half his time since redundancy on the dole.

The foregoing notwithstanding, we can sum up by saying that the redundancy of mid-1956 did not—in the great majority of cases—have any serious impact as far as further unemployment in the ensuing period is concerned. Though 18 per cent of the 1 in 10 sample had, over and above that experienced immediately after lay-off, undergone some further unemployment by the time of interview in the second half of 1958, mostly this was of short or fairly short duration. Only 22 of the 447 men, or 5 per cent, had suffered aggregate spells of joblessness of over one month, though these include several instances of real hardship. It might also be added that there is in any event a distinction between a time and a causal sequence; the periods out of work which chronologically followed dismissal from RJ cannot be assumed invariably to have resulted from the latter. Even, however, on the assumption that they did, the conclusion that the 1956 redundancy did not—overall—have any grave after-effects in the shape of recurrent unemployment is not in doubt.

REASONS FOR LEAVING INTERIM JOBS

As mentioned in the preceding section, nearly 18 per cent of those who had interim employment faced some further redundancy. In terms of posts, of the 478 first, second and third interim jobs combined, 64 or 13 per cent were terminated in this way.[1] Redundancy

[1] Reasons for leaving fourth and subsequent interim jobs were not obtained. However, as shown in Table 33, only 9 of the 447 men had four or more interim employers.

was not, however, the most important single ground for leaving: that honour goes to the more cheerful topic of 'returning to RJ', of which full details will be given in the next chapter.

As we shall there see, 226 of the 447 respondents in the sample were back at RJ at the time of interview, all except 15 of whom had some interim employment. The bulk of these 211 men actually gave as their reason for relinquishing their last (or only) interim job that RJ had sent for them, that they had applied for reinstatement, or simply 'to return to RJ', though in some cases more specific, additional or other factors were enumerated. However, as 'to return to RJ' could, clearly, cover a multitude of sins, any quantitative treatment of why other interim posts were abandoned is apt to be misleading. Since the majority did not enlarge on why they decided to go back, to tot up how many non-returning respondents left their interim boss for, say, pecuniary motives is unsatisfactory, as the decision to rejoin RJ is also likely frequently to have been made with an eye on cash considerations. Accordingly, we shall here content ourselves with a few further illustrations; we have of course had occasion to cite several already in other contexts.

Apart, then, from rejoining RJ and further redundancy, interim jobs were given up on such variegated grounds as adverse effects on health, dislike of Saturday morning work and other 'hours' grumbles, bad working conditions, a dispute over piece rates, low wages, wanting to return to 'the girl', and not passing a short training that was to have equipped the respondent to sell encyclopaedias. One man 'got sacked for insubordination', another downed tools in a foundry because it was 'filthy', while a third simply 'had a job off the union for better prospects'. Several others similarly moved to better themselves, though on the whole financial reasons did not figure as prominently as might have been expected in the light of the wages data reviewed earlier.

One respondent, who had commenced work a week after discharge but who revealed that 'it would have been difficult if I'd wanted to stay in my own trade', gave up his job as garage hand upon finding an opening in his own line. Another had to leave his firm of heating engineers, because he refused to scrub the office floor, while a landscape gardener's employment finished because of the rain. An Irishman—in a skilled post at RJ, but unable to get fixed up locally—took one in London as a shoe repairer, but quit after about four weeks because he could not settle in the metropolis.

A man who had landed a vacancy as engineering inspector following redundancy was discharged after 18 months over a dispute with a workmate. A second turned his back on British Railways at the end of seven weeks, because of—he had been a porter—'too much hanging around and late work'. A third, at large for some six weeks in mid-1956, then became a trainee miner; however, he left within a month having obtained 'what I thought was a better job'. This was in coal delivery, but it soon emerged that he could not cope with it; his third post was cut short by a dispute with the management. Yet another respondent, born in 1896, secured an opening as a storekeeper upon dismissal but when, after a year, his new employers left the district, he decided against moving with them.

A particularly unfortunate set of circumstances attended a young man in his middle twenties, who had made preliminary arrangements some months before redundancy to set up with a partner in the boot repairing business. Following his dismissal he went ahead with his plans, though they did not get going for about two months. After half a year, however, the whole project—in which he had sunk all his savings—had to be abandoned, since they could not procure sufficient custom to carry on. His average earnings in the period were less than £5 a week despite a 7 a.m. to 9 p.m. working day. He was unemployed for about a month after winding up the venture.

If we now turn to the 41 respondents who relinquished their first post-R job after three weeks or under, the same variety of factors is in evidence. Thus there was the man who left within two days because the journey was too long, as did a second on account of the wages (brickworks labourer), while a third was lured away from his trainee bus driver's post by a former employer whom he had given as a reference. A fourth, who had found refuge in a foundry, quit because of bad working conditions; yet another, because packing bags was both too boring and badly paid. One man, unemployed for four months following dismissal, then managed to obtain a placing as a plastic moulder; after one week, however, he received a letter from RJ inviting him back. We may add that the 41 respondents with a first interim post of not more than three weeks' duration comprise four where this was due to an offer of re-engagement from RJ.

Also among the 41 was a man in his early twenties, who ceased being a bread salesman after a fortnight simply because it did not appeal to him. A second, after the same time-span, was made redundant from a brickworks, while a third was dismissed as unsuitable. A fourth, unemployed for 16 weeks following redundancy, then became a male nurse in an old people's home; however, he left for 'more money' and 'no week-end working'. One post had to be abandoned 'because it was a closed shop and I wasn't in the union', while a respondent who had become a machine-minder in paper making and who had decided to move on for financial reasons, found that, while working off his notice, the new post had been filled.

Finally, there was the man who explained that he had applied to the Gas Board before discharge because he 'could see the red light'; when actually dismissed, he took a temporary job as a bus cleaner, until he heard from the boss of his choice that he could commence there.

Speaking generally, we can perhaps say that, in so far as interim jobs were given up voluntarily, the grounds for doing so were either that they were felt to be unsatisfactory in some 'absolute' sense, or because an opportunity for betterment presented itself or, again, because of a fortuitous change in working conditions in a post not otherwise disliked. Any attempt, therefore, to divide interim jobs into 'good' and 'bad' would be hazardous—in particular, as so many were cut short by an invitation from RJ offering reinstatement.

Chapter 6

THE PRESENT JOB

'BACK' AND 'NOT BACK'

In this chapter we are primarily concerned with the final industrial adjustment of the sample to the redundancy of mid-1956. The basic fact to carry with us is that on the day of interview 226 of the 447 respondents, or 51 per cent, were back with the firm from which they had been laid off—to wit, RJ. A further ten were with a different company of the same combine; these ten are being treated throughout as *not* back.

The 221 men, or 49 per cent of the sample, who were not back at RJ at the time of the fieldwork include six not then in employment, though all had had some work since mid-1956. One of the six had meanwhile retired owing to ill-health. The remaining five were unemployed—three for two weeks or less on the day of interview; one for seven weeks; though one, just under 65, for nearly four months.

Apart from those reinstated at the time of interview, a further twelve respondents had been re-engaged by RJ since dismissal, but had subsequently left again. Time back with the firm ranged from a fortnight to two years, though in only two instances was it longer than one year. These twelve men had a distinctly higher record of post-R job changes than the rest of the sample, seven having had four or more interim employers. We may add that if those who had an 'interim spell' at RJ are included, the total number who either were or had been back since redundancy is 238, or 53 per cent of the sample.

What were the characteristics of those who returned to the fold, as compared with their colleagues who did not? A breakdown by age of the total sample reveals that 53 per cent of those 30 years and under at the time of discharge rejoined RJ as their 'present boss', 58 per cent of the 31–40 year-olds, 46 per cent of the 41–50 group, but only 32 per cent of the over-fifties.[1] Age thus appears to have

[1] Of the 10 over-sixties in the sample, only 2 were back. It should be noted that the above and all ensuing breakdowns, being in terms of the men's 'present' employment, will treat as 'back' only ***the 226 respondents back at RJ on the date of interview***: the 12 who had an interim job there will be classed as 'not back'.

been a factor of considerable importance. In line with the foregoing figures, 59 per cent of those single when laid off, but merely 49 per cent of the married, were back with the firm at the date of interview.

As regards skill—taking the classification in force at RJ before dismissal—42 per cent of both the skilled and unskilled were back, but in the case of the semi-skilled, the proportion was 53 per cent. Of the 50 men who had completed an apprenticeship, the percentage re-engaged was 52, though it was higher for those who had both served an apprenticeship and held a skilled job prior to redundancy. As for length of service, of those who had been with the firm for not more than two years, exactly one half were back at the date of interview; of men with over two up to and including six years' service, 53 per cent had returned; but of those with over six years to their credit, only 45 per cent had done so. Both the skill and length of service breakdowns would appear in part simply to reflect the age data given earlier, though in the case of the skilled a special factor was also operative, in that a number of these were not invited back in the light of a subsequent understanding with the competent trade union. This, incidentally, affects not only the proportion of skilled men re-engaged, but also—though to a lesser extent—the total proportion re-employed, as well as the number *offered* reinstatement.[1]

When we come to place of residence, of the 299 respondents living in Birmingham at the time of discharge, 52 per cent were back at RJ when interviewed; of those residing outside but within 8 miles of the city, 49 per cent were back; while of those living at over 8 miles away, 47 per cent had rejoined the firm. While these differences are small, since—as we saw in Chapter 2—those living at some distance from Birmingham comprised relatively more young men, this suggests that distance was a factor in its own right, deciding some to seek their fortunes nearer home.

Relating the figures to place of birth brings to light that the proportion back at the time of interview ranged from 42 per cent of the small number born in 'England, other than Midlands' and 47 per cent of the 'Midlands, other than Birmingham' rubric to 63 per cent of the Irish and 68 per cent of the coloured/abroad category. In the case of the Brummies, just under one half had returned. It is clear, therefore, that there was no prejudice of any kind in the matter of re-engagement against those originating from overseas.

There were some interesting differences in the post-R experiences of the two groups. Thus of the 226 'backs', only 6 had been unemployed for upwards of three months, as compared with 19 of the 221 'not backs'. On the other hand, one-quarter of the last-named commenced work within three days of dismissal, as against 19 per

[1] See *post*.

cent of the 'backs'. More of the latter than of the former went after over forty jobs in an effort to get fixed up: the proportion was nearly 17 per cent for the 'backs', and just over 12 per cent for the 'not backs'. Similarly, the 'backs' were more mobile as regards the areas in which they searched for employment. In all, 61 per cent of the 'backs', as compared with 55 per cent of the 'not backs', considered it to have been difficult to obtain a post after redundancy—which is again significant, since the age breakdown quoted earlier would have led one to expect these figures to be reversed. We may also here add that of the 86 respondents who—as we saw in Chapter 3—cited 'anti-RJness' as a reason for their troubles in securing employment, 43 per cent were *not* back at the date of interview.

There is another intriguing set of figures throwing light on the question of who did, and who did not, return to RJ. They are set out in Table 49.

TABLE 49

Proportion Back at RJ at Date of Interview Relative to Pre-R Earnings at RJ

*Earnings at RJ, July–December 1955**	*Total in category*	*Back at date of interview*	*Earnings at RJ, January–June 1956**	*Total in category*	*Back at date of interview*
£ p.w.	No.	%	£ p.w.	No.	%
£10 and under	7	14	£10 and under	47	34
Over £10–£13	58	26	Over £10–£13	128	32
Over £13–£16	152	45	Over £13–£16	147	59
Over £16–£19	107	60	Over £16–£19	70	67
Over £19	57	70	Over £19	28	68
Misc./not clear	22	73	Misc./not clear	15	73
	403†	51		435‡	51

* Gross weekly average.

† The remaining 44 respondents were not at RJ in the period or were aged under 21.

‡ The remaining 12 respondents were aged under 21.

As indicated, there is a clear correlation between high wages at RJ before redundancy and rejoining the firm. The trend is evident both if we take the boom period of 1955 and the months of short-time in the first half of 1956, though it is more pronounced in respect of the former—which is also the more relevant in this context. These figures help to account for more of the younger men returning to the company from which they had been laid off, for an analysis of the July–December incomes shows that, while 49 per cent of those 21–30 and 47 per cent of those 31–40 years old earned over £16 prior to lay-off, the proportion was only 32 per cent for the 41–50 group and a mere 16 per cent for the over-fifties. The earnings data also go a considerable way to explain the different proportions back for the several firms in the sample: these proportions, we may point out, ranged from under 20 to over 70 per cent.

Being back at RJ was not of course solely a function of the men's personal actions and preferences, and we may now look at the other side of the penny—i.e. the degree to which respondents were given to understand in the first place that they would be taken back, followed by an examination of the extent to which they were actually offered reinstatement.

INTIMATIONS AS TO REINSTATEMENT AT THE TIME OF DISMISSAL

All respondents were asked 'When made redundant, were you told you might be taken back?',[1] and the replies spanned a fascinating spectrum ranging from 'oh yes, quite definitely' to 'no, no promises whatsoever'—with every conceivable nuance of emphasis in between. Typical answers were 'yes, when the work picked up'; 'yes, *if* the work picked up' or 'no, not definitely—they said that if things brightened up, they might send for you'. Then again there was 'yes, the chargehand told me'; 'no, but the chargehand . . .'; 'no, not in so many words, but it was implied'—with numerous variations on this theme. Some made clear that they were not told personally; others referred to there having been talk in the shop or that it was reported in the press that the dismissed would get preference when vacancies occurred. Yet others had had some information from trade union officials, or mentioned that it was union policy that the redundant should have priority in the matter of re-engagement.

An attempt to reduce the material into broad categories reveals that about three-fifths of the sample were either told—including unofficially or indirectly—or given to understand that they would or might be taken back if or when the situation improved. About 31 per cent were not told/given to understand, etc., while some 8 per cent were not sure or made miscellaneous remarks. An interesting point is that there was very little difference between the 'backs' and 'not backs' in this respect: the percentage who were 'told' and so on was almost the same, and while the proportion of 'noes' was

[1] Q. 17 (*a*) of schedule.

some $2\frac{1}{2}$ per cent higher among the 'not backs', there were more 'backs' making mixed comments.[1]

The 'authority' communicating the possibility of re-employment varied widely. Leaving aside newspaper reports, union officials and shop floor opinion, several levels of the firm's managerial hierarchy were involved—among them the undermanager, the night superintendent, the welfare officer, the chargehand and the foreman. The last two were the ones most frequently named, several respondents stressing that it was only the lower rungs of management who gave any indication as to future prospects. 'Yes, only by the foreman sort of thing', as one put it. Another, stating that they were all promised that they would be taken back at such time as RJ required them, resented the implication that the men should be ready to respond to the firm's 'beck and call'.

It would not be satisfactory to use the foregoing for measuring how the expectation of reinstatement affected the steps taken to secure work after dismissal. Thus one respondent countered 'no, but I knew they would', while a few others of those answering in the negative pointed out that they had been requested to leave their addresses. This shows that some of those simply saying 'no' may have also considered it likely that they would be asked back. Further, many of the affirmative replies were contingent not only on an improvement in RJ's economic fortunes, but on an additional 'if', such as the existence of a vacancy for the particular individual. In sum, the majority of the 447 respondents were given some idea as to the probability of re-employment, or were at any rate under the impression from one source or another that there would or might be an opportunity to return. But it is not the case that all the men either could or did assume that they would be readmitted: it was much less definite than that—especially as regards the crucial time element—and the vast bulk of the sample certainly looked for alternative employment. It is not incompatible with this that what was felt to be acceptable in this context was influenced in some way by the prospect of re-engagement.

[1] As indicated in Chapter 1, the official settlement reached between the B.M.C. and the trade unions at the Ministry of Labour on August 10, 1956—for an end to the strike which had broken out over the redundancy—included that 'the British Motor Corporation repeat their undertaking to offer re-employment to their ex-employees in appropriate vacancies which may arise'. The purpose of the question on the schedule was to find out what had been communicated to the men *before* their discharge (mostly end-June), though it cannot of course be ruled out that some unwittingly drew on subsequent press statements.

METHOD OF RETURNING TO RJ: THE 'BACKS'

How did it all work out in practice? Taking the 'backs' first, Table 50 outlines how the 226 men concerned actually came to rejoin the firm.[1]

As indicated, more than three-quarters of the 'backs' received a personal invitation offering reinstatement.[2] Not all accepted there

TABLE 50

Method of Returning to RJ

(All respondents back at RJ on day of interview)

	No.	%
Was offered re-employment by RJ	173	77
Applied himself for re-instatement: had not (at time of his application) been offered re-employment	44	19
Through trade union	5	2
Not clear	4	2
	226	100

and then; in a few cases men at first stayed put, but returned after a second or third communication. Also among the 173 respondents are eight who similarly thought it over, and who subsequently had to take the initiative themselves—one or two being readmitted only with some difficulty. Men were asked back by divers means including letter, telegram and verbal message; in one instance 'they sent a chap round in a blooming great Rolls'. One respondent emphasized that he did not himself make the first move, being an 'independent chap'; another expressed his appreciation that RJ, in contacting him, had kept to its promise.

As regards those who themselves set the ball rolling to gain re-employment, some might possibly still have been summoned at a later date; a few remarked that they were informed that this was so.[3] Others, however, had to make several applications before re-engagement: one, for example, succeeded only at the fourth attempt; a second 'kept on filling in forms and pestering them'. One respondent heard on the wireless that RJ were busy again and that ex-redundants would be given first option; a few read it in the press; one picked it up at the pub. Yet another, paid off from his interim job, tossed a coin: 'Heads, I would try . . .; tails, I wouldn't'. We may add that the 'backs' were not questioned as to why they had

[1] The figures are based on Q. 17 (*b*) and Q. 32 (*z*) of schedule.

[2] Announcements on the wireless, etc. are not, of course, covered by the figures.

[3] Two or three men similarly pointed out that the relevant communication may not have reached them, due to several changes of address on their part.

accepted the offer of reinstatement or themselves approached the firm, though a few revealed the secret that the motive was financial.

THE INVITATION TO RETURN: THE 'NOT BACKS'

Of the 221 respondents not back at RJ at the date of interview, 117 or 53 per cent had received an offer of re-engagement, while 101 or nearly 46 per cent had not.[1] It will be seen, therefore, that the proportion invited back was significantly smaller than for the 'backs'.

Taking the 117 men who had an offer of reinstatement—a number again received several—by far the most important ground for declining it was the fear of further redundancy or related reasons bearing on job security.[2] Fifty-four of the 117—46 per cent—mentioned this factor, at least three-quarters of the 54 giving it as the sole or main ground for their decision. Another 20 respondents replied to the effect that they had obtained, or had settled in, another post, and were content or preferred to remain there. A further 24 of the 117 were more specific, and accounted for their not responding to RJ's overtures by their dislike of some aspect[3] of the job in question; the item most frequently cited was 'nights' or the shift system—or appreciation that their new post did not entail this. Among the remaining 19 men were nine of those who actually returned to the firm, but who had left again by the time of interview.[4]

Comments by the 54 who did not go back for 'redundancy' considerations include 'too much risk of being out of work again'—with many variations on this theme, such as that the respondent would be certain to be affected again because of the 'last in, first out' rule. Several added that at their age they could not afford to chance it: 'Well, I'm over fifty, and I want more security now', as one put it. It is, however, of interest that of the 54 men in this group, by no means all were elderly; only 20 were born before 1920.

Other comments by the 54 were '. . . did the dirty on me—I didn't want to give them the chance again'; 'when you've had one dose, you're a bit wary'; 'they'd put us out again when it suited them'; and 'I don't like being pushed around'. One man explained that he did not wish to have a post 'where you might be slung out at any time; if I do my work well, I expect my job to be safe'. A

[1] In 3 cases the position was not clear. The figures are based on the replies to Q. 17 (*b*) of schedule.

[2] This and the following data are based on the replies to Q. 17 (*e*).

[3] Other than lack of security.

[4] The remaining 10 cases consist of 6 giving miscellaneous reasons, 3 'not clears', and 1 where the offer of re-employment was withdrawn.

second observed that RJ had been his first civilian employer after the Navy, and he decided that 'if this is industry, I don't want it'. He had therefore joined the fire service. One respondent, however, who received the summons about six months after dismissal, confessed that 'I could kick myself not going back', and one or two others similarly came to rue not having taken up the invitation.

Quoting briefly from the various other reasons for not accepting the offer of reinstatement, these comprised being satisfied or more content in the current post, having secured a better one, having rejoined an old boss, or feeling a sense of loyalty to a new one. Among those who were more specific, the dislike of night- or shift-work was, as indicated, the most important item advanced; others were the greater interest of the then job, less travelling, and a regular—even if smaller—income. A respondent who had become a bus driver had a week to go before obtaining his public service driving licence. A second—born in 1908 and out of work for three months after discharge—revealed that he more or less had 'to sign a peace treaty' in order to be taken on, i.e. he had to make a quasi-promise not to rejoin RJ. We may add that though the offer of re-engagement from the latter was received at various dates, the majority of the 117 men had by then already entered the company in whose service they were at the date of interview.

Taking now the 101 'not backs' who were not invited to return, 64 did not themselves at any time approach RJ for this purpose.[1] The remaining 37 men did, six being offered re-employment. Of these, three did not, in the event, take it up, while another three joined the firm but subsequently departed again. Thirty-one respondents thus applied for reinstatement but were rejected, 15 of the 31 making several unsuccessful efforts.

If we endeavour to sum up the foregoing—taking all 447 men—the position is that about 78 per cent either were back at RJ at the time of interview, had been back since redundancy,[2] or had at any rate received an offer of reinstatement. About 14 per cent had not been back, had had no offer, but had not themselves—for whatever the reason—taken any steps to secure one. A further 7 per cent of the sample—i.e. the 31 individuals just referred to—had not been back, had received no invitation to return, and had been spurned when themselves taking the initiative to this end.[3] These 31 include a number of real hardship cases, many of the men still hankering after RJ when interviewed. In fact, only one-third of them stated subse-

[1] Q. 17 (*f*) of schedule.

[2] Irrespective, in both cases, of whether they were *asked* back.

[3] The remaining 1 per cent was not clear.

quently that they preferred their present job—as compared with a substantially larger proportion of the remaining 'not backs'.

The other point which emerges is that the three most important factors in the context of the 'back/not back' theme were the receipt of an invitation to return—which varied as between those laid off from the several firms—the level of earnings in the pre-R period and age. Certain others were involved—such as the closer proximity of the new post, the dislike of the shift system at RJ, and the fear of further redundancy—but it would appear that, overall, the three cited had most weight. These three factors, moreover, worked hand in hand; for example, fewer of the old, relatively, were asked back, while at the same time they had less incentive to procure re-engagement in that—job security apart—the lure of the cash must have been less potent in the light of their earnings prior to dismissal.

DATE OF TAKING UP PRESENT JOB

It will be recalled that the great bulk of the sample—89 per cent—were made redundant on June 29, 1956, the remainder being laid off earlier in that month or during July 1956. Table 51 gives the other end of the story—i.e. the date on which the men joined their present employer.[1]

TABLE 51

Date of Taking Up Present Job

	Back at RJ		*Not back*		*Total*	
	No.	*%*	*No.*	*%*	*No.*	*%*
On or before 31.8.1956	12	6	100	47	112	25
Between 1.9.56 and 31.10.56	32	14	30	14	62	14
Between 1.11.56 and 31.12.56	30	13	9	4	39	9
Between 1.1.57 and 30.6.57	127	56	26	12	153	35
Between 1.7.57 and 31.12.57	20	9	24	11	44	10
On or after 1.1.1958	5	2	26	12	31	7
	226	100	215†	100	441†	100

† Six respondents were not working at the time of interview.

It will be seen that one-quarter of the sample were settled in a new, and to all intents and purposes permanent, job by end-August 1956, i.e. within two months of their dismissal.[2] Forty-eight per cent were so settled by the end of the year—that is, within six months of discharge[2]—while by mid-1957 all but 17 per cent had found their

[1] By implication, Table 51 ignores the small differences in the precise date of dismissal. These are, however, taken care of by the figures in Table 52.

[2] In the case of those laid off before June 29, 1956, the period could be fractionally larger.

new niche. Not surprisingly, though, there were considerable differences as between 'backs' and 'not backs'. The largest single group of the latter—nearly 47 per cent—were fixed up with their present firm within two months, while nearly two-thirds were taken care of by end-1956. In the case of the 'backs', on the other hand, only 6 per cent rejoined RJ in the two months following lay-off, though even here one-third were reinstated by the end of the year—and, as pointed out, not all men returned at the first opportunity. However, the peak period for reabsorption by RJ was January–June 1957, by which time the motor industry had recovered from the setbacks of 1956.

As a corollary of the above, the great majority (109) of those who had no interim job (124) are in the 'not back' category. Or putting it another way, approximately one half of the 'not backs' managed to obtain their present post without recourse to interim employment.[1] As for the 226 'backs', 15 returned without having had an interim job.[2] One other, whose first firm was RJ, left again after nine months, so that 16 men in all had RJ as their first boss after redundancy. However, only 8 of these were reinstated during July–August 1956, some of the rest being unemployed for lengthy periods.

A breakdown of the figures by age shows that, in the case of the 'not backs', the over-fifties took longest in finding their 'present firm': only 47 per cent had done so by end-1956, as compared with 73 per cent of the 41–50 year-olds, 70 per cent of the 31–40 group and 61 per cent of those 30 and below.[3] Similarly, one-third of the over-fifties joined their present employer after June 1957, the corresponding proportions being 18, 17 and 28 per cent for the 41–50, 31–40 and 30-and-under categories. As regards the 'backs', the picture is quite different: here the over-fifties—though they number only fifteen—were the quickest to be absorbed, nearly 47 per cent being re-engaged by end-1956, as against proportions of from 30 to 35 per cent for the three younger age-groups. Taking the sample as a whole, it was the 41–50 year-olds who had the highest percentage settled by end-1956; the proportion was 55 per cent—as against from 45 to 47 per cent for the rest.

On the subject of skill—using the grading at RJ prior to dismissal—only 39 per cent of the skilled had secured their present post by end-1956, as compared with 50 per cent of the semi- and 48 per cent of the unskilled. The skilled likewise had the highest proportion placed (present job) *after* June 1957—i.e. 29½ per cent, as against 14½ per cent of the semi- and not quite 22 per cent of the unskilled.

[1] The taking of an 'odd' job is not precluded.
[2] One of the 15 had a casual/part-time job.
[3] Age is as at date of redundancy.

As for the 50 respondents who had served an apprenticeship, only 34 per cent had found their present employer by end-1956, the proportion for the remainder of the sample being 50 per cent. This rather striking result reflects the fact that the skilled were on the whole less inclined to stay with their first post-R boss, if he was not to their satisfaction; it is also no doubt due to the apprentices containing a relatively large number of men in their twenties.

We have purposely deferred but may now perhaps consider a point rather fundamental to the discussion in our last chapter of the number and characteristics of interim jobs, and our review in the ensuing sections of the attributes of present posts. Partly, of course, the totals for what are being treated as interim and present employment are a function of the date when interviews took place: if the whole programme had been carried out twelve months earlier, the number of interim ventures for some individuals in the sample would have been smaller. Vice versa, had it been completed a year later—with corresponding repercussions on the identity, and date of taking up, of present jobs. Does this mean that what have here been classed as 'interim' and 'present' are merely chance aggregates, reflecting nothing more than the particular timetable of the interviewing programme?

The question can most usefully be looked at by comparing the time spent in present, with that spent in interim, jobs.

TABLE 52

Relative Duration of Interim and Present Jobs

	*Duration of interim jobs**		*Time in present job as at date of interview*	
	No.	%	*No.*	%
6 months and under	307	64	19	4
Over 6 months–1 year	128	27	32	7
Over 1–2 years	31 (Over 1–2 years and Over 2 years combined)	6 (combined)	255	58
Over 2 years			135	31
Miscellaneous/not clear	12	3	—	—
	478	100	441†	100

* All first, second and third interim jobs combined, but excluding fourth and any subsequent interim post.

† Six respondents were not working at the time of interview.

The first column of Table 52 covers all interim jobs, except the fourth and subsequent ones of the few (9) men in the sample who had over three such employers. As shown, 64 per cent of (the overwhelming majority of) interim posts lasted six months or less; 37 per cent, in fact, were of not more than three months' duration. By contrast, the great bulk of present jobs had, by the time of interview, been held sufficiently long for them to rank as the men's new niche in the labour market. Clearly, they may—for one reason or another—be abandoned at some stage, but this is merely part of the natural history of most industrial careers. Secondly, in so far as those back at RJ are concerned, it is reasonable to regard their return there as their final adjustment to the redundancy of 1956, with the corollary that employment prior thereto was 'interim' only. A further important consideration is that, as we shall see subsequently, a substantial majority of the sample made clear that they intended to stay with their present firm. It would thus seem that what have been respectively described as 'interim' and 'present' jobs are not meaningless entities, and can—taking the sample as a whole—lay some claim to that status.

A related item in this context is that, as men were interviewed over a period, the 'count' was not made at exactly the same point of time for them all. However, this is an unavoidable feature of most interviewing programmes; as 405, or 91 per cent, of the 447 respondents were seen in the five-month span July–November 1958, the matter is perhaps not tragic.

Before leaving this topic, we may also briefly revert to the comment in our introductory chapter that though from some points of view it would have been preferable to have interviewed the sample nearer the events of 1956, the relative lateness of operations has, equally, had its compensations. Thus 11 per cent of those back at RJ returned there after June 1957; 67 per cent did so after end-1956. If the fieldwork had been carried out at a date sufficiently early for the immediate effects of the dismissals to be studied in their 'red-hot' state, the more permanent impact of the redundancy in the matter of adjustment in the labour market could not have been accurately portrayed.

LOCATION

As Table 53 indicates, only two-thirds of those who had not returned to RJ were working in Birmingham at the time of interview, there having been a significant move outwards. Hence even in terms of the sample as a whole, the redundancy can be said to have led to a distinct shift away from the city in so far as the place of employment is concerned. That shift, moreover, may be understated by the figures, in that we do not know the fate of those persons in the

TABLE 53

Location of Present Job

	Present Job				First post-R job
	Not back at RJ		All respondents		All respondents
	No.	%	No.	%	%
Birmingham	141	66	367	83	62
Up to 8 miles from Birmingham*	26	12	26	6	8
Over 8–15 miles from Birmingham	38	18	38	9	20
Over 15 miles from Birmingham	7	3	7	2 (7 and 3 combined)	9
In Forces/Merchant Navy†	3	1	3		1
	215‡	100	441‡	100	100§

* But excluding Birmingham.
† 'Miscellaneous/not clear' in case of last column.
‡ Six respondents were not working at the time of interview.
§ 100 here = all 447 respondents.

original sample whose whereabouts could not be traced. At the same time, if we compare the location of all present with that of all first post-R jobs, the 'permanent' drift from Birmingham will be seen to be well below that occurring immediately after the dismissals.

INDUSTRY

Of the 215 men in employment at the date of interview but not back at RJ, four were working on their own account, one had a part-time post but was semi-retired, the rest being full-time employees. Details of the industry group in which they had landed—with the figures again combined also with the 226 'backs', and with comparable information for first post-R jobs—are given in Table 54.

The industrial grouping adopted is based on the 1958 edition of the Standard Industrial Classification. Referring to the first column of the table, item 'manufacture of motor vehicles and cycles' is designed to single out those remaining faithful to the car industry. It is, therefore, not co-terminous with the whole of S.I.C. Order VIII (Vehicles), but merely with its first two Minimum List headings; manufacture of aircraft and locomotives, for instance, have been classed as engineering.[1] As pointed out in this connection in Chapter

[1] See *Standard Industrial Classification* (H.M.S.O. 1958), p. 18. Those engaged by firms making cars plus other engineering products have, however, been classed as 'vehicles'. Two respondents in 'motor repairing and garages' are included under 'miscellaneous'.

TABLE 54

Industry Group of Present Job

	Present Job				*First post-R job*
	Not back at RJ		*All respondents*		*All respondents*
	No.	%	*No.*	%	%
Manufacture of motor vehicles and cycles (including parts and accessories)	37	17	263	60	13
Engineering;* metal goods; metal manufacture	69	32	69	16	35
All other manufacturing industries	28	13	28	6	11
Mining; agriculture	4	2	4	1	2
Construction	19	9	19	4	13
Transport and communications	20	9	20	5	10
Distribution	15	7	15	3	6
Miscellaneous†	23	11	23	5	9
	215‡	100	441‡	100	100§

* All branches other than motor vehicles and cycles.

† Includes gas, electricity and water; financial, professional and miscellaneous services; public administration and defence.

‡ Six respondents were not working at the time of interview.

§ The missing 1 per cent = 6 'not clears'. 100 = all 447 respondents.

5, in the case of those in accessory firms allocation as between the top two entries of the table is not altogether foolproof.[1]

Of the 28 individuals in 'other manufacturing industries', ten were in food and drink, the next largest category being in plastics. The handful in mining and agriculture includes three coalminers; it also covers a self-employed landscape gardener who, we are told, must be deemed to be engaged in 'agriculture'.[2] Of the twenty in transport and communications, nine were in municipal or public utility undertakings, four with British Railways, two with the G.P.O., one in the Merchant Navy, and four with private transport concerns.

The last item in Table 54 is made up, *inter alia*, of four in gas, electricity and water; two in insurance; two in the hospital service; one in a boys' remand home; three in catering; two in H.M. Forces; and one each in the police and fire service. As far as the 'public administration' element of the category is concerned, this is used

[1] The general *caveat* on p. 119 likewise applies to the present section.

[2] *Standard Industrial Classification*, Order I, 001/3 and Appendix.

purely in the S.I.C. sense of the term; it does not comprise those engaged in, say, transport or building under public service auspices. If the latter are included, the total in public employment at the date of interview was 37 men, or 17 per cent of the 215 'not backs'.

One of the main points emerging from Table 54 is that only about one half of those not at RJ at the time of interview were still in the vehicles, engineering and metals group—and the engineering and metals entry covers rather a 'mouthful', ranging from iron foundries and steel works to aircraft and nuts and bolts.[1] Even therefore taking into account—as does the second column of the table—that 51 per cent of the sample had rejoined RJ, the 1956 discharges can be said to have resulted in a fairly sizeable industrial redistribution of those involved. Further, if those in metal manufacture are held to be in an industry as dissimilar from that of RJ as, say, those in plastics or furniture, the proportion found to have transferred to a fundamentally different field will be correspondingly higher. Finally, it follows that where the phenomenon of returning to RJ is absent or less prominent than in the dismissals here investigated, redundancy may be expected to lead to a much more substantial redeployment of manpower. However, this is too big a subject to explore in these pages: the causes of such redundancy, the state of the industry, the industrial structure of the locality, etc. etc., would all, clearly, be crucial considerations.

TIME PREVIOUSLY WORKED FOR FIRM

TABLE 55

Present Job: Time Previously Worked for Firm

(All respondents not back at RJ)*

	No.	%
Nil	167	78
1 year or under	6	10
Over 1–4 years	17	
Over 4–7 years	6	3
Over 7 years	13	6
Self-employed/in H.M. Forces	6	3
	215	100

* But working on day of interview.

[1] In view of the difficulty of distinguishing clearly, on the basis of the available particulars, between metal manufacture, metal goods and engineering, it was felt best to put them into one category.

As indicated by Table 55, 42 respondents or almost one-fifth of the 'not backs' were, at the time of interview, with an employer by whom they had already been engaged prior to dismissal. For 22 of the 42 men this pre-R boss was their only one since redundancy, and for 16 of these 22, he was also the one in whose service they had been immediately before joining RJ. In all, there were at least 23 respondents who, when interviewed, were with their immediate pre-R employer, though in one case he was merely of part-time standing.

It will be clear that the time previously worked for the firm differed greatly, and in general we can say that the significance of the 'old boss' element varied widely—more so, perhaps, than the figures suggest. Thus there was the man who returned to a concern with whom he had formerly spent 39 years—in fact, his entire working life apart from his spell at RJ. By contrast, a second had merely passed one month with the company previously, and came to work for it after lay-off through the good offices of an employment exchange.

TRAINING RECEIVED AFTER REDUNDANCY

All 'not backs' were asked whether they had received a new formal training from their present employer,[1] and their replies are summarized in Table 56.

TABLE 56

Training Received: Present Job

(All respondents not back at RJ)*

	No.	%
Nil	167†	78
2 weeks and under	14	6
Over 2 weeks–1 month	12	5
Over 1–3 months	6	3
Over 3 months	10	5
Self-employed/in H.M. Forces	6	3
	215	100

* But working on day of interview.

† Including one whose occupation (skilled) at present firm was originally the same as at RJ, who agreed to be trained for a *less* skilled job as an alternative to further redundancy.

[1] Q. 31 (g) of schedule.

About one-fifth of the 'not backs' received some sort of training from their present firm; in most instances this was fairly short. Those who had the benefit of more than three months' instruction include a Gas Board retort operator (24-week course); three municipal bus drivers (5–9 months); a National Coal Board underground road repairer (2 years); an apprentice electrician undergoing a five-year apprenticeship; and a former semi-skilled transfer machine operator, who had meanwhile become a skilled toolmaker. A rather different brand of training was a correspondence course on human relations in branch management, taken by an assistant manager in a co-operative food store.

A few of those answering in the negative made remarks such as that they already had the training or knew how to do the work. Others, that no instruction was necessary or that 'you just pick it up as you go along'. A number of men observed that they were shown the ins and outs of the job by a foreman or workmate, while a handful had one or two days' breaking in. All these were treated as 'nil' for purposes of the table.

Some of these comments, however, again highlight the difficulty which exists in this context—namely what precisely constitutes 'training'? The word 'formal' was included in the question solely so that the real thing might be distinguished from the just-being-shown-what-to-do variety; the intention was not to exclude genuine on-the-job instruction merely because it was informal. As it was not possible to ask the men to enlarge on the matter, some allowance must be made for the vagaries of interpretation. But though this might affect the totals somewhat, it is unlikely to alter the general picture—i.e. that the great majority of 'not backs' received no training from their present employer.

We might here point out that a question re training was not put in connection with respondents' interim employment, though a limited amount of information could be gleaned from related answers. Thus three men had interim jobs as trainee miners, in which they persevered for from three to five weeks; a would-be salesman left after about a fortnight, because the training proved to be beyond him. Others had interim posts respectively as trainee bus driver, trainee bender (engineering), trainee polisher and trainee moulder (aircraft). One respondent was given a ten-week drill as a British Railways signalman; a second, formerly in that occupation, participated in a six-week refresher course on his return there after redundancy. An inspector, who abandoned his boss to attend a course as an electronics engineer, subsequently joined a different branch of the company as an electronics inspector.

There were a handful of other references to training in the context of the men's 'interim' history, though in the absence of a specific question on the topic, no definite statement is warranted as to the extent to which such training was received. As far as probabilities go, it is likely to have been considerably less than that given by present employers, if only because the proportion in labouring occupations was higher in the interim than in the present job period.

Though the fact that the great majority of 'not backs' received no training from their present employer is not in doubt, and though that given on all first post-R jobs is unlikely to have been any more extensive, it is difficult to know what to make of this. In so far as men had served an apprenticeship or participated in other forms of instruction earlier on in their industrial career, or had previously acquired the requisite experience, or belonged to a group of semi-skilled mass production workers for whom formal technical teaching is not necessary or usual, there is really no reason why they should have had a fresh training after lay-off. The scantness of training received becomes a matter for comment *à propos* of redundancy only, if it can be shown that respondents had relatively more difficulty in finding work because they were not trained and, further, because would-be employers were unwilling or unable to train them. In the present investigation—as we found earlier—the skilled were not necessarily better off than the less skilled, while as the men themselves saw it, lack of training and experience were only a minor factor at the time. Some indeed indicated that the trouble was that only openings for labourers were available, from which one could conclude that, had they been in that category, theirs would have been a smoother path. This is in no way to imply that the question of training is of no consequence—either in general or in the context of a wider redundancy policy: it is merely to say that training is not *ipso facto* the crucial factor in the equation.

OCCUPATION AND SKILL

Table 57 shows how the 215 'not backs' had distributed themselves occupationally by the time of interview. As pointed out in Chapter 5, prior to lay-off over four-fifths had been in the metal, engineering, etc. category—with, we may add, few differences only between 'backs' and 'not backs'.

Although the 215 men had landed in a wide variety of occupations, the proportion in the different groups is very similar to that given in Table 41 in respect of first interim jobs. This is of interest not merely because, of the 323 respondents covered by the earlier figures, about 65 per cent had meanwhile returned to RJ, but because one might have expected a rather greater divergence in the matter between

TABLE 57

Occupation of Present Job

(All respondents not back at RJ)*

	No.	%
Workers in metal, engineering and allied trades†	102	47
Other occupations in productive processes	14	7
Construction occupations‡	15	7
Transport occupations‡	16	7
Warehousemen, storekeepers, packers	9	4
Labourers, etc.	18	8
Shop assistants, salesmen, roundsmen	8	6
Sales managers, insurance agents, shopkeepers	4	
Barmen, restaurant workers	4	2
Miscellaneous§	25	12
	215	100

* But working on day of interview. Note* on p. 122 likewise applies to this table.

† Including vehicle building occupations, but excluding labourers.

‡ Other than labourers.

§ Includes crane drivers, miners, a gardener, a fireman, 2 in Forces, 3 clerks, etc., as well as 6 'not clears'.

the more temporary and the more permanent posts. However, there is one such difference, for only 8 per cent of the 215 'not backs' were engaged as labourers at the time of interview, as compared with 15 per cent of all first interim job-holders. This of course reflects the fact that labouring had to be resorted to in the immediate post-R period, but was got out of subsequently wherever circumstances permitted. Which brings us to the related topic of skill changes in general.

TABLE 58

Skill Status before and after Redundancy

(All respondents not back at RJ)*

	At RJ, pre-R: Actual grading by RJ	*At RJ, pre-R: Grading by RJ according to respondent*	*At present job: Grading by firm according to respondent*
	%	%	%
Skilled	16	25	45
Semi-skilled	78	66	28
Unskilled	6	6	12
Not known/inapplicable, etc.	—	3	15
	100	100	100

* But working on day of interview, i.e. 215 respondents.

The theme of Table 58 is the skill rating of the 'not backs' before and after redundancy. The first column shows the *de facto* grading in force at RJ prior to discharge; these are the figures we have used throughout in our various 'skill' breakdowns. The second column comprises the men's answers to how the occupation held when laid off had been rated by RJ as regards skill, while the third column contains the replies to the exactly parallel question as to how their present job was classed by their present employer.[1] As previously pointed out, the extent of overrating on the part of respondents was relatively small as far as their occupation at RJ is concerned.[2] Though it may have been somewhat greater *à propos* of present jobs in that these were less universally of semi-skilled status, it seems reasonable to assume that the ranking given is not widely out of line with that actually operative. We can take it, therefore, that the differences between the second and third columns of Table 58 represent what is at any rate a genuine trend.

In terms of individual 'not backs', 106 of the 215 men—49 per cent—thought that the official skill grading of their present post was the same as that of the occupation from which they were dismissed.[3] Nineteen respondents[4] (9 per cent) stated that their current ranking was lower, while 50 men[5] (23 per cent) believed that their present calling enjoyed a superior classification.[6] The remaining 40 cases primarily consist of those who did not specify or know their skill status in respect of one period or the other. Frequently this was because they felt that the question was currently inapplicable, being no longer engaged in industrial or manual pursuits.

Of the 19 respondents maintaining that their present job had an inferior ranking, 14 said that while that at RJ had been semi-skilled, their current one was only unskilled. One stated that he had dropped from skilled to unskilled, and four that the change was from skilled to 'semi'. Included in the group are an inspector who had become a destructor attendant in a municipal refuse department, a car finisher who had been transformed into a hospital ward orderly, and a machinist downgraded to labourer. Some of the rest, however, who described their present rating as unskilled were in occupations actually qualifying as semi-skilled at certain of the RJs—an indication of the precarious nature of the whole subject.

[1] Q. 10 (*e*) and Q. 31 (*e*) of schedule.

[2] See p. 43 *ante*.

[3] Of the 106, 22 had not known their correct skill grading at RJ.

[4] Including 2 who did not know their correct skill grading at RJ.

[5] Including 3 who did not know their correct skill grading at RJ.

[6] These figures are in terms of movements between skilled, semi-skilled and unskilled; the few who commented that they had moved *within* one of the three standard categories are not included.

Of the 50 intimating that their official grading was superior to that before redundancy, all except two defined their current duties as skilled—as against semi-skilled at RJ. Among these 50 was a car wirer who had become a servicing engineer; an electrician's mate who had graduated to G.P.O. maintenance technician; several operatives who had returned to painting and decorating; an engine rectifier who had become a laboratory technician; and a labourer who had risen to train fireman. Also included are a number of respondents still in the same calling as at RJ, but now carrying it out at a more advanced and highly-ranking level. On the other hand, a few men commented on changes in job content *not* reflected in its formal classification: for example, a skilled inspector (RJ) but on a different type of skilled task at the time of interview remarked that the latter, unlike the former, was 'first-class' work.

Use made of previous skill and experience: Asked whether the skill and experience gained at RJ were of use to them in their present work,[1] only 47 of the 215 'not backs' or 22 per cent said 'yes', while 158 or 73 per cent replied in the negative.[2] These figures are startling as, indeed, are the ensuing ones, namely that of the 168 men who did not answer the first question in the affirmative, 99 stated that some of their *other* (i.e. non-RJ) experience was currently of benefit to them.[3] At the same time, 61 of the 215 'not backs' were, as they saw it, neither drawing on the skill and experience acquired at RJ nor on that gathered anywhere else. One respondent in this group, observing that none was needed for his then job, added bitterly that he had wasted three years at the college of technology.

It ought perhaps to be pointed out that, in the case of both sets of replies, a variety of factors may have accounted alike for some of the 'yes' and some of the 'no' answers—just as these covered varying degrees of useful- and uselessness. Thus a handful responded in the negative because 'they knew it all before going to RJ'. Again, some of those who by implication were wasting the know-how acquired at the latter, were from among the category who were actually on more highly skilled tasks at the time of interview. What does, however, stand out is the sizeable number reporting that they were utilizing experience accumulated *prior to* joining RJ rather than that gained *at* the latter. The figures in fact understate the position, in that the 47 respondents saying that their RJ-gathered knowledge was currently coming in handy were not questioned as to the recourse being had to any of their earlier skills.

[1] Q. 31 (*v*) of schedule.

[2] The remaining 10 (5 per cent) were miscellaneous/not clear.

[3] Q. 31 (*w*) of schedule. Six of the 99 men were referring exclusively to experience gained in the 'interim' period.

Another interesting point is that those drawing on their non-RJ experience were well over twice as numerous as those who had found their way back to a former employer. In other words, a good many 'not backs' had not merely rejoined a previous boss, but over and above the 42 in that category, had returned to a trade or occupation in which they had spent some part of their earlier industrial career. All in all, then, while some of the 'not backs' had landed in a less skilled job than that performed prior to discharge, a larger total considered that they had graduated to more highly skilled pursuits, while a significant proportion can be said to have gone back to their old girl after a shorter or longer flirtation with RJ.

OCCUPATION, SKILL AND TRAINING: THE 'BACKS'

TABLE 59

Whether Doing Same Job as before Redundancy and, if not, whether Previous Skill and Experience of Use in Present Work*

(All respondents back at RJ)

	No.	%
Doing the same job as before R	154	68
Doing broadly the same job	29	13
Doing different work, but pre-R experience at RJ of use	19	8
Doing different work; pre-R experience at RJ of no use, but other experience is	6	3
Doing different work; not making use of any earlier experience	18	8
	226	100

* Based on replies to Q. 32 (*a*), (*c*), (*v*) and (*w*) of schedule.

As shown by Table 59, 68 per cent of the 226 men back at RJ at the time of interview were doing the same job as before dismissal, while another 13 per cent were on broadly similar work. As to the distinction between the two, 'broadly the same' covers those who were, say, spot welders or assemblers both prior to and after redundancy, but on different operations; or machinists then and now, but on a different machine. However, too much importance should not be attached to the distinction, the main point being that approximately four-fifths of the 'backs' were performing precisely or broadly the same work as before lay-off.

This four-fifths includes small numbers who (*a*) were doing the same job as some time, but not immediately, before dismissal; (*b*) who at the date of interview were on analogous duties as prior to discharge but who, on first returning, had done something different; and (*c*) those initially going back to their old post but who had since been shifted elsewhere. We may here point out that it is common practice among the firms concerned to move their semi- and unskilled labour over a range of related occupations. As the questions were designed to ascertain whether redundancy had resulted in any waste of acquired skills, that someone was in the same post as some time, rather than immediately, preceding lay-off is immaterial. Likewise, that another went back as a driver until his production-line job was available again or, conversely, returned to his former tasks but was subsequently transferred for some fortuitous reason, could hardly be considered as 'waste' due to the dismissals.

Of the 43 'backs' neither doing the same nor broadly the same work, 19 stated that the skill and experience gathered at RJ prior to discharge were currently of (varying degrees of) use to them. Six maintained that they were not, but that skill and experience gained elsewhere were. Only 18 of the 226 were of the opinion that none of their earlier knowledge was now of any service to them.

Of the 24 replying that the skill, etc. acquired at the firm pre-R were of no use, about half a dozen had either received a fresh training since their return, or were engaged on more highly skilled processes. One need not, therefore, shed any tears because they were not drawing on previous know-how. In any event—and this of course also applies to the 'not backs'—'no' to whether past skill and experience were of use may simply mean, say in the case of the unskilled, that these are not—nor were prior to lay-off—required for the particular task. At the same time, a few (mostly older) respondents revealed that they were now on labouring or otherwise less skilled operations as compared with pre-mid-1956: it is these who, as far as job-content among the 'backs' is concerned, are the main victims of the redundancy.

As for training, only those 'backs' not on the same job as before dismissal were asked whether, on returning to RJ, the latter had given them a new formal training.[1] Of the 72 men in question, 7 persons had had the benefit of such instruction.[2]

SHIFTS

Table 60 sets out—for both 'backs' and 'not backs'—the shifts worked during the final half year preceding dismissal, as well as

[1] Q. 32 (*g*) of schedule.

[2] One other, who had returned to his old post, was later transferred to different work, for which he was given a two-week course. Three answers were not clear, the remaining 61 replying in the negative.

those put in in the present job during the six months[1] previous to interview. We may point out that, in the matter of shifts at RJ, those during the boom conditions of 1955 were on the whole very similar to those in the half year immediately before lay-off, given below.

TABLE 60

Shifts Worked before Redundancy and in Present Job

	All respondents back at RJ on day of interview		All respondents not back on day of interview	
	Last 6 *months before R*	*Last* 6 *months: present job*	*Last* 6 *months before R*	*Last* 6 *months: present job*
	%	%	%	%
Days	27	26	32	79
Nights	14	9	16	5
Week about/fortnight about/ month about	48	58	46	4
Days and nights: other; 2-, 3- or irregular shifts	11	7	6	11
	100	100	100	100*
No. in category	226	226	221	215†

* The missing 1 per cent = 2 respondents in Forces.
† The remaining 6 men were not in employment on day of interview.

As will be seen, there were some differences already between 'backs' and 'not backs' before redundancy, though they were not very pronounced. As far as present jobs are concerned, however, the contrast is striking: while of the 'backs' almost the same proportion were on days in the two periods, when we come to the 'not backs', the percentage jumps dramatically from 32 to 79—a fact materially contributing to the satisfaction of the 'not backs' with their current lot. A small offset against this increase in day-workers was the rise in the proportion of 'not backs' doing odd shifts; included here are a number of those who landed in transport occupations, some of whom expressed disapproval of their new daily routine.[2]

[1] Or since joining present employer, if less. The figures are based on Q. 11 (*i*) and Q. 33 (*i*) of schedule.

[2] It should be noted that respondents doing (*a*) days plus overtime or (*b*) days plus *occasional* night work—'occasional' being defined as less than a fifth of the total—have been treated as 'days'. But where early morning or evening work formed part of the *regular* shift, they are included under the fourth item of the table.

HOURS OF WORK

We now turn to the subject of hours, those at RJ prior to lay-off and those in present jobs during the six months preceding interview being detailed in Table 61. Cumbersome though it is, it is again necessary to give two sets of figures in respect of the pre-R period.[1]

TABLE 61

Net Average Weekly Hours Worked before Redundancy and in Present Job

	All respondents back at RJ on day of interview			All respondents not back on day of interview		
	July–Dec. 1955	*Jan.–June* 1956	*Present job**	*July–Dec.* 1955	*Jan.–June* 1956	*Present job**
	%	%	%	%	%	%
40 hours and under	4	32	11	5	35	8
Over 40–45 hours	49	41	65	53	43	40
Over 45–50 hours	23	12	16	26	13	24
Over 50–55 hours	16	11	4	8	4	7
Over 55 hours	4	2	2	7	5	19
Misc./not clear	4	2	2	1	—	2
	100	100	100	100	100	100
No. in category	211†	226	226	206†	221	215‡

* Average during last 6 months (or since joining present employer).
† Fifteen respondents were not at RJ in the period.
‡ Six respondents were not working on day of interview.

It will be noted that the differences as between 'backs' and 'not backs' were relatively minor only prior to discharge. However, as regards present jobs, while only 22 per cent of the 'backs' were, on average, working more than 45 hours and a mere 2 per cent over 55 hours a week, for the 'not backs' the corresponding proportions were 50 and 19 per cent. Six per cent of the 'not backs', or 13 men, were in fact putting in upwards of 60 hours during the six months preceding interview; of the 'backs', only one solitary individual was in that category. Another interesting point is that the proportion of 'not backs' reporting above 55 hours is actually slightly higher than that recorded in Chapter 5 in respect of first interim jobs.[2]

[1] *Cf.* p. 125 *ante*. See also p. 126 for definitions of *net* and *average* hours, etc., which likewise apply to the present section.

[2] See Table 42 *ante*. The proportion doing more than 50 hours was, however, higher for first interim jobs.

How did these changes affect individuals? As compared with the last six (boom) months of 1955, approximately one-third of both groups had the same working schedules in the half year previous to interview—if differences of two hours in either direction are ignored. Eight per cent of the 'backs', but 37 per cent of the 'not backs', were doing upwards of two hours longer; 14 per cent of the latter were putting in over ten hours more per week in their present post than in the boom months at RJ in 1955. As a corollary, 53 per cent of the 'backs' were doing over two hours less when interviewed than in 1955; of the 'not backs', 24 per cent only were in this position. As compared with the slack half year immediately before redundancy, 60 per cent of the 'not backs' were currently working more than two hours harder—including 48 per cent more than six, and 30 per cent over ten, hours longer.

It should perhaps be pointed out that although the foregoing statistics refer to average weekly hours over a six-month time-span, they are nevertheless influenced by the accident—as it in many ways is—of whether the firm (or department) happened to be on short-, standard or overtime. This is true, in particular, of the 'backs' for whom, in view of the nature of the industry, no one period can claim to be 'typical'; the qualification applies in lesser degree only to the 'not backs'. The other general comment called for is that whether long hours are regarded as an advantage or drawback varies considerably; as is well known, the opportunity to do overtime in order to increase income is greatly valued by many. In one sense, therefore, the arduousness of the working week acquires its proper significance only when related to the earnings which are 'purchased' thereby—a topic with which we deal in the next section.

Before leaving the subject, however, it is of interest to record how the men themselves summed up the change wrought in their working schedules by redundancy. In Table 62, therefore, we present the answers of the 'not backs' to 'Do you find your present hours and shifts more convenient or less convenient than at RJ before your R?'[1]

Although replies were given with the usual gradations of emphasis, it is worth mentioning that 20 men stressed that hours and shifts were *much* more convenient in their present job, while of the 'less convenients' only two considered them *much* less so. As for what lies behind the figures, it is clear that the change from nights/shifts to days provides the main explanation. For as we just saw, hours for the 'not backs' were more arduous at the time of interview than before redundancy—drastically so, as compared with the immediate pre-R

[1] Q. 34 (*b*) of schedule. (The figures in Table 61 and in the preceding paragraphs of this section are based on Q. 11 (*j*) and Q. 33 (*j*).)

TABLE 62

Whether Present Hours and Shifts More or Less Convenient than before Redundancy

(All respondents not back at RJ)*

	No.	%
The same/about the same	30	14
Less convenient now	40	19
More convenient now	117	54
More convenient in some ways, less convenient in others	17	8
Miscellaneous/not clear	11	5
	215	100

* But working on day of interview.

period, but longer even as compared with 1955.[1] By contrast, as shown by Table 60, there was a dramatic switch from shift- to day-work, so that there is little doubt—it is plain also from the comments made by the majority of those expanding on the topic—that the large-scale substitution of days for the pre-R régime involving nights is responsible for the preponderance of favourable verdicts. A subsidiary factor probably was the journey to work. Although not formally included in the question, it is of course relevant to the length of the working day, and as we shall see in Chapter 7, there was a gain here likewise for the 'not backs'.

We might add that although day-time duties were on the whole much more popular with the men, this was not universally so. Thus a few of the 'less convenients' are in that category because they preferred the nights at RJ, while one liked his current set-up better because he regarded permanent nights as superior to a 'month about'. In a few instances, it became apparent that husband and wife did not see eye to eye in the matter.

EARNINGS

Table 63 shows the gross average weekly earnings[2] of 'backs' and 'not backs' in the two six-month periods at RJ prior to dismissal and during the half year preceding interview. As pointed out earlier in this chapter, there was a high correlation between pre-R remuneration and rejoining RJ, which is of course another way of

[1] And, as will be shown presently, the earnings 'purchased' therewith were lower than before redundancy.

[2] The data are based on Q. 11 (*k*) and Q. 33 (*k*) of schedule. Where earnings differed for days and nights, the figures represent a weighted average.

TABLE 63

Distribution of Gross Average Weekly Earnings before Redundancy and in Present Job

	All respondents back at RJ on day of interview			All respondents not back on day of interview		
	July–Dec. 1955	*Jan.–June* 1956	*Present job**	*July–Dec.* 1955	*Jan.–June* 1956	*Present job**
	%	%	%	%	%	%
£10 and under	1	7	1	3	14	14
Over £10–£13	7	19	8	22	41	44
Over £13–£16	34	39	19	42	28	24
Over £16–£19	31	21	38	22	11	8
Over £19–£22	16	7	26	7	4	7
Over £22	3	2	5	1	—	1
Misc./not clear	8	5	3	3	2	2
	100	100	100	100	100	100
No. in category†	205	221	226	198	214	211

* Average during last 6 months (or since joining present employer).
† The 'missing' respondents were not at RJ in period (1955), not working on day of interview, or aged under 21.

saying that the 'not backs' had considerably smaller pay packets already before redundancy. Taking the boom months of 1955, for instance, merely 8 per cent of the 'backs' were in the '£13 and under' range, while nearly one-fifth were making over £19 a week. In the case of the 'not backs', on the other hand, one-quarter were drawing £13 or less, while only just over 8 per cent had incomes in excess of £19.

Nevertheless, there is no doubt that, in monetary terms, the 'not backs' lost heavily by not returning to RJ. Granted that due to inter-firm differences, age and other factors, their earnings potential was lower than that of the 'backs', the gap between them and their erstwhile colleagues had substantially widened by the time of interview. Thus fully 61 per cent of the 'not backs' had incomes in their present post below those at RJ (1955), while nearly 48 per cent were worse off as compared even with 'RJ, 1956'. Taking the 'backs', the corresponding proportions are 29 and 15 per cent. Similarly, only 30 per cent of the 'not backs' were, in the six months preceding interview, making more than at RJ (1955)—i.e. some three years previously; of the 'backs', 52 per cent had enhanced wages by the latter date.[1] Further, and most important, while for those who had

[1] As compared with January–June 1956, 44 per cent of the 'not backs', but 70 per cent of the 'backs', had higher earnings in their present job (6 months preceding interview).

rejoined RJ there was a fall in the proportion working over 50 hours as between pre-R and present, the opposite is true of the 'not backs'.[1] We will revert to the hours aspect later; meanwhile, we may look at the actual extent of the drop/rise in remuneration for the individuals in the two groups.

TABLE 64

Gross Average Weekly Earnings in Present Job as compared with those at RJ before Redundancy

Earnings in Present Job =*	*As compared with RJ, July–Dec.* 1955			*As compared with RJ, Jan.–June* 1956		
	Back	*Not back*	*Total*	*Back*	*Not back*	*Total*
	%	%	%	%	%	%
Same ±£1	24	25	25	21	32	26
Over £1–£4 higher	30	17	23	32	18	25
Over £4 higher	15	3	9	31	12	22
Over £1–£4 lower	14	29	21	6	25	15
Over £4 lower	6	21	14	3	9	6
Misc./not clear	11	5	8	7	4	6
	100	100	100	100	100	100
No. in category†	205	196	401	221	208	429

* Average for last 6 months (or since joining present employer).

† The 'missing' respondents were not at RJ (1955), not working on day of interview, or aged under 21 (in either or both periods).

Table 64 will speak for itself. As far as the 'not backs' are concerned—who are of course of primary interest in this context—we may add that 28 per cent were making over £1 *less* in their current employment than in the *lower* of their two earnings periods before discharge, while only 16 per cent were earning over £1 *more* than in the *higher* of the two.[2] In view of the upward trend of wages in the interval, these figures are striking.[3]

Basically, the above data simply reflect the different standards of reward obtaining at RJ and elsewhere; no great subtlety is needed for purposes of interpretation. A contributory factor, however, was

[1] See Table 61.

[2] In some cases, earnings were, of course, the same in the two periods.

[3] Average weekly earnings for men, 21 years and over, in the industries covered by the Ministry of Labour's bi-yearly earnings inquiries were 222/11d. in October 1955, 235/4d. in April 1956, 253/2d. in April 1958 and 256/8d. in October 1958 (*Ministry of Labour Gazette*, February 1959, p. 46). It will be recalled that the great bulk of interviews were carried out in the second half of 1958, a few being conducted early in 1959.

the switch from shift- to day-work; as is well known, 'nights' in industry are paid for at augmented rates, and these no longer accrued to the majority of 'not backs' in their new posts. The change from nights to 'fortnight about', incidentally, no doubt contributed to some of the 'backs' having lower present job takings.[1]

As a corollary of the major cause responsible for the reduced incomes of the 'not backs'—and as in the case of interim earnings—the most important determinant of whether individual wage packets rose or fell after redundancy was their actual cash level prior to the latter.[2] The figures are set out in Table 65; we may add that the picture is similar if the exercise is done on the standards ruling at RJ in the first half of 1956.

TABLE 65

Drop/Rise of Present Job Earnings* Relative to Level of Actual Earnings before Redundancy (July–December 1955)

(Respondents not back at RJ)†

	Earnings in Present Job =					
	Over £1 above RJ	*Same ±£1*	*Over £1–£4 below RJ*	*Over £4 below RJ*	*Total*	*No. in category*
Earnings at RJ (July–December 1955)	%	%	%	%	%	
£13 and under	31	45	24	—	100	49
Over £13–£16	16	26	40	15	100‡	82
Over £16–£19	19	9	24	48	100	42
Over £19	12	17	12	59	100	17

* Gross weekly average during 6 months preceding interview (or since joining present employer).

† The table covers all 'not backs', except those not at RJ in 1955, not working on day of interview, or aged under 21. Six respondents whose 1955 earnings were not clear are also omitted.

‡ The missing per cent = 3 'not clears'.

We have seen that the gap in incomes between 'backs' and 'not backs' widened materially as a result of the lay-off and that, further, this went hand in hand with a lengthening of hours for the latter but a shortening of those for the 'backs'. Table 66 shows the combined effect of these two trends.

[1] *Cf.* Table 60.

[2] The breakdown of the figures by e.g. age was much less 'telling'. While it showed that the proportion with present job earnings in excess of those at RJ fell with advancing years, the relation between age and a reduced income did not emerge clearly.

TABLE 66

Present Job: 'Backs' and 'Not Backs'
Gross Weekly Earnings by Net Weekly Hours*

		Hours Worked					
		–40	Over 40–45	Over 45–50	Over 50	*Total*	*No. in category*
Earnings		%	%	%	%	%	
£13 and under:	Back	14	48	24	14	100	21
	Not back	7	43	27	22	100†	121
Over £13–£16:	Back	14	57	19	10	100	42
	Not back	4	31	26	39	100	51
Over £16–£19:	Back	13	68	15	3	100†	87
	Not back	17	50	5	28	100	18
Over £19:	Back	7	74	12	7	100	70
	Not back	12	41	18	29	100	17

* In both cases, weekly average during 6 months preceding interview (or since joining present employer). The table covers all 447 respondents, except 6 not working on day of interview, 4 aged under 21, and 10 whose earnings were not clear. † The missing 1 per cent = 1 'not clear'.

Perhaps the chief features of Table 66 are the diverging totals in the different earnings ranges, and the fact that the proportion having to put in more than 50 hours to gain any particular wage was significantly higher for the 'not backs'. However, those (few) of the latter who drew above £16 a week contain a larger percentage working short-time than the 'backs' in the comparable income bracket. *Within* each of the two categories, it is of interest that superior earnings were not necessarily associated with more arduous hours; in this respect the figures for the interim period were distinctly more 'ethical'![1]

All in all, then, not having returned to RJ has meant a sizeable pecuniary sacrifice. By the time of interview, the level of earnings had of course recovered from the depths reached immediately after redundancy. As we saw, nearly 77 per cent of first interim job-holders made less than they had done in the six months leading up to the lay-off, while the proportion of 'not backs' worse off in their present post as compared with the same period was not quite 48 per cent. The contrast in both instances is considerably greater if we take the boom months at RJ (1955) as our base date—just as, again in both cases, the fall in hourly standards was more serious than that in weekly incomes. By definition, however, the present job situation is of more permanent consequence than that obtaining temporarily, and here the question resolves itself into whether the 'not backs'

[1] *Cf.* Table 47 *ante.*

have found some compensation for their straitened financial circumstances or whether, alternatively, these have soured their satisfaction with their current lot. It is to this topic that we devote the next section.

JOB PREFERENCES: THE 'NOT BACKS'

TABLE 67

Whether Prefers Present Job or that at RJ

(All respondents not back at RJ)*

	No.	%
Prefers present job	130	61
Preferred RJ	48	22
Preferred RJ in some ways, present job in others. Non-committal/not sure	29	14
In Forces/not clear†	8	3
	215	100

* But working on day of interview.

† Includes 5 stating that satisfied/happy in present job, without expressing a view on the relative merits of the two posts.

Asked 'In general, can you say which you prefer—your job at RJ or your present one?',[1] 61 per cent of the 215 'not backs' stated that they preferred their present post, while 22 per cent expressed a preference for RJ. Fourteen per cent felt that the two were much about the same, that they were equally content in both, or that it was a case of 'fifty-fifty'.

The question on job preferences was preceded by two, respectively requesting the men to sum up how average earnings in their present post compared with those before redundancy, and whether current hours and shifts were more or less convenient than at RJ.[2] In the case both of those declaring for their present post as in that of those opting for RJ, the majority did so although they had just made clear that the less-liked of the two had certain advantages. This is not to say that these men were necessarily any less enthusiastic about the job of their choice than their colleagues. All the 178 recorded as

[1] Q. 34 (*c*) of schedule.

[2] Q. 34 (*a*) and (*b*) of schedule; these were distinct from Q. 11 and Q. 33, which asked for actual facts and figures on these topics. While the two preceding sections are (with the exception of Table 62) based on Q. 11 and Q. 33, any references in the following pages to hours and earnings are based on Q. 34 (*a*) and (*b*), since it is these which are here immediately relevant.

preferring either the one post or the other committed themselves in that direction, the waverers comprising the third group of 29 individuals, set out separately in the table.

A breakdown of the figures by age reveals that the proportion preferring their present employment fell with advancing years. Thus 77 per cent of men aged 30 and under at the date of interview expressed themselves in favour of their current post, though only 57 per cent of the 31–40 and 41–50 year-olds and merely 51 per cent of the over-fifties did so. Conversely, the proportion preferring RJ increased with age—from one-tenth for those 30 and below to one-third of the over-fifties. One reason for this seems to be that those who made several unsuccessful attempts to secure re-employment and who, so to speak, continued to pine for RJ, contain a relatively high proportion of the elderly. A related factor is that those with over ten years' service with the firm when dismissed were the least satisfied with their current lot: only 43 per cent preferred their present boss, as compared with 68 per cent of those with two or less years' service.[1]

As regards industry groups, if we leave aside those absorbing only a handful of men, manufacture of motor vehicles and cycles boasts the biggest proportion preferring their present job, i.e. 73 per cent. For those who had landed in engineering (other than vehicles) and metals, the corresponding percentage was 61, for construction 58, and for those who had joined transport and communications 55. In the case of the 15 respondents who had found a niche in distribution, two-thirds gave their vote to their present employment; of the three in coalmining, incidentally, all did. What does come as a surprise is that of the 42 'not backs' who had rejoined a former boss, only 57 per cent—i.e. a somewhat smaller proportion than of other 'not backs'—preferred him to RJ, a relatively large number of the 42 describing themselves as 'fifty-fifty'.

As for earnings in this context, those with the highest current income—i.e. more than £19 per week—contain the smallest proportion directly hankering after RJ. However, the relationship between earnings and job satisfaction was not entirely straightforward, and it is the 'over £13–£16' category which shows the largest percentage—just under 73—preferring their present post, as against 67 per cent of the 'over £16–£19' group, not quite 71 per cent of the 'over £19' men, and 48 per cent of those making £10 or under. Those with low wages, we may add, again include relatively high numbers summing it up as 'fifty-fifty'.

More immediately relevant, in strict logic, to the question of

[1] Of those with 'over 6–10 years' service', however, 62½ per cent preferred their present job.

preferences is the *drop/rise* in earnings as between RJ and present. Here it is of interest that, while the handful of respondents who were more than £4 up on RJ (1955), all declared for their present firm, in numerous other instances the change in finance was *not* decisive in shaping verdicts. Thus though 63 per cent of those with enhanced standards in their present job preferred the latter, as against 54 per cent of those 'down' by comparison with RJ (1955),[1] this difference is surprisingly small. Further, of those whose current earnings were the same ±£1, 68 per cent—i.e. a *higher* proportion than of those who had bettered themselves—expressed themselves in favour of their present employment. Again, the figures for those 'over £1–£4' up on RJ (1955) and 'over £1–£4' down are practically identical.

If we relate the answer on job preferences to the more limited topic—dealt with in Table 62—as to whether present hours and shifts were more or less convenient than those before dismissal, it emerges that 68 per cent of those finding the current arrangement more to their liking, also preferred their present job, as against 45 per cent in the case of those considering their present hours, etc., less suitable. Of the latter, fully 42½ per cent declared for RJ—an unusually big proportion. Another noteworthy fact is that of the 50 respondents who thought that the skill grading of their new occupation was superior to that from which they had been laid off, 72 per cent gave their present job as 'favourites'—as compared with 57 per cent of their colleagues.

Of those 'not backs' who had spurned RJ's offer of re-employment, 68 per cent opted for their present post. Overall, therefore, they had no regrets, though at the same time they were not 'conspicuously happier' than the rest of the 'not backs'. An exception are the 31 men who, as we saw, were not invited to return and who were rejected when they themselves took steps to that end. Of these 31,[2] merely one-third preferred their present employment, while of the 15 respondents[2] who made several unsuccessful attempts to secure reinstatement, only one did so.

If the foregoing statistics are suggestive rather than conclusive, this is because jobs were liked and disliked for a wide multiplicity of reasons, some of which escape the net of any of the more formal breakdowns. There were, for example, quite a number who cited 'work' factors in this context, and these were not necessarily associated with any official change in skill status. Thus several explained that they enjoyed the greater variety of their present duties; 'the other was the same thing day in, day out', as one put it. A second reported that in the two years' experience he had had with his new firm, his

[1] 'Enhanced' and 'down' both here mean *by more than* £1 per week.

[2] Of whom 1 was not working on the day of interview.

knowledge of engineering had much increased; he preferred it although his wages had dropped by £3–£4 a week. A third, similarly worse off, observed that 'you do the job from start to finish now', while a respondent who had become a salesman in a retail store remarked that 'if I'd stayed at . . . , I would have turned as dull as ditchwater . . '. Again, a food shop assistant manager declared for his present employment—not for the money, which was half that at RJ, 'but for my own satisfaction', while a mobile servicing engineer commented *inter alia* that now 'I can see the results of my work'.

A different type of 'work' reason for preferring present jobs was that they were cleaner, healthier or less hard. Thus several referred to the speed of the track at RJ—like one who remarked that it built up tension, while the shift system entailed a loss of sleep. Many others mentioned approvingly the change from night or shift duties to a day-time régime; illustrations of this have already been given.

Another ground for preferring present posts was the 'human element': several men emphasized that at RJ 'you are just a number', and that they liked their present *environs* better because they were more of an individual there. Frequently, this went hand in hand with having found a niche in a smaller concern, where there was more direct contact between management and workers. These various strands were well combined in the reply of one respondent: 'I have more satisfaction with my work; I don't feel just a number. The present firm has no canteen or such facilities, but the general atmosphere is better than at . . . . Now I am relied upon as a person.'

Then there were those who declared for their present employment because it did not entail the risk of redundancy—an aspect, again, not reflected in the cross-tabulation of specific variables. Thus a respondent in his middle thirties, who had landed an unskilled job with a local authority and whose earnings were about half those at RJ, explained that 'you may get big wages at . . ., but you never know how long it will last; I've got a job for all my working life and a pension at the end'. A skilled engineering inspector, again 'definitely not earning so much', likewise confessed to feeling much safer. A third, who had become a British Railways goods guard, observed that 'as regards to the hours, I'd rather work in a factory, but you need the security'.

Among other/miscellaneous reasons adduced was appreciation of a reduced journey to work—to which topic we return in the next chapter. A latter-day driver was more contented, because he was subject to less direction. By contrast, a second expressed his approval of there now being better supervision, while a third—still in the car industry—gave vent to the view that RJ was 'a proper jungle; this isn't such a mad-house'. A man whom the events of 1956 had turned into an insurance agent unhesitatingly commended his new calling, because 'you mix with better people', while one who had become a fireman explained that, though the money was less, it was *inter alia* healthier and more interesting, and there was more comradeship, more security, and the chance of a career.

Despite the variety of motives and the gradations of emphasis with which preferences were stated, one theme can be detected as running through the majority of replies of those favouring their present post. This is that a large number of men were more content in the latter although it was yielding them an inferior, or even substantially inferior, income. In many instances there was felt to be compensation in the change from nights/shifts to days, in a shorter journey, in the greater interest of the work, in the less depersonalized atmosphere, or in enhanced security. In other cases there was no obvious off-set, though there were of course also some who had gained financially, like one who had graduated to sales manager and who was currently paying as much in income tax as he had earned at RJ—an undoubted feat. What is striking, however, is that so many should have voted for the job providing them with a reduced, and often much reduced, standard of living.

Turning now to those who confessed to a soft(er) spot for RJ, these include a bus driver who found his current hours and shifts very inconvenient; an industrial civil servant whose earnings, among other things, had fallen from £18 to £11; and one who had landed in a foundry where the work was arduous. One respondent felt that 'I haven't done any good at all since I got stopped from . . .', a second remarked that his then job was the worst ever, while a third preferred RJ 'every time'. Yet another, who had rejoined the industry in which he had passed his entire previous working life, pointed to the happier hours spent at RJ; his present industry was 'dreary' by comparison.

A respondent whose new occupation was that of stock control clerk and who definitely preferred RJ, complained of very poor working conditions and lack of interest in his duties. His earnings were also much curtailed. Another case concerns a man currently employed elsewhere in the motor industry. Though his wages were higher and his shifts more suitable, he considered his pre-R job better—partly because it was less strenuous, but also because his new firm was 'behind the times with regard to method'. A skilled respondent similarly extolled RJ, because 'the administration' there was the best he had ever been under.

A rather sad illustration is that of an erstwhile skilled arc welder whose occupation with his present company was at first the same, but who had to agree to be retrained as a fitter as an alternative to further redundancy. Although still classed skilled, he was no longer rated 'top skilled', and he described his current duties as 'only more or less like labouring'. He disclosed that he greatly preferred RJ, and half considered throwing in his hand and emigrating. Our final example is that of a man who had ended up in the hospital service, training mental defectives in upholstery tasks. He favoured his old job among other things because he was then working with normal people, and he indicated that he would return to RJ, if given a guarantee of continuous employment. Quite a number of others in the group were willing to rejoin the firm without such a guarantee.

As for those feeling that the pros and cons of the two posts about balanced each other, these comprise a few who were equally content in both, and one who was not too enamoured of either. A skilled man stated that as regards workmanship and being happy, he preferred his present employment, though he would probably get more cash at RJ. A second—a warehouseman in a wholesale concern and about £6 per week 'down'—similarly made clear that, financially, he preferred RJ but, occupationally, his present firm. A bus driver explained that though RJ had many advantages, he could not face the insecurity, while a builder's labourer at the time of interview summed it up as 'I'd prefer the factory for winter and the building for summer'.

Of the four respondents working on their own account at the date of interview, one—who had become a car body repairer—expressed a distinct preference for his 'present firm': his finances were much improved, it was almost on his doorstep, and 'I know better where I stand as I'm my own boss'. The second, however, who had set up in radio and TV repairs a few weeks previously, preferred his driver's job at RJ, one of several reasons being that the present involved too much worry. The third in this group, who had started up as a landscape gardener, also declared for RJ 'where it is winter and summer work', while the fourth, a decorator, was in the 'fifty-fifty' category.

We may conclude with two general comments, the first being that preferences are of course relative. Thus a 'vote' for the present job did not necessarily mean that RJ was disliked—as some specifically underlined—nor did one for RJ invariably imply that the individual wished to return there or that, more generally, he was eager to depart from his then employer. How many in fact wanted to stay put and how many were anxious to leave will be dealt with in the next section.

The second point is that it is of course good to know that well over half of the 'not backs' preferred their present employment to that from which they were axed in such dramatic fashion in 1956. At the same time it cannot be denied that, except among the professional pessimists, there is a common tendency to make the best of a job; in this case this tendency might have operated both literally and metaphorically. A person who is tolerably happy in his work and who, for any number of reasons not excluding inertia, does not intend to move, will often fasten on the good features of his post and decide—or gently persuade himself—that it is, all in all, superior to the old. A certain amount of this kind of rationalization no doubt takes place in the shaping of preferences, and it is as well that it does.

While this consideration might be borne in mind in looking at Table 67, there is no wish to exaggerate its importance. The conclusion still is, on the basis of the figures, that in so far as preferences on the part of the 'not backs' are concerned, the honours go to 'present job'. As regards the total sample, on the other hand, if those who preferred RJ are added to those who actually returned (and stayed) there, the evidence is equally clearly that 'RJ has it'.[1]

WANTING TO STAY WITH PRESENT EMPLOYER

TABLE 68

Whether Wants to Remain in Present Job

	Back at RJ		*Not back*		*Total*	
	No.	%	*No.*	%	*No.*	%
Yes	206	91	168	78	374	85
No	8	4	31	14	39	9
Not sure	10	4	14	7	24	5
In Forces/not clear	2	1	2	1	4	1
	226	100	215*	100	441*	100

* Six respondents were not working at the time of interview.

All respondents—irrespective of whether or not they had returned to RJ—were asked 'Do you want to stay in your present job?'[2] As shown by Table 68, the great majority answered in the affirmative, though the proportion was significantly higher for the 'backs' than for the 'not backs'.

Those men who replied in the negative were asked, further, whether they were actually planning a change. Of the 39 individuals concerned, 21 or 54 per cent were planning such a move or had even reached the stage of actively searching for a fresh opening. Of these 21, all except two were 'not back'.

[1] i.e. $\frac{48+226}{447} = 61$ per cent of sample either preferring, or back at, RJ.

[2] Q. 35 (*a*) of schedule.

Relating the figures in Table 68 to those given in the preceding section, of the 'not backs' preferring their present employment 94 per cent also wanted to stay in it. Of those who had declared for RJ, on the other hand, only 48 per cent wished to remain with their new boss; 44 per cent did not.[1] As for those stating that they preferred RJ in some ways but their present job in others, 62 per cent were keen to stay put, 21 per cent were not, while 17 per cent were not sure.

Generally speaking, those wishing to stay were decidedly more numerous than those preferring their present job. This is because 'wanting to stay' in some cases meant genuinely wanting to, but in others merely intending to do so—say, *faute de mieux*, because of advancing years, or for other reasons dictated by prudence or circumstance rather than by positive attachment to the post. It follows that answers were again given with varying degrees of enthusiasm, some of those answering in the affirmative—both 'backs' and 'not backs'—indicating that they would not be averse to bettering themselves, should the opportunity arise. We may add that of the 'not backs' who were disinclined to remain with their present employer, several intimated yet again that their goal was to return to RJ.

VIEWS AS TO 'PERMANENCE' OF PRESENT JOB

As a follow-up to the question about respondents' intentions regarding staying with their present employer, all men were asked 'Do you think your job is likely to last?'[2] A broad grouping of their replies is given in Table 69.

TABLE 69

Whether Thinks that Present Job is Likely to Last

	Back at RJ		*Not back*		*Total*	
	No.	*%*	*No.*	*%*	*No.*	*%*
Yes, will last/has a fair chance of lasting/thinks he is 'all right' for the present	91	40	159	74	250	57
No, will not last/unlikely to last/fears further redundancy	36	16	16	8	52	12
Can't tell/hard to say/position uncertain	94	42	31	14	125	28
Miscellaneous/not clear	5	2	9	4	14	3
	226	100	215*	100	441*	100

* Six respondents were not working at the time of interview.

[1] Eight per cent were not sure.

[2] Q. 35 (*d*) of schedule.

One of the main points of interest of the figures lies in the contrast they paint between 'backs' and 'not backs'. Though the total of out-and-out pessimists was relatively small for both, the difference in the number feeling secure or at least reasonably so is substantial as between the two groups. Over and above this, the nature of the 'yes' of the 'not backs' was more positive on the whole than their ex-colleagues', a sizeable and significantly larger proportion of the 'backs' replying with a qualified affirmative. To which we might add that, as with all opinion questions, the attempt to reduce the material to a few manageable categories does less than justice to the several dimensions of some of the views advanced.

To give a few illustrations, comments from among those feeling 'safe' included 'they'll always want a loaf'; 'I've got a job for life as long as they keep drinking beer'; 'there's no fear of redundancy on the buses'; and 'yes, of course—as long as people throw out the refuse, there will be refuse collectors'. Another—who had likewise joined a local authority—pointed out that his post was superannuated; a second remarked that he was now with a firm who 'never sack anyone through lack of work'. A few observed that they were secure provided they did their part: 'As long as I keep my wits about me and keep on my toes' and 'unless you commit a felony' are examples. One respondent commented that redundancy was unknown in the printing industry: 'A bloke has to drop dead before an apprentice gets on to a machine.' Several men stressed that it was just because their job *was* likely to last that they were in it.

Among those countering with a qualified 'yes' were those who thought that they were all right for the time being, or who realized that in a dynamic setting there was always an element of uncertainty. This feeling, as indicated, was much more pronounced among the 'backs' who, understandably, were inclined to have reservations even if on the whole hopeful.

Those answering in the negative comprised one who declared that his firm—in the engineering industry—'could easily go bust tomorrow'; a second, who had landed with a concern of electrical contractors, and who stated that in that field 'you can be in and out as soon as the contracts finish'; and a third, a painter and decorator, who explained that 'we only do it in the summer'. Among 'backs' considering that their job would not last, some based their misgivings on the spread of automation; some, more generally, on the speed of production; and some on developments in export markets, likely to hit the demand for British cars. Others were worried by the presence of short-time, by rumours and opinion on the shop floor, while one foresaw the cancellation of orders owing to the prevalence of strikes.

Of the large contingent of 'backs' in the 'hard to say' category, many stressed that in the car industry one could not tell from—to quote—one week/day/hour/minute to the next. 'It's rather precarious up there—you can't really bank on anything', as one put it. A second respondent pointed out that since the redundancy there was a fear at the back of every worker's mind that it would come again or, to cite a third, 'I don't expect any immediate eruption, but I am very much on guard'. One man revealed that 'we are reorganizing at the moment, and everybody is on tenterhooks . . .'; others, that since the 1956 dismissals had come quite unexpectedly, current prospects, however favourable, were no guide. A West Indian made clear that he would return home immediately in the event of another lay-off; a skilled and fully apprenticed sheet metal worker wished he had had a better education—so as to escape what he regarded as a risk endemic in all factory employment. But the typical retort of the 'backs' in this group was that 'you can never tell in the *car* industry'. The men, clearly, had balanced the net advantages of the latter against its disadvantages in the sphere of security.

Chapter 7

FINANCIAL AND FAMILY ADJUSTMENTS

In this chapter we retrace our steps, chronologically speaking, and look at the financial effects of the redundancy on the domestic situation and kindred topics. By way of putting matters into perspective, Table 70 relates the length of post-R unemployment to the burden of dependency of the men in the sample.

TABLE 70

Unemployment after Redundancy of Respondents Grouped by Marital Status and Number of Children*

	Unemployment					
	2 *weeks and under*	*Over* 2 *weeks–* 1 *month*	*Over* 1– 2 *months*	*Over* 2 *months*	*Total*†	*No. in category*
Marital status, etc.	%	%	%	%	%	
Single	48	21	16	10	100	73
Married:						
No children	53	13	8	22	100	105
One child	57	16	11	14	100	126
Two children	62	19	8	9	100	77
Three or + children	46	12	19	21	100	52
All Married	56	15	10	17	100	363

* The table covers all 447 respondents with the exception of 11 widowed, divorced, etc., while 3 respondents (no. of children = not clear) are included in the last line of the table only. Marital status is as at date of redundancy; wholly dependent single children only are included. Unemployment = time elapsed between leaving RJ and commencing next job.

† The missing percentages in each case are accounted for by respondents whose length of unemployment was not clear.

As shown, the percentage commencing work within a fortnight of discharge was 48 for the single but 56 for the married—with the proportion *rising* with the number of dependent children,[1] except in the case of those with the largest families. On the other hand, only 10 per cent of the single were unemployed for more than two months,

[1] All references in this chapter to the no. of children cover *wholly dependent single* children only.

while the overall proportion for the married was 17 per cent. These figures require some comment—though the correlation with age and other variables discussed in previous chapters must be borne in mind in this context.

Taking the first column of the table, the data suggest that the single were under less domestic and financial pressure to accept a job immediately after dismissal than were those with heavier commitments. This view—plausible anyhow on common-sense grounds—is in line with the fact that, as we shall see, a significantly smaller percentage of single than of married men suffered serious financial difficulties after dismissal, though at the same time a slightly bigger proportion of the former than of the latter drew on their savings. That those respondents with three or more children do not fit into this pattern is to a small extent at any rate due to the rather higher admixture of coloured families in this group.

The above helps to explain our earlier finding[1] that, although unemployment increased with age, it was the 31–40 rather than the 30-and-under category which had the largest proportion settled in a new post within a fortnight of lay-off. In other words, the men in their twenties—a considerable number of whom were single—were able to bide their time to some extent, while their comparative lack of know-how may have been a contributory factor on the demand side. The 30–40 year-olds, on the other hand, tended to have family responsibilities and were thus more anxious to get placed without delay; they were also—with one or two exceptions—not yet handicapped by their age as were their seniors, while they had more experience to their credit than their juniors. However, while domestic considerations made the question of obtaining work quickly one of special urgency for the family man, this differential factor no longer operated in the matter of extended unemployment, and the difference here between single and married appears to be one primarily of age. For even the single, with savings in the bank and no mouths to feed, could not have relished being 'out' for prolonged periods. The elementary law of the labour market—that its movements are, in however imperfect a fashion, the result of the interplay of demand and supply—thus seems to have been in action: pressures and preferences on the supply side, no less than the requirements of employers, had a bearing on the relative speed of absorption.

ADDITIONAL SOURCES OF INCOME AT TIME OF REDUNDANCY

We shall now deal with some of the subsidiary sources of income available to the men at the time of redundancy. First, while of the

[1] *Cf.* Chapter 3, Table 18.

363 married respondents 67 per cent had wives who were wholly dependent on them, in 32 per cent or 117 cases the wife was working.[1] This figure of 117 covers all those women who did *some* paid work; they by no means all held full-time jobs, many being in part-time and some merely in casual employment. Though these particulars were not asked for, it is clear from information volunteered that the wife's contribution to the household budget was quite modest in some instances, so that it does not follow that those with working spouses were necessarily better off than those without. Several respondents did, however, indicate that they managed due to their good ladies; one, for example, at large for five weeks but whose wife was earning just over £6 weekly, revealed that it was this and his savings which kept them going after redundancy. We may add that the 117 women were engaged in a variety of occupations, and included shop assistants, a bookkeeper, a chocolate packer, a midwife, a typist, one likewise at RJ though escaping the axe, and a number of cleaners. One was running her own hairdressing establishment.

Leaving aside the working wives—as also the earnings of any adolescent children—21 men or 5 per cent of the total sample stated that, at the date of lay-off, they had some subsidiary form of income.[2] In twelve cases this was derived from their own part-time or casual job; five of the remainder were in receipt of a disability pension; one was being paid £20 a month in respect of his previous service with the G.P.O.; one had about £2 a week from a smallholding.

Of the twelve whose additional income stemmed from a part-time post, the majority continued with this after redundancy. One—who while at RJ had busied himself at week-ends as a self-employed body repairer—made this his main livelihood immediately after discharge, and was still so engaged when interviewed. A second—a barman—turned this into his whole-time vocation subsequently. Another spare-time barman stepped up his earnings from that source from 30s. to £3 a week, this being his only occupation during his seven months' unemployment following dismissal. Among other sidelines was playing in a dance band, window-cleaning and relief coach driving; there was also a singer averaging £3 a week, a club waiter, and one who had resorted to cabinet-making when placed on short-time a few weeks before lay-off.

Not counting those already having some part-time pursuit, 26 men—6 per cent of the 447 respondents—*took on* an odd job following redundancy in order to make some cash.[3] As pointed out in

[1] In 3 cases the position was not clear.

[2] Q. 44 of schedule.

[3] Q. 45 (*a*) of schedule. In two or three cases there was some reluctance to give details of casual jobs, and it is possible that a handful were not reported.

Chapter 5, however, the line between a casual and a temporary job is somewhat blurred, and the handful going in for the more substantial kind of stop-gap post are not here included, as we have treated these as 'interim' employment.

Some men commented that there were no odd jobs to be had; others, that they were too busy searching for regular work or that they did not want anything of a casual nature. A few reiterated that they had no cause to seek this sort of outlet, one explained that he was preoccupied decorating his home, while yet another remarked that 'you couldn't because of the Labour pay'.

The odd jobs taken lasted from one day to 'on and off for twelve months'. Their duration did not normally coincide with the period of unemployment, being frequently considerably shorter, though others lasted much longer, being retained to supplement the inferior level of post-redundancy wages. As for type of job, this included gooseberry picking, plastering, gardening, building, odd electrical and motor repairs, helping in the same shop as the wife, driving, and an eight-day Christmas-time spell with the Post Office to relieve an otherwise unbroken eight months on the dole. The amount earned from these activities was equally various.

All those married at the time of lay-off were also questioned whether, because of their redundancy, any member of their family had taken on either a regular or a casual job; of the 363 men concerned, 25 (7 per cent) answered in the affirmative.[1] Of the 25 wives coming to their husbands' rescue, 20 were not then gainfully occupied; of the remaining five, three changed from part- to full-time employment, while one—already a whole-time barmaid—started putting in extra hours.[2] Among the posts taken by the other wives was assisting with school dinners, charring work of various descriptions, a few factory jobs, while one served in a shop until her husband had found a niche. Another turned to outwork in sewing, which she subsequently built up into a flourishing business of her own.

One husband stated that his missus accepted an assignment against his will; a second, whose wife went out potato picking, amplified that she did so merely to pick up the gossip. Some of the jobs were held temporarily; others, on a permanent basis. A few men explained that their wives could not come to their aid because of children—actual or expected; others, that their spouses were already in employment. A West Indian with serious financial difficulties after dismissal disclosed that his wife was made redundant at the same time as himself; another respondent—unemployed for four

[1] Q. 45 (*e*) of schedule. The rest replied in the negative, with the exception of 6 men (2 per cent) where the question was inadvertently not put.

[2] In one case it was not clear whether the wife already had some employment.

months—reported that his wife tried but could not find anything. We may add that no members of the family other than spouses were involved, though one man revealed that his eldest boy promised to do a paper-round but, in the event, could not get up early enough.

The proportion of working wives—as previously defined—was higher at the date of interview than at that of lay-off, having risen from 32 to 36 per cent. Though the majority did not change their status in this respect and while a variety of factors must have been at play, nevertheless over and above the wives entering employment as an immediate effect of their husband's dismissal, there may have been others doing so subsequently by reason of their menfolk's reduced earnings. However, such cases were possibly not regarded as jobs taken *due* to redundancy, which means that the total of wives drawn into the labour market—directly or indirectly, and temporarily or permanently—may be somewhat greater than the 7 per cent indicated.

UNEMPLOYMENT BENEFIT

As mentioned in Chapter 4, 325 of the 447 men registered at an employment exchange after lay-off. All these were asked whether, when declared redundant, they had collected unemployment benefit,[1] their replies being set out in Table 71.

TABLE 71

Whether Drew Unemployment Benefit after Redundancy

(All respondents registering at an employment exchange after R)

	No.	%
Yes	205	63
No	116	36
Not clear	4	1
	325	100

The proportion drawing benefit varied of course significantly with length of unemployment. Thus just under 27 per cent of those embarking on a new post within a fortnight of discharge collected the payment, while for those commencing work more than two weeks after, but within one month of, dismissal, the percentage rose to 75. Of those at large in excess of one month, the overwhelming majority—96 per cent—had recourse to benefit.

Of those who did draw, some stated that they did not receive the

[1] Q. 46 (*a*) of schedule.

full rate or did not collect for the whole period. Others took the opportunity to express the view that the scale of insurance was inadequate. Of those who did not draw, the bulk explained that they were not out of work long enough; others, that they did not qualify because of the week-in-lieu and holiday money, etc. from RJ; yet others—including some who appear to have been eligible—that they 'didn't bother' on that score. A few were too busy looking for a job or expected to find one quickly; one respondent thought that 'the fuss and palaver was too much'. A second—unemployed for seven weeks—remarked that if he had collected the payment, 'I would probably have had to accept jobs offered by the Labour, and I wasn't prepared to do that'. A third had actually been disqualified on that ground.

One man made clear that he did not register until his return from holiday, after which he was soon fixed up; several others seem to have been in a similar position. In a few instances there were difficulties over stamps: thus a former self-employed baker of 35 years' standing had not sufficient contributions to his credit to entitle him to benefit during his four to five months 'out'. A number of respondents mentioned that they had drawn money while on short-time before lay-off, but not following the latter. We may here add that of the total sample of 447, less than half—i.e. 46 per cent—received unemployment benefit after redundancy.

The foregoing particulars are concerned only with the period preceding acceptance of the first post—and not with any benefit granted during subsequent spells of joblessness. As we saw in Chapter 5, 83 respondents had some—or some further—unemployment in the 'interim' period. Of these 83, 34 per cent drew unemployment benefit, the proportion being 17 per cent for those out of work for not more than one month, and 77 per cent for those at large for longer. Too much should not, however, be read into these percentages since, as pointed out, 'interim' unemployment was again frequently short or consisted of more than one spell, while some had voluntarily relinquished the post and were thus disqualified from availing themselves of the payment.

NATIONAL ASSISTANCE

Respondents were asked next whether they had made use of National Assistance facilities—either immediately after redundancy or subsequently.[1] Of the 447, only 13 men or 3 per cent had had recourse to Assistance in the period following dismissal; of these, three individuals also did so on a later occasion. Of the 433 'noes',[2] ten

[1] Q. 47 of schedule.

[2] One answer was not clear.

men likewise applied for National Assistance in the 'interim' period, though not immediately after lay-off.

Of those not drawing Assistance, a few stated that they had endeavoured to obtain help but were not eligible, or that the scale of aid—or that to which they would have been entitled—did not make it worth while. A rather larger number, however, gave vent to their dislike of the whole institution, and made clear that they would turn in that direction only as a last resort or not even then. 'No fear', 'I wouldn't go near it', 'never'—or 'never again' will convey the flavour of some of the comments. One man observed that 'there is no such thing for Englishmen—it is only for the "darkies"'; another expressed himself similarly, though in more forceful terms. By contrast, one or two of the coloured had not been aware of the existence of National Assistance. We may add that a handful of men also made adverse remarks regarding the desirability of drawing unemployment benefit.

SAVINGS

All respondents were questioned next whether, following their dismissal, they had drawn on any savings to tide them over.[1] Their replies are summarized below.

TABLE 72

Whether Drew Savings after Redundancy

	No.	%
Yes	208	47
No	222	50
Miscellaneous/not clear	17	3
	447	100

The first comment called for is that the term 'tide over' was very liberally interpreted by the men. In other words, recourse was had to savings not merely for subsistence requirements, but also simply in order to maintain customary standards of living. The dividing line here is in any case blurred, but a number made quite plain that savings were used for other than necessaries. Some, again, drew so as to be able to honour H.P. and similar commitments, and while incurring the latter may not have been a necessity, the honouring of such obligations was. Further, a few who turned to their reserves mentioned that an addition to the family was about to take place or

[1] Q. 48 of schedule.

that there was illness; here we cannot be certain whether these contingencies would have, in any event, involved resorting to the bank. On the whole, therefore, the figures may somewhat overstate the extent to which savings were depleted strictly as a result of redundancy, though several affirmative answers were—in the light of the supplementary information offered—treated as 'miscellaneous'.

Secondly, savings were drawn upon not merely during the period of post-R unemployment, but also to augment the frequently much-reduced earnings once a new opening had been secured. Thus one respondent, who commenced work two days after lay-off, confessed that it was such a business accustoming himself to half-pay that he spent all his savings; he had averaged £18 a week in the six months prior to discharge, but began his first interim job at £8, subsequently increased to £9.[1] A second, unemployed for one week, drew about £100: his first niche was with British Railways where he started at £7.5.0.; though this was raised by 10s. after a spell of training, his income at RJ had been well over double. Again, a man who the day after dismissal embarked on his present job, helped himself to £2 a week for some six months—until he had adjusted his mode of expenditure to his straitened finances. He was still 'about £6 per week down' when interviewed. Finally, a respondent who became a hospital porter working sixty hours in return for £11.15.0., raided his reserves to the tune of £2 weekly during the twelve months he occupied the post.

These illustrations are by no means exhaustive, though this is not to say that meagre interim wages were the sole or main ground for resorting to savings. Some i.e. turned to the latter both during their spell of unemployment and their first post-R job, while others did so during the former only. Thus a single man—at large for ten weeks—had to fall back on his reserves because it was 'hard to live on Labour pay'. A second—unemployed for six weeks—drew on them for the same reason but, finding they were dwindling, bought some welding gear with the remainder, making a little cash that way. A West Indian spent around £20 travelling north in search of work; another, who tried his hand in London, commented that all the travelling broke him, while a number stated that they continued to pay their wife the usual housekeeping money and depleted their capital to that end. As for the nature of the savings, in one instance an insurance policy happened to mature, in a second it was the wife's reserves, in a third it was funds available through cancelling the holiday, while a fourth drew on what he described as 'a tidy bit in the bank' destined for the purchase of a house. One respondent revealed that he had been putting money away for just such an

[1] These and subsequent earnings figures are *gross*.

eventuality, and was therefore in no particular hurry to look for a fresh opening.

Those spending savings were not specifically asked to what extent they had done so, though a good many added the relevant figure. Thus of the 208 respondents concerned, 36 had drawn up to £25—with another 18 indicating that it was a matter of a few pounds or not a great deal. Seventy had taken out between £26 and £75, while 39 had helped themselves to more than £75—including 17 to over £125.[1] A number had used up all they had. Of the 39 men drawing in excess of £75, 14 were unemployed for upwards of three months.

It will be clear that the resort to the bank depended on several different factors; consequently, the breakdown of the material by our standard variables did not show an entirely consistent pattern. Thus the proportion calling on savings tended to fall with increasing domestic responsibilities—partly, no doubt, because those with families had had fewer opportunities to accumulate them—48 per cent of the single, 46 per cent of those married with no dependent children, 44 per cent of men with one child, and 42 per cent of those with three or more offspring drawing on them. Of those with two children, however, 51 per cent did so.[2] At the same time—ignoring those not giving the requisite details—the proportion spending above £75 was higher in the case of married than in that of single men, and was greatest for those with three or more children. Taking now one of our other favourite variables, the proportion of the sample turning to their reserves rose with length of unemployment, not quite 32 per cent of those out of work for a fortnight or less making use of them, as against 80 per cent of those without job in excess of three months. Here, again, the proportion for men in the 'over 2 weeks–1 month' group, i.e. 72 per cent, was unexpectedly large.

Of the 222 respondents answering the question in the negative, well over one-quarter let it be known that they had no savings at the time, though this is not necessarily the total in this category while, conversely, not all those making this comment necessarily needed to draw on them. Several of the 'noes' simply explained that they were not out of work for long, or that the problem did not arise because of the payments received from RJ. Others managed by cutting down on things or somehow 'scraped through'. An Irishman revealed that all his reserves were 'with M. & B.'; a Pakistani who badly required some, but did not possess any, borrowed some money most of which he sent overseas to his family. A few mentioned

[1] The remaining 45 men made miscellaneous comments but gave no figure.
[2] The proportion for 'all married' was 46 per cent.

that they did not touch their capital after redundancy, but had done so while on short-time. We may here add that 161 of the 222 men, or 72½ per cent of those who did not spend any savings, commenced work within a fortnight of dismissal, though 40 of the non-drawers were unemployed for over one month.

Generally speaking, there is little doubt that savings were a great boon to the men after discharge. Although the proportion of the sample respectively having recourse to savings and unemployment benefit was practically the same, it is clear from the considerable number pointing out that their savings pulled them through, and the very few only singling out the unemployment benefit for special mention, that the availability of the former was the more important item. This is not to suggest that a flat-rate national benefit *can* perform the role that savings are capable of performing, nor is it to ignore the succour given to those without reserves of their own: it is merely to convey the collective flavour of the comments made by respondents. The value of putting something by for a rainy day is indeed one of the lessons which many of the men subsequently stated that redundancy had taught them.

RENT, H.P. AND OTHER COMMITMENTS

All respondents were asked whether, at the date of lay-off, they had any regular commitments such as rent, mortgage, H.P. or similar weekly or monthly payments and, if so, whether they had fallen behind with any of these as a result of their dismissal.[1] Their replies were as follows:

TABLE 73

Extent of Arrears on Contractual Commitments

	No.	%
Had no regular commitment	68	15
Had regular commitment:		
Fell behind	52	12
Did not fall behind	324	72
Not clear	3	1
	447	100

The figures refer essentially to those who had a formal or contractual commitment; they do not, for example, include a married man's obligation to provide for his family. Thus if a husband gave

[1] Q. 49 of schedule.

his wife less housekeeping money, this is not covered—nor is any curtailment in allowances to dependent parents in the case, say, of single men. Many of the latter living at home in fact regarded themselves as having no commitment—which explains the relatively large number in that category. These were not, that is, all owner-occupiers.

It will be seen that 52 persons, or 12 per cent of the sample, fell into arrears with one of the more formal types of payment; as a proportion of those having a commitment, the percentage is 14. Of the 52, 12 fell behind with miscellaneous payments, some type of insurance or their mortgage; 18 with their rent; and 36 with some variety of H.P. A few men were in difficulties with several items or under more than one head. We may add that though hire purchase was the biggest single cause of arrears, it was not of course the most widely diffused 'commitment'; this was, almost certainly, rent.[1]

The arrears were by no means all very serious. For instance, of the 36 who got into trouble over their H.P., all except four kept the article concerned, the firm permitting them to reduce the amount of the instalment, while some were excused payment altogether for given periods. Only three reported that they had to part with the goods in question, while one respondent—with a wife and five children and unemployed for eleven weeks—was sued in connection with a debt on clothing. A *caveat* should here perhaps be sounded in that where shops or dealers were 'decent about it'—as several respondents testified that they were—and without being awkward agreed to instalments being spread over a longer time-span, some men conceivably may not have considered this as 'falling behind'; the same could be true of temporary rent reductions secured from sympathetic landlords. Hence it is possible that a few men answered the question in the negative, even though some accommodation was received. At the same time, this demonstrates that incurring arrears must not be automatically equated with a visit from the bailiff armed with an eviction order, and though 10 of the 52 men had to resort to National Assistance following redundancy, it is pertinent to record that a substantial minority of the 52 did not feel that they had had *serious* financial difficulties.

Not surprisingly, the 52 respondents falling into arrears experienced much longer periods of post-R unemployment than the rest of the men, only 27 per cent commencing work within two weeks of discharge—as against 54 per cent of the sample as a whole. Similarly, 29 per cent of the 52 were without job for over two months, the

[1] Precise figures cannot be given, as details of commitments were only asked for where respondents had fallen behind. However, a considerable number of those with no arrears volunteered the nature of their commitment, the one most commonly mentioned by far being rent.

corresponding proportion for all 447 respondents being 15 per cent. The 52 did not diverge from their colleagues as regards age, and the extent to which they drew on savings was also very similar. However, there was a significant difference in so far as marital status and number of dependent children are concerned. Thus single men constituted only 8 per cent of those incurring arrears after redundancy, though they then accounted for 16 per cent of the sample. Conversely, while the fathers of three or more offspring represented 12 per cent of the sample at the time, they contributed 35 per cent to the 'fell behinds'.

Of those with commitments but no arrears, some simply remarked that they had no difficulty in meeting their obligations. Others, however, admitted to something of a struggle or at any rate to a tightening of belts, several emphasizing that the rent had to come first. Quite a few made clear that it was in order to maintain their payments that they had drawn on their savings: one respondent, for instance, spent practically all he had—more than £200—on his mortgage instalments, while another reduced these to the amount he was obliged to forward under his contract, having consistently sent more than this previously. One or two took the opportunity to stress that they 'did not believe in H.P.'—or at least kept within a limit. On the whole, however, it can be said that the men behaved with a sense of responsibility; they used up their savings or trimmed their expenditure rather than 'fall behind'.

THE EXTENT OF FINANCIAL DIFFICULTY AFTER REDUNDANCY

As the final item in this series, respondents were asked whether, all in all and taking, say, the first three months after redundancy, they had had some—or serious—financial difficulties.[1] The question was designed to ascertain how the men themselves summed up the situation, and Table 74 consists of a broad grouping of their verdicts.

It is emphasized that too fine a degree of precision must not be imputed to the table, as in the grading of this type of material there is clearly some overlap between adjoining categories. Similarly, answers are liable to be influenced by character and attitude: some are inclined to shrug off having to do without certain creature comforts, while others view this in a more serious light. Nevertheless, the figures give a broad indication of the extent to which the lay-off was felt to have imposed financial strain in the short and medium

[1] The precise question (Q. 50 of schedule) was: 'All in all, taking, say, the first three months after redundancy, would you say you had *some*—or *serious*—financial difficulties?'

TABLE 74

Extent of Financial Difficulty after Redundancy

	No.	%
None	161	37
Nothing much; no, though had to economize, etc.	50	11
Some financial difficulties	131	29
Serious financial difficulties	87	19
Miscellaneous/not clear	18	4
	447	100

run; the phrase 'the first three months after redundancy' should not be taken too literally.

Of the 'nones', almost a quarter countered in terms such as 'no difficulties whatever' or 'none at all'. The 'nothing muches', by contrast, qualified their remarks in some direction. Many of those with no or no real pecuniary headaches added comments to account for this: these ranged from being single to having a working wife, while a Pakistani had none because—as his interpreter confirmed—when one is in trouble, compatriots come to the rescue. Again, a respondent in his fifties and out of work for some six months answered the question in the negative, but made clear that he had depleted his savings.

One man observed that, not having 'got used to the big money', he managed; others, that it was a case of cutting out luxuries or lowering their standard of living somewhat. One husband related that 'it stopped me going out a bit, that's all'—with an aside from his wife that 'a bit' meant 'never'. A second explained that, working on the railways, he anyhow had not much time to spend money. A third confessed to merely having the *fear* of financial worries, adding that the women probably suffered more from this. On the other hand, a respondent securing employment immediately after lay-off said that he was possibly rather better off in these three months, since he was working sixty hours a week; there were of course others in this position.

Among those describing themselves as having had *some* difficulties was one—unemployed for six weeks—who had to sell an endowment policy before maturity. A second's problems were due to the fact that a week before discharge he had moved to another house—with both a higher rent and articles to be bought. A third reported 'just slight difficulties', though these included three months' arrears with his H.P. instalments on a camera. A single man, at large for five weeks, similarly fell behind with his payments on a tape recorder, as well as exhausting his savings of about £40.

Before quoting from the case histories of the 87 respondents with serious—ranging from fairly to very serious—financial troubles, it may be pertinent to scrutinize their characteristics *in toto*. As regards age, they tended to contain somewhat higher proportions of the elderly. Thus taking all 447 men, 17 per cent of those 30 years and under had pronounced difficulties; 21 per cent of those between 31 and 40, 19 per cent of the 41–50 group, but 26 per cent of those over 50. Nevertheless, age is unlikely to have aggravated pecuniary hardship directly; indeed, some of the factors responsible for it primarily affected the younger men. The rather bigger proportion of over-fifties experiencing financial embarrassment would appear to be a corollary simply of the greater difficulty these men had in finding work and their consequently more prolonged spells of joblessness.

On the subject of skill, 21 per cent of those graded skilled by RJ had serious money problems, 18 per cent of those classed semi-skilled, but in the case of the unskilled the proportion rose to 38 per cent. This last figure, however, is most probably swollen by the fact that 10 of the 19 respondents in the sample born in India, Pakistan, West Indies or 'other abroad'—a high percentage of whom were un-skilled—had pronounced cash worries.

Not surprisingly, family responsibilities were an important item in this context. Thus only 4 per cent of the single felt that they had been seriously embarrassed—as compared with 23 per cent of the married. Within the latter group, the proportion was 19 per cent of those with no dependent youngsters, 22 per cent of men with (both) one and two children, but of the 52 fathers with three or more off-spring, 33 per cent encountered grave financial difficulties. Again, however, the three-or-plus child couples contained a somewhat higher sprinkling of coloured respondents.[1]

The overwhelming majority of the 87 men—94 per cent—also had a rough passage securing a job after lay-off, three-quarters considering the search for work to have been 'very difficult'. By contrast, of the 259 persons who—as we saw in Chapter 3—found it hard to obtain a placement, only 32 per cent had serious monetary problems. The position as regards post-redundancy unemployment is detailed in Table 75 (page 196).

Though the 87 individuals clearly had a very different record from the rest of the sample in the matter of post-R unemployment, approximately one-fifth of the former nevertheless commenced work within two weeks of lay-off. This is because financial problems at the time were due to a variety of causes; for example, the 87 comprise a comparatively large number of men with greatly-reduced 'first

[1] The coloured, that is, accounted for about 3 per cent of the total sample, but for about 8 per cent of those with three or more children.

TABLE 75

Length of Post-R Unemployment of Respondents with Serious Financial Difficulties, Compared with Rest of Sample

	Men with serious financial difficulties after R		*Remainder of sample*	
*Unemployment**	*No.*	%	*No.*	%
2 weeks and under	18	21	226	63
Over 2 weeks–1 month	12	14	58	16
Over 1–2 months	20	23	32	9
Over 2–3 months	20	23	23	6
Over 3 months	14	16	11	3
Miscellaneous/not clear	3	3	10	3
	87	100	360	100

* i.e. time elapsed between leaving RJ and commencing next job.

interim' earnings. All the same, it can be seen from the table that long unemployment was not co-terminous with pecuniary complications of the more grave kind: the sample of 447 consists, in all, of 68 respondents out of a job in excess of two months; of these, one half had serious financial difficulties.

As regards resources available to them, 61 per cent of the 87 men had recourse to savings, as compared with 43 per cent of the rest of the sample. The former also drew on them more heavily, at least[1] 13 per cent using more than £125—as against 2 per cent of the remaining 360 respondents. In some ways, though, it may seem surprising that the divergence was not more pronounced, but this can be explained by the fact that not all those in need of savings possessed them and, secondly, that the latter were spent for other than strictly 'tiding over' purposes. We may add that 12 of the 87 men, or 14 per cent, resorted to National Assistance in the period following lay-off.

As for some flesh-and-blood illustrations from among the 87, there was the 40-year-old Brummie with a wife and four children, who could not find a job until three months after redundancy. He used up his savings, applied for National Assistance, and dropped behind with his H.P. payments. In a nutshell, his trouble was that he had to keep his family on £6 a week, as compared with the £10 he had averaged prior to discharge. A second case concerns one likewise with five dependants, unemployed for ten weeks. This man had

[1] As previously indicated, the amount of savings drawn was 'voluntary' additional information and not supplied in all cases.

to maintain his household on 'just over £5 Labour pay'; he incurred some seven weeks' arrears on his rent and had to part with his TV set.

Our third example is a man with spouse and three children at the time of dismissal, following which he was without livelihood for six weeks. He was compelled to have his H.P. instalments reduced and had recourse to National Assistance, while his wife took a part-time job to ease matters. This respondent had earned £24.10.0. weekly in the half year preceding lay-off; he found himself without savings when the axe fell though, as he put it, he 'learned the lesson since'. Yet another with a wife and four offspring, but no resources, became unemployed for five weeks after holding a skilled post at RJ. When he was *inter alia* threatened with eviction for defaulting on his rent, he sold his bedroom suite—losing heavily on the deal. On obtaining work, his wages were £12 as against £18 before discharge; in his own words, after the first month it was 'one gigantic struggle'. A respondent with four dependants, and out of work for six weeks apart from a casual job, likewise had severe trouble although drawing £80 of savings. Among other things, the family had to dispose of their van, sewing machine and shed.

While in the preceding instances the accent is on unemployment plus a sizeable family, in the following it is on unemployment combined with heavy contractual commitments. An illustration here is a man in his early forties, without children though one was on the way, who spent between £150 and £200 of his savings during his four months 'out'—primarily so as to maintain his mortgage. A second, unemployed for three months apart from an odd job and also with a mortgage to keep up, got through about £300 worth of reserves; his wife entered the labour market, whereupon he was disqualified from National Assistance. This man described the position as not too bad to begin with, but later 'came towards the end of his tether'. A respondent unplaced for eight weeks stated that things got desperate the last month, because of the weight of his hire-purchase debt on furniture.

Commitments caused difficulties also in the absence of both unemployment and a big family. An interesting example is a respondent in his middle thirties—without children and a wife in full-time employment at the date of redundancy. He commenced work after a fortnight at £8 a week, his average pre-R earnings having been £20. He had mortgage payments to meet and, in addition, owed about £200 privately for the deposit on his house, which he had to continue repaying. He used up approximately £30 of his savings and his wife put in some overtime; 'terrible' is how he summed it up. Again, a man with two dependants and unemployed for one week only, found his wages reduced from £15 to £8.10.0.; having commitments on a caravan and house totalling some £15 per month but no savings, he fell temporarily behind with his instalments. We may add that one man disclosed that it took about twelve months to clear off his arrears of rent.

We see then that whether or not serious financial difficulties ensued depended on a considerable variety of circumstances. Perhaps we can define the problem as three-dimensional, in that the crucial items in the equation were, first, the fall in income resulting from unemployment and/or reduced earnings; secondly, the men's total commitments—using the term now in the sense both of the burden of dependency and contractual obligations. Thirdly, there was the question of resources to meet the situation—the wife's wages, the number of other earners and the extent of their net contribution to the household budget, odd jobs or other forms of minor income, whether unemployment benefit was collected, National Assistance resorted to, and the availability of savings. Over and above these, there were also special complications such as, say, illness or the arrival of a baby. Tempting, therefore, though it may be, it would be inaccurate to force the data into the strait-jacket of one or two factors as the sole generators of monetary worries at the time—just as there is no simple measure of their severity. Thus falling behind with an H.P. debt was not invariably equivalent to having pronounced trouble; to some degree this depended on the ease with which accommodation could be gained from the dealer. The spending of savings, similarly, does not clinch the matter. Quite apart from the fact that this course is possible only where reserves have been accumulated in the first place, how serious their depletion is is a function not merely of the total drawn, but also of the total possessed, the care with which funds have been built up, and the purposes for which it was planned to use them. In general, the data show that even a comparatively mild redundancy, such as that of mid-1956, causes a not insignificant amount of hardship. This lends urgency to the question of making financial provision for the more drastic varieties of the genus that are now upon us.

CHANGE OF ACCOMMODATION

All respondents were asked—turning our back now on financial topics—whether they had moved to new accommodation since discharge and, if so, the reasons.[1] The purpose of the question was to ascertain how many such moves were a direct result of the dismissals, though the replies were rather 'disappointing'. For while 127 of

[1] Q. 52 of schedule.

the 447 men had changed their address, in only six cases was this specifically due to the lay-off.[1] This latter figure does not include those *temporarily* living in alternative accommodation—i.e. while holding an interim job away from home. Similarly, those who, on returning from such sojourns, took lodgings with a different landlady have not been counted, as the change of home here was merely incidental.

Of the six whose move was a direct consequence of redundancy, two had changed house within the Birmingham area in order to be nearer their new job. A West Indian, being unable to obtain employment, had left the city altogether and since August 1956 was living and working at a dozen or so miles' distance. When queried on the subject,[2] he explained that the finding of fresh accommodation had not proved difficult—though his wife having to look for another post, as well as himself, had. The move also entailed separation from a brother and friends.

The remaining three men had all changed addresses to get cheaper accommodation, one of them having quite a history of travelling behind him. This respondent, following dismissal, could no longer afford the rent of his flat; after a week's unsuccessful search for work, he took his family home to Ireland for a fortnight's holiday. He then journeyed to London alone, where he had his first interim post; separation apart, his stay there involved an added financial headache since he had to keep himself, forward money to his wife and child, and save for their eventual return to England. However, finding it impossible to settle in the metropolis, he returned to Birmingham after a few weeks, and on securing a new boss as well as a cheaper flat, was able to send for his family.

The great bulk of moves were due to the usual factors—being offered a council house, eviction, to have a place of one's own, or simply to take up more suitable accommodation. Possibly, the redundancy played a part in the background in isolated cases. For instance, the desire to get away from in-laws may conceivably have been heightened by strained tempers in the post-R period. But this is rather stretching a point, and it is clear that, though there was a substantial amount of moving, it was by and large independent of the 1956 lay-off. It needs, however, to be added that the picture might be altered somewhat, had the 'left-without-trace' fraction of the original sample proved less elusive than it did.

JOURNEY TO WORK

We now come to the impact of the dismissals on the journey to work, details for the 'not backs' being set out in Table 76.

[1] In 8 cases the precise reason was not clear.

[2] Q. 53 of schedule.

TABLE 76

Journey to Work before and after Redundancy

(All respondents not back at RJ)

	To RJ		*To Present Job*	
	No.	%	*No.*	%
5 minutes and under	8	4	24	11
6–15 minutes	50	23	59	27
16–30 minutes	83	38	77	36
31–45 minutes	45	20	25	12
46–60 minutes	23 }	14	10 }	7
Over 60 minutes	9 }		4 }	
Varies/miscellaneous*	—	—	14 }	7
Not clear	3	1	2 }	
	221	100	215†	100

* Includes travelling salesmen, self-employed decorator, servicing engineer and similar. Also those in Forces/Merchant Navy.

† Six respondents were not working at the time of interview.

As indicated, journeys for the 'not backs' were shorter, overall, at the time of interview than before the discharges. On the face of it, this could be due either to respondents having moved nearer to their place of employment or because they had found a post in greater proximity to their home, though it is clear that in this instance the latter is the case. For while one-third of the 'not backs' had a present job outside Birmingham[1] and despite the considerable number changing addresses, very few respondents had actually moved out of the city; in fact, the vast majority were, at the date of interview, living in the same distance range from Birmingham as when made redundant. Thus of the 299 persons then residing in the city, 290 were still living there when interviewed, while of the 125 residing at defined distances from Birmingham—the reader is referred to Table 7—all except four had remained in that 'distance belt'. Seeing that present journeys were briefer, on average, than those to RJ, this means that a good many 'not backs' had exchanged RJ for a boss closer to their doorstep.

Before looking at the shortening of journeys as it affected individuals, we might point out that the reduction is reflected also in changes in the mode of travel as between pre- and post-R. Thus 33 'not backs' were currently walking to their place of work, as compared with 23 prior to lay-off; likewise, 30 were cycling—as

[1] *Cf.* Table 53 *ante.*

against only 14 doing so while at RJ. Again, those having to resort to two buses, or a coach and bus (or similar), fell from 13 to 4 men. We may add that the total travelling by car (including friend's car, etc.) went up—from 28 persons (RJ) to 41 (present)—the number using bus or coach having dropped sharply by the time of interview.[1]

The changes in the method of transport—like the mass of, in the context of the project, fortuitous moves—complicated the attempt to measure just how many men had a slower or faster trip to work as a result of redundancy. Thus where someone had found a post round the corner—entailing a 5-minute walk as compared with a 30-minute bus ride—the switch in the means of transport followed naturally from that in distance. Where, however, a respondent reported a 20-minute car run currently as against a 40-minute one by coach to RJ, this could be simply because he had meanwhile acquired a car or for some reason had decided to use it daily. In such instances, it would be misleading to link the time saved to the change of employment occasioned by dismissal. Accordingly, for purposes of Table 77 overleaf all schedules were scrutinized, and those 'not backs' who had either moved house on grounds unconnected with the lay-off, or where the change in mode of travel was such as to make a comparison only doubtfully relevant, were eliminated. This left 129 'not backs' in respect of whom it appeared reasonable to contrast the length of journey to their present workplace with that to RJ prior to discharge.[2]

As compared with those rejoining RJ, the 'not backs' had more extended journeys previous to lay-off, though the differences were not pronounced: for example, 9 of the 221 'not backs', but only 6 of the 226 'backs', then had over an hour's travelling. Further, taking the 'backs' as a whole, there were only marginal variations in the length of their trips before and after redundancy, and as a result—by the date of interview—the 'not backs' were better off *in re* travelling time than their erstwhile colleagues. Thus 38 per cent of the

[1] In the case of the 'backs', the total travelling by car similarly increased from 26 (pre-R) to 42 (present)—with a corresponding reduction in the numbers going by bus/coach. There were only few other differences in the backs' mode of travel between the two dates.

[2] More precisely, from the 221 'not backs' were eliminated (*a*) 56 who had moved house for reasons unconnected with redundancy; (*b*) 17 who were not working at the time of interview or where the journey varied/was 'not clear' (RJ or present job); and (*c*) 19 where the difference in the mode of travel made the comparison dubious. By and large, these were switches involving the use of a car at one date only, and though these may have been due to R (lower/higher earnings, for example), it was not possible to tell. Where, however, it seemed reasonable to compare the two journeys despite the changed means of transport, the schedule was included for purposes of Table 77.

TABLE 77

Change in Journey to Work for Individual Respondents

(Respondents not back at RJ)

	No.	%
Journey to present job the same as to RJ ± 5 minutes	32	25
Journey to present job longer than to RJ:		
By 6–20 minutes	14	
By 21–40 minutes	16	27
By more than 40 minutes	5	
Journey to present job shorter than to RJ:		
By 6–20 minutes	21	
By 21–40 minutes	28	48
By more than 40 minutes	13	
	129	100

former, but only 27 per cent of the 'backs', had a 15-minute journey or under to their present employer, while merely 7 per cent of the 'not backs', as against 14 per cent of the 'backs', needed more than ¾ hour in order to reach him.

Chapter 8

FROM TRADE UNIONS TO THE 'INEVITABILITY' OF REDUNDANCY

In this chapter we deal with a few miscellaneous topics, beginning with a series of trade union subjects about which questions were addressed to the sample.

TRADE UNION MEMBERSHIP

TABLE 78

Whether a Member of a Trade Union at Time of Redundancy

	No.	%
No	76	17
Yes: rank-and-file member	358	80
Yes: shop steward, branch official, etc.	13	3
	447	100

Trade union membership at the date of discharge is set out in Table 78. There were wide variations in the matter according to firm (RJ), the proportion of non-members among those laid off from the several companies ranging from nil to 47 per cent. In this instance, the differences between the four B.M.C. concerns were almost as large as those between all six firms in the sample. Three major unions accounted for nearly four-fifths of those affiliated.[1]

Of those not belonging to a trade union when dismissed, only 36 per cent were back at RJ at the time of interview; of the 371 respondents who did belong, 54 per cent had returned. The causal connection is not, however, entirely clear; there is, amongst other things, no precise correspondence between the proportions reinstated by individual concerns and the extent of unionization. All the same, of those laid off from the firm with—in terms of the redundant population

[1] The figures are based on Q. 15 (*a*)–(*d*) of schedule.

—100 per cent union membership, by far the highest proportion was back.

Replies by those who did not belong ranged from 'I was lapsed' to 'I don't believe in trade unions'. One man had been a member until becoming a chargehand, with his wife explaining that these were 'on the firm's side'. A second had thrown in his hand because the unions were getting him 'browned off'. Other reasons were a temporary or permanent dispute—or simply not having been approached/enrolled. Comments by those who were affiliated covered an equally wide span—from 'I've been a member all my life' to 'I joined it because we had to'.

Among answers to whether respondent was a branch official or shop steward were 'not at the time', 'no, but I've always been an active trade unionist', 'no, thank you' and 'wouldn't have that for a pension'. One man countered 'never on your life—too many bloody communists for me'; a West Indian remarked that he would not be given such a position. An ex-branch treasurer and shop steward pointed out that, in the latter capacity, 'you are a friend of neither management nor men'. We may add that the fact that only 13 respondents, or 3 per cent of the sample, had held office—including, in some cases, quite minor office—makes it unlikely that the discharges were employed to get rid of troublesome office-holders, though only 4 of the 13 had found their way back to RJ.

T.U. HELP IN THE SEARCH FOR WORK

Of the 371 respondents in membership of unions at the time of lay-off, 33 or 9 per cent had some help from this source in their search for work, while 90 per cent stated that they had not.[1] However, as we saw in Chapter 4, merely one-fifth of unionists *applied* to their trade union for details of vacancies; of those who sought such aid, therefore, nearly 45 per cent received it.[2] On the other hand, as in the case of the employment exchange, obtaining help includes being the object merely of 'helpfulness': of the 33 persons who had some assistance in this context, only 12 actually secured their first post-R job via their union.

The extent to which trade unions provide employment services for their members varies—as of course does the existence of a closed or quasi-closed shop for individual trades. The bulk of those who

[1] One per cent of replies was not clear. The figures are based on Q. 15 (*g*) of schedule (*minus* the phrase 'or any other way').

[2] This proportion is not comparable with the 30 per cent who received help/'helpfulness' from the employment exchange (*cf.* Table 32)—*inter alia* since the latter had to be computed as a per cent of all those registering at an exchange, not all of whom applied for assistance.

were succoured were sheet metal workers or in various vehicle building occupations, and a relatively high proportion were skilled men. Comments include 'oh yes, they got me a job', 'yes, they sent me to several jobs', while some expressed appreciation that their trade union maintained a list of openings and firms. One respondent related that his union secretary 'would ring up factories for you to find out if any jobs were going'. Another, that he was apprised of vacancies and that particulars were also being given at branch meetings. One of the skilled sheet metal workers summed it up as 'we have our own organization for that; all men are registered, and firms apply to the society for good men'.

It will be clear that a negative reply to whether help was received covered several different situations. Typical answers were 'I never bothered them, as I dropped into a job straight away'; 'well, I didn't ask them—I've no doubt they would have done'; and 'no, they offered to, but I'd already got a job'. Then there was 'it would have been useless . . . there were so many out'; 'they were overburdened with labour, you couldn't get near the office'; and 'I applied, but it was no good'. Next, 'no, I never went to them . . . they had my address', and 'no, they are a wash-out'. One respondent kept away 'as I felt they hadn't done enough at the time'; a second burned his membership card, as he had been forced into belonging—in his view, most of the men were in that position. A third—who had suffered from 'anti-RJness'—held the unions responsible, while one said that his T.U. had hindered him in that he was refused a card for a post of his choice.

T.U. UNEMPLOYMENT BENEFIT

Of the 371 respondents in membership of a union at the date of redundancy, 28 or 8 per cent received some payment from that source during their unemployment following lay-off, while 91 per cent did not.[1] Those who drew benefit again include a relatively high proportion of skilled craftsmen, 11 of the 28 also having had help in their quest for work. The rate of benefit was mostly between 10s. and 15s. per week, though it did not necessarily accrue for the whole period of joblessness.

Several of the 'noes'—some of whom, it will be clear, were not unemployed—had not inquired about the matter. Others disclosed that they had not been a member sufficiently long, while one or two admitted to being in arrears with their subscriptions and so disqualified. One man, at large for 16 weeks, was not eligible, as he had not paid the special contributions for the purpose, while

[1] Q. 15 (*f*) of schedule. One per cent were not sure, etc.

one or two others with lengthy spells on the dole also explained that it was 'their fault', in that they had not claimed their entitlement.

Leaving aside the question of help in the search for work and the granting of benefit, a sizeable minority referred to various general measures—or attempts at such—taken by the unions at the time.[1] These comprised the holding of meetings with management, the endeavour to introduce more short-time or otherwise stave off the dismissals, the attempt to ensure they were fair, the calling of a strike and the obtaining of compensation. Only a handful mentioned that their union had intervened with a view to procuring their removal from the fatal list, though by and large the men did not expect such action—both because of the 'last in, first out' rule and because of the suddenness of the operation.

CHANGE OF UNION SINCE REDUNDANCY

TABLE 79

Whether Has Changed Trade Union since Redundancy

(All respondents who were trade union members at time of R)

Position at time of interview	*No.*	%
Still in same union	230	62
Now in another union	61	17
No longer in any union	78	20
Not clear	2	1
	371	100

As shown,[2] 62 per cent of those belonging to a union when made redundant were still in the same organization at the date of interview. A few of these indicated that they had left temporarily or had entered another body to match their interim employment, but that they were now back in their old T.U. All these are recorded as 'still in same union'.

Of the 61 men in another union, some 43 had changed because they were currently in a different job/industry, or because they were now in a closed shop, or because all their mates were affiliated to the new body, or similar. Examples are having joined the N.U.R., the Post Office Engineering Union, or the N.U.M. Also included are

[1] Q. 15 (*e*) of schedule. As this question was very variously interpreted, precise figures are not being given.

[2] Table 79 and the following paragraphs are based on Q. 15 (*h*) and (*i*) of schedule.

those making less radical changes of employment, but who explained that 'the firm I'm at now has a different union'. Further, the group comprises a few 'backs' who had transferred their allegiance along with their job/shop, or who did so to fall in with their colleagues.

The remainder had switched to an alternative organization on miscellaneous grounds, such as 'just chance really' or being promoted. One 'back' was enrolled by the trade union first to approach him after reinstatement; a second was anxious to avoid the arrears of dues accumulated during the 'interim' period. One or two thought their new union better in some respect, while one had made the move for political considerations. What is of interest is that only a handful of the 61 changers adduced dissatisfaction over services rendered *à propos* of the redundancy.

Turning now to the 78 respondents who *no longer belonged* to a union when interviewed, the overwhelming majority—72 men—were not back at RJ. Some 35 (of the 78) gave as their reason that there was currently no need to be affiliated, or similar. Thus 'I'm working for a non-union firm now'; 'because very few are in the union at . . .'; and 'the trade what I'm in, there's no union'. Again, 'I have a staff position now'; 'I'm not in one since I've been a labourer'; and 'not because I have anything against the unions—I now work with a very small firm'. One man intimated that membership was unnecessary because 'we have no complaints against the boss'; a second, that they received the full rate plus a generous bonus for good time-keeping. Two respondents revealed that they were in the employ of a company that would not tolerate a union on the premises.

Of the 35 individuals just dealt with, some made neutral noises subsequently when asked to comment generally about trade union activities or policy at the time of redundancy, some made favourable ones, but some made adverse remarks. The distinction between the group and our next one—i.e. 31 men who accounted for their no longer belonging by their dislike/disapproval of unions—is not, therefore, a hard and fast one. Illustrations from this second category are 'I don't believe in unions—at . . . I was forced to join', and 'I was only in . . . because it was a closed shop'. Again, 'I've no interest'; 'I don't hold with all these strikes'; and 'I haven't got any time for them'. One respondent thought that the trade unions were too powerful, a second felt they were merely out for themselves, while a third went so far as to say that they should be done away with. One man considered that the employers he had known were more reasonable in their attitude to the workpeople than were union officials, though he made clear—as did several of the critics—that opposition was to defined T.U. practices, rather than to unionism *per se*.

It will be seen that the majority of those dropping out for reasons of hostility, etc., objected to unions on general grounds rather than as a result of grievances arising from their handling of the redundancy. A few, however, intimated that their disenchantment dated from the lay-off—like one who lost faith over the 'last-in, first out' principle, while a second observed that after paying 1/7d. a week for two years, he had not got his money's worth. A third was dissatisfied because he was not given help in finding alternative employment, while yet another considered that he should not have been dismissed and *inter alia* bore his union a grudge on that score.

The final 12 of those no longer in membership had miscellaneous motives such as 'just not bothering'; one of these had been at large for eight months following dismissal, and had not troubled to join since. Another indicated that he was merely a part-time worker now, a second was in the Forces, while a third intended to belong again once he was properly established in his post. A fourth remarked that 'there's no point in the building trade—the union isn't strong enough', while one in a government naval depot likewise felt that while at RJ one got 'satisfaction', little was to be gained by affiliation currently.

PRESENT POSITION OF NON-MEMBERS

Of the 76 respondents who, as shown by Table 78, did not belong to a trade union at the time of lay-off, 37 had not enrolled since, though 39 had. The 76 comprise 27 men who had meanwhile returned to RJ; of these, all but 5 had become members. Of the 49 'not backs', on the other hand, only 17 had joined in the interval.

Of the 39 who had affiliated since dismissal, 3 had left again or were intending to do so. Twenty-two had signed up for reasons such as that they were now in a closed shop or because virtually everyone else belonged. One of these revealed that he had himself been converted to the merits of the closed shop; a few, more generally, commented on the advantages accruing from membership, though one stated that it was a case of 'Hobson's choice'. The remaining 14 respondents had become unionists on a variety of grounds, several explaining that their non-membership when discharged had been more or less an accident. One—back at RJ—admitted that at the date of lay-off 'I wished I had been in'; among other things he had now joined because the unions 'got a fair deal for the redundant men'.

In conclusion, it can be said that though the dismissals led to a considerable change in trade union affiliation, by and large this did not result from the activities or policies pursued by the unions at the time. It is a commonplace that the strength of unionism is to a significant extent a function of industry and plant: that, by the date of interview, there was a net loss of membership is not surprising, since relatively few of the 'not backs' are likely to have transferred to more highly unionized enterprises. Also, though some hard feelings were certainly voiced by those no longer in membership, on the whole these were of pre-R origin and of a general kind. Both the switch of allegiance to another organization and the cessation of membership altogether did not, in broad terms, flow from any specific dissatisfaction over the unions' handling of the redundancy.

VIEWS ON 'FAIRNESS' OF THE 1956 DISCHARGES

TABLE 80

Whether Thinks that Method of Selecting those to Be Laid Off Was Fair

	No.	%
Fair	175	39
Unfair	193	43
Fair in some ways, unfair in others/hard to say/not sure/miscellaneous	79	18
	447	100

All respondents were asked 'Do you think the method of selecting those to be laid off was fair?',[1] their replies being summarized in Table 80. It is pointed out, first, that this particular question was confined to the ethics of the selection procedure, and did not extend to the handling of the redundancy as such. Secondly, both the major verdicts were given with different degrees of emphasis, though the 'unfairs' tended to be more definite. Another item to be borne in mind is that some answered in general terms, while others did so primarily from a personal point of view. Yet others tried to cover both aspects, though several stressed that they could only speak for their own section or shop.

Of those countering 'fair', 47 per cent were back at RJ at the date of interview; of both the 'unfairs' and those making mixed comments, 53 per cent had returned. Another interesting fact is that the proportion of 'fairs' fell with age—being 45 per cent for men aged 30 and under, 40 per cent for the 31–40 year-olds, 37 per cent for the 41–50 category, but only 21 per cent for the over-fifties. An unusually high percentage of the last-named felt it was a case of 'fifty-fifty', so that the largest proportion actually saying 'unfair'—i.e. one half—was among the 41–50 group.

[1] Q. 14 (*a*) of schedule.

The mode of selection varied according to the identity of RJ, one of the crucial factors being the weight given to the 'length of service' criterion. In brief, the range was from this being the sole consideration to it merely being the determining factor *other things being equal*, with—in that event—ability, etc. as the pivotal item. Speaking in broad terms, length of service was the main guide as far as the present sample is concerned, though an important point is that the latter can be, and was, calculated in divers ways—of which more anon.

Meanwhile, we may record that the proportion answering 'fair' ranged from 36 to 75 per cent for the several firms in the sample, while the percentage replying 'unfair' varied between 12½ and 49. What may come as something of a shock is that the company using ability as the primary principle is the one where those affected came out with a 75 per cent 'fair' vote. This is certainly an achievement, even though it is probable that the verdict here was due to factors other than the basis of selection. We might also add that some men stated that the latter was largely decided by the trade unions, so that 'fair' or 'unfair' was in these instances directed at the unions as well as, or rather than, at the firm.

The proportion declaring 'fair' was not quite 31 per cent of those graded skilled prior to lay-off, 33 per cent of those classed unskilled, but 41 per cent in the case of the semi-skilled. The percentage of 'unfairs', however, was almost as high for the semi- as for the skilled—i.e. 43½ against 45—though it was only one-third for the unskilled. Somewhat surprisingly, perhaps, there were no material differences in the matter between those who were and those who were not trade union members at the time.

TABLE 81

Views on Fairness of Method of Selection by Length of Pre-R Service at RJ*

	Thinks that method of selecting those to be laid off was				
	Fair	*Unfair*	*'50:50' etc.*	*Total*	*No. in category*
Length of Service at RJ up to time of R	%	%	%	%	
6 months and under	57	29	14	100	28
Over 6 months–2 years	42	41	17	100	181
Over 2–6 years	42	40	18	100	152
Over 6–10 years	31	52	17	100	46
Over 10 years	11	64	25	100	36

* The table covers all 447 respondents, except 4 whose length of service was not clear.

The relation between the men's views and their period of employment at RJ up to the date of dismissal is dealt with in Table 81. As will be seen, length of service made a significant difference, which is not of course to be wondered at, since the expectation of staying on must have increased according to the time already spent with the firm. What is rather odd, therefore, is the similarity between the figures in the second and third lines of the table.

To give some flesh-and-blood illustrations, many of those answering 'fair' based themselves on what they regarded as the essential equity of the 'last in, first out' rule—L.I.F.O., as it was frequently called. As one man put it, 'if I was doing it, I'd do it the same way . . . I can't see anything fairer myself'. Another gave most convincing proof of the probity of the whole exercise: his father, a foreman at RJ, 'could have pulled strings to get me kept on, but he stuck to his principles and I was paid off'. Some of the 'fairs', however, had certain misgivings, feeling that though the method was fair, it was not necessarily the best from the firm's standpoint.

As for those in the 'unfair' camp, these include both those disagreeing with 'last in, first out', and those approving of it but who considered that it had not been properly interpreted. A very common criticism was that L.I.F.O. had been applied to the section (or line/track) rather than to the firm (or shop) as a whole, and numerous examples were given of how inequitably this had worked out in practice. As one explained, on some sections men with 28 years' service were sacked because their colleagues had 30 or more, while on other tracks those with merely two or three years with the firm stayed on, because the rest had still less. He added that the worst cases were where men had been moved a short time previously, one or two respondents suggesting that such transfers had been deliberate. One man cited the fate of a workmate, shifted after an industrial accident; although a long-service worker, he was laid off since he was now last in his section. A second remarked that those who had trained newcomers had to leave, while their charges with fewer years to their credit were retained because they happened to be on a well-selling model when the axe fell. The respondent who summed it up as 'definitely wrong; it was L.I.F.O. on the section; it should have been done on service with the firm' was typical of many.

There is no denying that there was a good deal of this kind of inequity. Although the 'section' basis—it was not applied by all the companies—was actually in line with a trade union decision, there is no doubt that it involved much injustice as between individuals. 'Last in, first out' which means in practice that men with 15 years' service are dismissed in one case, while those with two years are kept on in another becomes relatively beside the point—in particular, when the definition of a 'section' is rather loose and when, as it appears, there was no complete consistency in just how seniority was calculated. At the same time, some men approved of the 'section' method while, at the other extreme, a respondent in his late forties felt that even 'L.I.F.O. on the firm' was not enough. He regarded the whole procedure as unfair because, although only having some eight months with RJ, he had been in the trade since age 14, while others had merely two or three years behind them. He was echoed by several colleagues who resented that those only relatively recently attracted to the car industry had been able to remain in their posts.

As for the men opposed to L.I.F.O. altogether, some held that it worked unfairly against those with long periods in the Forces, while a few commented in terms such as 'it doesn't give a young chap a chance to settle down'. Primarily, however, those in this category were of the opinion that skill, merit, ability and so on should be given weight. Thus a fully-apprenticed carpenter and joiner described it as wrong for a poor workman to be retained and a skilled one thrown out—'that isn't what you learn a trade for'. Or as another put it, speaking for many, 'I think they should take quality of work into account'. Among miscellaneous complaints were that those on the night shift had been discriminated against, that 'with some of the blokes, it wasn't what they knew but who they knew', while a few believed that they were dispensed with because they were non-unionists. By contrast, one suspected that in his shop the 1956 redundancy served as an opportunity for management to eliminate those supporting an earlier strike over the dismissal of a union leader.

As pointed out, Table 80 consists of the replies to the specific question as to the fairness of the mode of selection. As a follow-up, all respondents were asked 'Have you any other comments about the firm's handling of the redundancy?',[1] their answers ranging from 'callous' and 'criminal' to 'no, they were very good about it really'. What might be stressed is that a verdict of 'fair' on the selection issue was by no means always associated with a like one on the general handling of the discharges, many both among 'fairs' and 'unfairs' heavily criticising the firm over the abruptness of the lay-off. Others did so because of the numbers involved or because of the lack of staggering the dismissals, while their timing just before the holidays and the smallness of compensation also came under fire. Some felt that the sackings could have been entirely avoided, like one who referred to them as 'silly' since he was summoned back after only a week, while a second stated that 'mass redundancy is not human'. A third observed that the firms had become overstaffed in the months

[1] Q. 14 (*b*) of schedule.

preceding lay-off: 'If they had been more careful about setting on labour, there need not have been so many out.'

By far the most common general criticism of RJ, however, was over the absence of notice. 'Ham-handed' as one called it, while a second described how the foreman came round with the list 'and we were in or out, just like a load of cattle'. He added that 'it was only a few hours before we had to leave; if there had been a mass fire there, we could have understood'. In this connection, several commented that RJ must have known well in advance who was going to be made redundant in that the cards and wage packets were ready; yet it was this lack of notice which caused all the confusion at the employment exchange.

On the other hand, one man held that if an enterprise had not got the work, it could not keep its employees and was entitled to dismiss whom it pleased. Another, that not much could be said about the firm's handling of the lay-off, as it was governed by the unions in that respect. An ex-shop steward felt that on the whole RJ had stuck to its agreements with the trade unions, especially as regards reinstatement; he also paid tribute to the extent of short-time working during the six months leading up to discharge. Again, there were those who thought that the whole issue had been one for the higher counsels of the corporation rather than for their immediate employer, while a few considered that it was the Government who were behind it, so that here again the men's strictures were not invariably directed against the firm. Finally, some of those replying 'unfair' to the selection question took the opportunity to express appreciation of particular features of RJ's activities both *à propos* of, and apart from, the redundancy.

METHODS OF SELECTION FAVOURED IN ANY FUTURE REDUNDANCY

(*a*) *Length of Service versus Skill, Ability, etc.*

More or less turning our back now on the past, all respondents were asked 'Where a redundancy is declared, what do you consider the fairest method for selecting those to be laid off?'[1] Just over 62 per cent of the 1 in 10 sample suggested length of service, 220 men or 49 per cent mentioning no other method. Thirty-four per cent cited skill, ability, time-keeping, etc., 101 respondents or 22½ per cent again doing so exclusively. All other alternatives were put forward by an insignificant number only; for example, a mere 5 per cent

[1] Q. 57 (*a*) of schedule.

thought that the list should be compiled in (or *inter alia* in) the light of family commitments.[1]

If we relate these figures to those in the preceding section, of those favouring L.I.F.O. *à propos* of any future redundancy, 57 per cent also felt that the system of picking those laid off from RJ had been fair. Of those who wanted any future contingency to be handled on a skill etc. basis, by contrast, only 16 per cent adjudged the 1956 operation to have been equitable.[2] In terms of the back/not back theme, of the 226 men who had rejoined the firm as at date of interview, 53 per cent gave length of service as the fairest means of choosing those to be discharged in the event of another lay-off; for the 221 'not backs', the corresponding proportion was 46 per cent. As regards age, those opting for L.I.F.O. tended to be slightly younger than the sample as a whole, while those declaring for skill, workmanship, time-keeping, etc., contained relatively more over-forties.

A number of respondents, before committing themselves in any direction, emphasized that the prevention of redundancy must be the main aim or stressed the importance of adequate notice. As for those commending L.I.F.O.—many of whom specified how this was to be computed—some pointed out that it would cut out all favouritism, particularly in a large firm where it was difficult to rate everyone individually. Others, thinking primarily in terms of RJ, preferred L.I.F.O. because 'everyone is only a glorified labourer, so skill doesn't come into it'. One man remarked that any alternative basis would put 'older men, whose life has been in the job and who couldn't change their ways, out of work'. We may add that while some favoured length of service, as it were *faute de mieux*, one or two made clear that they were underwriting it although it would once again adversely affect them.

As for those proposing skill, workmanship, time-keeping, etc., these were placed in one category, even though these criteria are not of course identical. However, comments about them and related methods were made in so many combinations and so often intertwined—for instance, there were references to loafers and slackers, containing elements of both inferior workmanship and poor time-keeping—that it seemed best to treat them as one. Actual replies included 'sack the bad workers, keep the best'; 'they should judge

[1] Another 6 individuals mentioned personal circumstances/need and may have meant the same thing.

[2] These and the following percentages in this paragraph are a breakdown merely of the 220 men who exclusively mentioned L.I.F.O., and of the 101 who exclusively cited skill/workmanship, etc., as the fairest method to be employed where a redundancy is declared. Those favouring other, or a combination of, methods are excluded.

you on your merits'; and 'they should look at the workmanship of a man and at his value to the firm'. One man retorted 'first get rid of the slackers—there are plenty at . . .—and keep the most highly-skilled till last'; several others also referred disparagingly to some of those who had found a niche at RJ. Yet another had 'seen it time and again—they lose some real good men over this service lark'. Some respondents perceived a basic conflict between what was fair from the standpoint of the men/unions and that of the enterprise, but others believed that ability, etc. as the main principle was in the best interests of all.

Some saw a way out of the dilemma in suggesting a combination of length of service and skill, while one was of the opinion that 'in a small firm it should be done on merit, but in a large firm . . . it would have to be L.I.F.O.' Leaving aside for the moment the few spontaneously urging the claims of the family man or analogous criteria, various miscellaneous methods were also put forward. Thus four respondents held that the fairest system was by ballot, while one remarked that 'they ought to get rid of some of the office staff first'. A second wanted the unfit and the elderly to go, but others were worried by the ethics of such a course, a few stating that there simply was no equitable way of performing the operation. Another handful refused to be drawn altogether, because 'nobody should be laid off'. Generally speaking, there were many thoughtful replies, some men at any rate having given much consideration to the pros and cons of the several alternatives.

Following the question as to the fairest method favoured for choosing those to be laid off in any future redundancy, all respondents were asked whether certain additional factors—other than those already cited by them—should also be taken into account.[1] The items were length of service, skill and quality of work, time-keeping, and number of children.

Of the 220 respondents who, as we saw, had proposed a length-of-service basis and who had not spontaneously mentioned any other, 136 or 62 per cent stated, when specifically asked, that both skill/quality of work and time-keeping should also enter into the reckoning. In some instances, the 'yes' was not very positive, though in others it was. Thus 48 of the 136 *definitely* wished to see at least one of these criteria being given weight. As against this, only about 7 per cent of the 220 respondents replied 'no' to both, while a further 27 per cent said 'yes' to one but were non-committal or negative vis-à-vis the second. Putting it another way, of the 220 commending L.I.F.O. but no other principle, 83 per cent were, when questioned, in favour of some notice also being taken of time-keeping, while of

[1] Q. 57 (*b*) of schedule.

the same 220 individuals two-thirds were, when asked, in favour of skill and quality of work being given greater or lesser weight. Only 11 per cent of the group said 'yes' to neither.

As for the 101 men who, in response to the first question, had described skill, quality, time-keeping, etc. as best, 57 per cent stated, when queried, that length of service[1] should likewise be taken into account. Twenty-four per cent held that it should not, while the remainder were not sure. As in the case of the L.I.F.O.s admitting to also favouring skill, those replying in the affirmative include some who were inconsistent, or who had at any rate not thought through the implications of their particular prescription. But by no means all were in this category, for both the enthusiasm with which the original principle was put forward and the emphasis with which the 'also' method was subscribed to varied widely. Further, it no doubt would be possible to devise a 'points' system under which both length of service and merit, etc. are given their due, so that it is legitimate to express approval of two potentially contradictory régimes. Judging from the comments made, however, some men were plainly inconsistent, and it appears that rather more of the 220 L.I.F.O.s than of the 101 advocating skill, etc., were so guilty.

(*b*) *Number of Children*

As indicated, all respondents were asked whether various criteria, other than those spontaneously suggested, should also be given weight, the last of these being the number of children. Thirty-eight per cent of the total sample[2] were in favour of their being considered, 55 per cent were opposed, while 7 per cent were undecided and so on. What is of special interest is that the single comprised a bigger proportion than the married willing to see allowance made for the family man: of the 54 respondents without spouses at the time of interview, 44 per cent felt that the number of children should also be a criterion, while of the 378 married[3] only 37 per cent thought so. As for age, the small band of over-sixties[4] contain the largest percentage—i.e. 53—willing to show consideration to the *pater-familias*, followed by the 41–50 group (45 per cent in favour) and the 30-and-under category (41 per cent in favour). The 31–40 and 51–60

[1] Length of service has been defined throughout as meaning employment with one firm; those favouring service to an industry/trade as the best criterion have been regarded as being in a different category.

[2] The figures are here being related to the whole sample, as the total spontaneously suggesting 'number of children' as the primary method of selection was insignificant.

[3] Which excludes 15 widowed, divorced or separated at the time of interview.

[4] There were 15 men aged 61 and over at the time of interview.

year-olds were comparatively hard-hearted—with only about 32 per cent holding that the number of offspring should enter into the reckoning.

The percentage opposed to family commitments being taken into account in the drawing up of redundancy lists can be regarded as significantly high. For in one sense it did not 'cost' anything to assent to a series of subsidiary methods also being given weight and, as we saw, sizeable proportions of those spontaneously advocating L.I.F.O. and skill readily agreed, when queried, to the claims of the rival principle. In the case of 'number of children', however, there was a strong feeling that this was a man's own business; by far the most frequent comment of the 'noes' was to that effect, only very few objecting to it because, say, it conflicted with L.I.F.O.

Typical replies were 'that's nothing to do with the firm'; 'if people go in for children, they know they have to bring them up'; and 'no, that's your own affair'. A few pointed out that family and income tax allowances were designed to deal with the matter, while one feared that 'there are some that would hide behind that'. One respondent remarked that he had four little ones himself but would not expect to be kept on on that score; a second, that fathers of several children should make it their duty to be in a regular job, so that the prospect of redundancy would not arise. Of those who approved of the number of children being considered, most emphasized the greater need or predicament of such men, while others felt that the children should not suffer: 'It's better for one to go hungry, and not four or five kids.' Some, finally, were of the opinion that dependants should count, but only 'other things being equal'.

All respondents were asked next whether they thought that, in the event of a lay-off, certain groups should be requested to go first, irrespective of their length of service and similar considerations.[1] Below we deal with their views in so far as married women, men over 65, and coloured and foreign workers are concerned.

(*c*) *Married Women*

TABLE 82

Whether Thinks that, in Event of Redundancy, Married Women Should Be Asked to Go First, Irrespective of Length of Service, etc.

	No.	%
Yes	392	88
No	26	6
Hard to say/depends/miscellaneous, etc.	29	6
	447	100

[1] Q. 57 (*c*) of schedule.

The verdict of the sample was overwhelmingly that married women be dispensed with first, irrespective of their service and analogous factors. At least one-fifth of the 447 respondents were *definitely* in favour of such a course, though approximately another fifth qualified their answer, countering in terms such as 'yes, if husband is working', 'yes, unless a widow' or similar. It is necessary to add at once that the large proportion of 'yeses' reflected the opinion of many that married women ought not to be at work in the first place.

Actual replies included 'they're not the breadwinners', 'their husbands should support them', 'they're mostly only after pocket money' and 'I'd rather a woman be out than a man'. Again, answers such as 'their place is at home', 'I wouldn't have a married woman in a factory', and 'any time—not just redundancy' were put forward by considerable numbers, although here the point of the question was to some extent lost in a wider issue. A few expressed disapproval of the quality of women's work or of the amount of money earned by them, though one urged equal pay—so as to remove their attraction as a source of cheap labour. One respondent believed that there were always plenty of alternative openings available for them.

The 'ayes' who were less adamant primarily made allowance for those married women who are not in fact typical of their *genre*, i.e. they held that married women ought to be dismissed first unless they were the main breadwinner due to their husband's unemployment or sickness, or because they were widowed, deserted and so on. In a few cases such consideration for defined categories produced replies such as 'yes, unless she has to work': here it was not altogether clear whether the reference was to the same type of factor or whether the intention was to make some concession also for the woman who, though equipped with a working spouse, was helping towards the household budget. These answers were therefore treated as 'miscellaneous'. We may add that a number of other respondents commented in terms such as 'yes, if they are doing a man's job'.

As for the small band opposed to women being discharged *ipso facto*, some took their stand on principle. They regarded such a policy as straightforward sex discrimination or as in conflict with a L.I.F.O. or 'skill' basis of selection, while one described it as 'a form of escapism—it's taking the easy way out to solve the unemployment problem'. Others gave examples of the different circumstances impelling married women to seek work, and generally took the line that these were so various as to make it wrong automatically to single them out for the sack.

One of the most interesting features of the replies lies in the contrast they provide to those to the 'number of children' question. The typical feeling of the sample was that number of offspring was a man's private affair, that work and domestic matters ought to be kept strictly apart, and that if a man was in greater need by virtue of the youngsters he had acquired, that was his own business. In the case of married women, on the other hand, the argument in favour of their prior dismissal rested very largely on their lesser need: here, that is, personal circumstances were, without qualms, felt to be a legitimate—indeed the crucial—factor in the equation. Be that as it may, the verdict of the sample is not in doubt.

(*d*) *Men over* 65

TABLE 83

Whether Thinks that, in Event of Redundancy, Men Over 65 Should Be Asked to Go First, Irrespective of Length of Service, etc.

	No.	%
Yes	281	63
No	122	27
Yes and no/not sure/miscellaneous, etc.	44	10
	447	100

As shown, more than three-fifths of the sample were of the opinion that, in the event of a lay-off, men over 65 should be requested to go first[1] irrespective of length of service and similar considerations. As might have been expected, the proportion holding this view fell with age, though the differences were not very marked: while 68 per cent of those 30 years and below favoured the prior discharge of those above pensionable age, the corresponding percentages for the 31–40 group, the 41–50 year-olds and the over-fifties were 64, 60 and 55. For the small number of over-sixties, the proportion rose again to three-fifths.

One of the stock responses of the 'ayes' was that men over 65 should retire. Some emphasized the desirability of this quite apart from any imminent redundancy—a blurring of the issue parallel to that come across in the preceding section. Thus one respondent felt that the old ought to enjoy the last years of their life, a few taking the line that people should down tools already at 60. More

[1] Strictly speaking, it is not, of course, possible for several categories to be asked to go *first*. However, the point of the questions was to ascertain the men's views as to whether defined groups should be discharged automatically, i.e. before L.I.F.O. or whatever principle of selection was favoured was put into operation. The order of precedence as between these categories was considered as of relatively minor interest and ignored for purposes of the questions.

frequent was the reference to the over-sixty-fives' eligibility for a pension from the state, their firm, or both, while others pointed out that such men no longer had any domestic commitments. 'They've got the pension and they've had their chance'; 'I don't think anybody should work after that age'; and 'they should make room for younger men' are typical.

While a considerable number of those replying in the affirmative seemed somewhat brutal in their comments, this was by no means true of all. Thus several respondents thought that the work was too arduous or the pace too fast for the elderly—especially in the car industry—while one was worried by the greater likelihood of accidents. Others, however, held that men over 65 were not much good any more, while yet others suggested that a part-time or odd job would be more suitable. Several believed that by that age a man ought to have saved enough to be able to withdraw from the scene, particularly if he had been at RJ. In the words of one, 'they've earned their money, or should have done'. A second contrasted the two pensions that could frequently be picked up, with the unemployment benefit alone available to a younger man on dismissal. On the other hand, several were uneasy because of the inadequacy of the pension, and coupled their 'yes' with a plea that this—state and/or firm—should be more generous. Generally speaking, then, those of the opinion that men over 65 should be dispensed with first *à propos* of any lay-off include both those anxious about the welfare of the old and those, by contrast, whose concern was primarily for the young.

As for the respondents opposed to men over 65 being discharged automatically, many answered in terms such as 'not if they can do the job', while some described the elderly as being better or more conscientious at their tasks. Others remarked that it was difficult for them to obtain alternative employment, or that the national pension was insufficient. Only relatively few specifically based their reply on L.I.F.O. etc. considerations, though the fact that a policy of dismissing the elderly indiscriminately may well be in direct conflict with 'last in, first out' might possibly have weighed with some of those not going into details. An interesting point is that it should have been felt that the old ought not to be sacked first *provided* they could still do a good day's work—a test not otherwise demanded or even regarded with disfavour by many.

Among actual replies from the 'noes' were 'their job means more to them than to most young chaps'; 'they might need it—people don't work for fun'; 'I think they ought to find them light work'; and 'they've got to live, and the pension's inadequate'. One man commented that the Government was in fact encouraging the elderly to postpone retirement; a second, that 'if the poor old soul wants to die working, it's up to him'. A third observed that 'it's all some men live for', and cited the case of an ex-colleague in his late sixties, who was well and happy until—but not beyond—the redundancy of 1956.

(*e*) *Coloured and Foreign Workers*

TABLE 84

Whether Thinks that, in Event of Redundancy, Coloured and Foreign Workers Should Be Asked to Go First, Irrespective of Length of Service, etc.

	No.	%
Yes	201	45
No	182	41
Yes and no/not sure/miscellaneous, etc.	64	14
	447	100

Table 84 shows that, on the issue of coloured and foreign workers, the sample was much more evenly divided than on the parallel questions relating to married women and the old. Though the replies revealed a fundamental cleavage of opinion—covering the whole spectrum from naked prejudice to expressions of impeccable egalitarianism—the coloured might derive some comfort from the fact that they were at any rate vastly more popular than married women, as well as distinctly more so than those over retirement age.

While the 1 in 10 sample contained no married women and no men aged over 65 at the date of redundancy,[1] it did comprise a number of coloured and foreign-born respondents—i.e. 19 stemming from India, Pakistan, West Indies and 'other abroad', as well as 35 Irishmen whose status as between an Ulster and Eire origin was not ascertained. More generally, there were some differences of attitude according to place of birth, those born in the Midlands outside Birmingham including the highest proportion—53 per cent—saying that the coloured and foreign should be dispensed with automatically in the event of a lay-off. Next came the Brummies with 47 per cent; the small contingent of Welsh and Scots with 44 per cent; 'England, other than Midlands' with 35½ per cent; the Irish with 34 per cent; while of the 19 coloured/abroad, one answered in the affirmative. As for age, the proportion feeling that the coloured etc. ought to be discharged first rose from 40 per cent of the 30-and-

[1] It is likely, however, that of the 15 men over 60 years at the date of interview, two or three had reached or passed age 65.

unders to 58 per cent of the 51–60 group, though of the over-sixties only one-third favoured such a policy.

Inevitably, perhaps, comments tended to centre on coloured rather than on foreign workers, and here again the question was willy-nilly merged into a much broader issue. In other words, a substantial number of those wishing to see the coloured depart first *à propos* of any lay-off made clear that they did not approve of their being here altogether, or at any rate that not so many should have been allowed into the country. Others went so far as to say that they ought to be sent straight home, or should be so dealt with in the event of a redundancy. At the same time, another sizeable number of 'yeses' pointed out that they had nothing against coloured people, but felt that Englishmen should have preference; many in this category were at pains to stress that they had no prejudice even though advocating discrimination. As for the 'noes', the majority of those enlarging on the topic objected to any differential treatment on principle, though a minority, having registered their 'no', likewise took the opportunity of questioning the wisdom of an open-door immigration policy.

To give some illustrations, there was 'they shouldn't let them in in the first place'; 'this happens to be our country, and they can live on National Assistance better than we can'; 'they shouldn't be kept on at the expense of an Englishman'; and 'if you can find one out of ten that will do any work . . . you're lucky'. One thought that 'their being here is a big cause for redundancy', while a few referred to the fact that many of those from overseas had been retained during the 1956 lay-off. Several replied that the coloured were merely labourers so that the problem did not arise, adding that if they were on production, they should leave first. Others singled out particular groups for their special displeasure, one stressed that foreign included 'southern Irish', while a second had the order of dismissal neatly worked out: first to be sacked should be the Irish, then the Pakistanis, and lastly the Jamaicans. We may add that, here and there, there was also an undercurrent of feeling against English non-locals obtaining employment in Birmingham.

Turning to those opposed to any discrimination, comments comprised 'they should be the same as us'; 'every man's equal'; 'everyone's got to earn a living—black or white'; and 'they often cause less trouble than some of the natives'. Several replied that they did not believe in the colour bar and that there was 'good and bad in every lot'; one remarked that there were whites with decent jobs in Africa; a second, that 'if they were good enough to fight with us, they're good enough to work with us'. A third maintained that 'if they're allowed to enter the country, they should be allowed to work', while another view expressed was that if their employer had been satisfied until then, there was no reason to mete out special treatment at the time of lay-off. Some reiterated that the L.I.F.O. or 'ability' test should apply; in the words of one, 'if a fellow knows his job, it doesn't matter whether he's black, white or pink'. One man observed that the majority of the foreign were British subjects, 'and if you treat them well, it does help to hold the Empire together'.

As for the last item in Table 84, this covers those who were undecided—like one who was torn between his natural inclination and a desire to be fair. Then again there were several wishing Commonwealth and colonial citizens to be retained but not the foreigners, or who wanted the coloured to be kept but not the southern Irish, or the Jamaicans but not the Indians. The group also comprises about a dozen countering in terms such as 'no, they are mostly labourers—they're not competing with us'; these were recorded as 'miscellaneous', it being considered—as in the case of parallel replies concerning married women and the over-sixty-fives—that these were not genuine 'noes'. That this is so is borne out by the fact that in two instances, where a diligent interviewer posed the supplementary as to what should happen if the coloured *were* doing semi-skilled work, the retort was promptly that in that event they should go first.[1] We may add that one or two were at a loss for an answer, feeling that the coloured were doing jobs unacceptable to Englishmen.

By way of concluding this whole subject, a few general comments may be in place. First, as regards a formula such as 'last in, first out', this is potentially something of a shibboleth, for it can be applied in divers ways—with very different results. Thus it may mean total service with the firm, with the whole of the works taken as one unit; or it may signify total service, but with each shop or department treated as self-contained; or it may mean total service with the enterprise in so far merely as the men on any one section or track are concerned[2]—with effects of the kind described. Then again, where the shop or section is the unit, seniority in the latter only may be reckoned—lending still greater significance to previous accidental inter-plant transfers. Further, 'total service' itself requires definition: it may or may not include former (disparate) spells of employment; it may or may not cover time spent in the Forces; while in a large combine, subject to bouts of reorganization, there is also the matter of employment with no-longer-existing companies. The question of service 'to the trade' is likewise a difficult one. What is important

[1] As pointed out earlier, there were also quite a number answering 'yes, if on production' or similar.

[2] These problems would not, of course, arise in small firms.

to realize is that the application of L.I.F.O. can be a fairly meaningless exercise, in that while it may deprive a firm of some of its best workers, it does not necessarily ensure any real equity between those of the same seniority.

As for the method of selection favoured *à propos* of any future lay-off, the present sample was not of course picked so as to be representative of the generality of workers, and no claims of any kind are made that the figures given are typical of the latter. At the same time, there is no special reason to regard them as a-typical; moreover, they are of interest in that all the men had themselves been the victims of redundancy, and had frequently—inconsistencies notwithstanding—given much thought to the subject. Nor is there any evidence to suggest that their experiences warped their judgment. What should, however, be pointed out is that though the intention had been to get away from the events of 1956 in so far as the men's attitudes to the handling of any future contingency are concerned, it is likely that many of the replies were framed with conditions at RJ or in the car industry primarily in mind. Thus a number of those holding that skill, ability and good workmanship should not be taken into account in drawing up redundancy lists based this on the view that on the track there was little scope for their display; similarly, some favoured L.I.F.O. chiefly because in very large factories a more individual assessment is fraught with complications. On the whole then, answering with, as it were, one eye on RJ has probably introduced a pro-L.I.F.O. bias;[1] it is all the more significant that a sizeable minority of the sample should have spontaneously pleaded the merits of skill etc. as the principal mode of selection.

Further, even in the case of those declaring for 'last in, first out', the majority—when questioned—stated that skill, time-keeping etc. should also be given weight. And while in many instances there was no contradiction, in others one got the impression that L.I.F.O. had become something of a *cliché* or stock reaction, in that some conceded, with distinct enthusiasm, the claims of good workmanship and time-keeping, when they had just made clear that 'last in, first out' should reign supreme. Again, as we have seen, large numbers of those regarding the latter as the most equitable method were prepared to see it put into cold storage, when it came to special categories such as married women, the old and the coloured. Thus of the 220 respondents originally commending L.I.F.O. as the fairest way of choosing those to be laid off in any future redundancy, 86 per cent

[1] Similarly, when asked whether those over 65 should go first irrespective of other considerations, some of those in favour referred to an agreement to that effect now operative at RJ. This may have increased somewhat the number of 'yeses' among the 'backs'.

nevertheless were of the opinion that married women should be asked to go first, 63 per cent that men over 65 should, and 42 per cent that the coloured and foreign should. Fully 26 per cent of the 220 men held that all three should be dispensed with in such a contingency *before* L.I.F.O. was to operate, while nearly 43 per cent believed that at least two of the three should. By contrast, only 2 per cent countered with a consistent 'niet' in the case of all three groups.

This is not to deny that 'last in, first out' was much the most popular single method put forward, nor is it to suggest that its adherents were, all in all, more inconsistent than their colleagues. For while the 101 respondents recommending skill etc. as the primary principle of selection were somewhat more reluctant to admit the claims of the system most immediately at variance therewith, when it came to the three categories of married women, the over-sixty-fives and the coloured, the 101 men were even less prepared to let these stand or fall simply on the strength of the criterion posited by them.[1] Finally, while on a question such as the treatment of the coloured *à propos* of a redundancy it is unlikely that the gulf between the 'ayes' and the 'noes' can be bridged,[2] it may well be that on the 'L.I.F.O. versus skill/workmanship' issue a considerable consensus of opinion might be achieved by some form of 'points' scheme designed to do a measure of justice to both.

THE 'INEVITABILITY' OF REDUNDANCY

Table 85 (overleaf) sets out the answers given by the sample to the question 'Do you think redundancies could be prevented altogether, or would you say they are bound to happen from time to time?'[3]

A considerable number of respondents—'not backs' as well as 'backs'—linked their remarks specifically to the motor industry: of those believing that lay-offs were bound to happen, for example, roughly 30 per cent expressly referred to the world of cars. However, this was perhaps 'inevitable'.

There was a certain difference of outlook between those who had and those who had not returned to RJ, 43 per cent of the former but nearly 52 per cent of the 'not backs' saying that redundancies must of necessity occur. As for age, the proportion holding that dismissals

[1] i.e. nearly 30 per cent of the 101—as against 26 per cent of the L.I.F.O.s—wanted all three categories to be discharged *ab initio*.

[2] We are, of course, referring to relatively isolated redundancies. In the event of extensive unemployment throughout the economy, there is little doubt that the clamour for the prior dismissal of the coloured would reach very high proportions.

[3] Q. 58 of schedule.

TABLE 85

Views on Inevitability of Redundancy

	No.	%
Redundancies are bound to happen	211	47
Redundancies could be prevented	119	27
Redundancies can't be prevented altogether, but their frequency/scale could be reduced	87	19
Question not answered/miscellaneous/not sure	30	7
	447	100

must be expected fell from 51 per cent of the 30-and-unders to 39 per cent of the 41–50 year-olds, though of the over-fifties just above 55 per cent regarded them as unavoidable.

Quite a number simply answered—a little fatalistically perhaps—'well, they're bound to happen', or similar. Others cited trade recessions; 'you're bound to get a fluctuation in the markets for one reason or another', as one put it. Some implied that periodic discharges were more or less inherent in the laws of supply and demand, while one based himself on the 'multiplier' effect of any one lay-off. Yet another ascribed it to the human element; managements, like individuals, 'have quiet spells followed by a rush'. Many realized the international dimensions of the problem, while others concentrated on the position facing a firm with no orders: 'They can't pay you for doing nothing.'

A fairly common view was that redundancies were certain to be with us because of mass production; there was a distinct feeling that productive techniques had become a kind of self-propelling force, flooding the market independently, and in excess, of the state of demand. There were also several references to automation: thus 'it's frightening when you come into contact with it'; 'automation is doing people out of work'; and 'I think it [redundancy] is inescapable, especially since the introduction of automation'. As indicated, many related their comments to the motor industry, which was judged to be specially vulnerable in view of its seasonal nature, its being a 'luxury' trade, because cars 'are quicker to make than to sell', foreign competition, and because 'in the car industry it's always been the same and always will be'. One or two added a reminder that 'it used to happen every year at one time'.

Turning now to the 119 respondents believing that it was possible to avoid redundancies, approximately two-thirds thought that this could be achieved by—or *inter alia* by—more short-time, a reduced working week, an evening out of production schedules or kindred solutions. Typical replies were 'they could largely be prevented—there should be more short-time'; 'yes, definitely—if they kept it to a 44-hour week and stopped stock-piling'; and 'the only way is to cut out overtime and spread the work over a 12-month period'. One man observed—*à propos* of any threatened contingency—that 'even if we had a couple of pounds a week less, it would be better'; a second, that the car industry made sufficient profits to retain all its employees on a reduced wage; a third, that short-time would be practicable, if no work were put out to sub-contractors. Generally speaking, the feeling that 'sharing is better than redundancy' was very widespread among this group.

Some stressed that a more long-term cure would be a permanent reduction of the standard week, one or two believing this to be particularly necessary in view of developments in the sphere of automation. Others put the emphasis on the control of manpower: to quote one who had rejoined RJ, redundancies 'could be prevented altogether by the firms making use of a smaller labour force . . . doing overtime or short-time as the situation dictates'. Some 'backs' referred to the fact that such an agreement had actually been concluded following the 1956 dismissals, one maintaining that it had been broken by the men's unwillingness to put in the requisite overtime, though a second testified to its success in his firm. Several of those urging more careful manpower budgeting expressed the opinion that this had been absent in 1956, in that 'they were starting blokes just a few weeks before', and 'were only about two months and they were starting people back'.

Coupled with the proposals for more short-time and a regulated labour intake, but also independent of it, there was the view that more planning and foresight on the part of management were called for. In the words of one, 'these large firms know how the orders are going; they should be able to plan the work better'. It was felt, in particular, that a big company ought to find it feasible to see ahead, while one remarked that the policy of an enterprise should be directed to steady rather than to quick profits. Some thought that these matters were the responsibility of employers only; others, that the trade unions or the Government also had a part to play. Thus one commented that 'under the present system an employer can decide he has made enough profit and close down; there should be some planning at a national level'. A second likewise felt that a wider approach was needed—as otherwise redundancy in one factory would merely be exported elsewhere. This respondent added 'it's out-dated, this idea of employers getting all the work out of them and then throwing them on the scrap heap', ending with the rhetorical question 'they didn't do that in the feudal system, did they?'

In some instances, then, the demand for more planning at plant level imperceptibly merged into one for government or political action, while several respondents exclusively concentrated on the latter. Thus 'there is nothing that can be done to stop it, unless the Government takes off the tax from cars'. Again, redundancies 'are bound to happen unless the Government is determined to have full employment at all costs'. And again, 'they're unavoidable under the present capitalist economic system; they could prevent them with more planning'. Others similarly urged the case for more controls or for less competition between car producers, while a few thought that redundancies could only be eliminated if all industry were nationalized. A handful—more hesitantly—hazarded into the realm of fiscal and monetary measures.

Among other proposals were that the Government should lift the ban on trade with Iron Curtain countries, while one suggested a fund, which could be drawn on in times of slack trade, adding 'they put money aside for machinery replacements, so they should put money aside for the workers, who are at least as important'. There were also references to American practice in the matter of a guaranteed annual wage. Finally, a few felt that redundancies could be prevented only if there were a change of Government. Two comments may be added. First, it was only a relatively small minority who specifically pinned their faith on Government or political action. Secondly, the gap between the latter and those saying that lay-offs were bound to happen was in some cases surprisingly narrow, in that both regarded them as likely, taking things as they are. The difference was mainly that some respondents were prepared to venture beyond the *status quo*, and against the background of such a broader canvas, declared that redundancies were preventable.

Of the 87 respondents who held that dismissals, though not in the last resort avoidable, need not be as frequent in occurrence or as large in scale, the chief method favoured for reducing their incidence or mitigating their severity was, again, short-time and analogous prescriptions; nearly three-fifths of the 87 commented to that effect. On the whole, the suggestions put forward tended to be fairly similar to those already described, except that the various remedies were considered to be of lesser potency and at any rate incapable of eradicating redundancies. Thus some believed that the latter could not be done away with in small companies, but that big concerns ought to be able to prevent them; others, that discharges below a certain size were probably inevitable but that mass lay-offs, like those of 1956, need not occur. One idea expressed was that 'if the firm let you know about the condition of the market well in advance . . . a good many would leave of their own accord', while a second was of the opinion that 'far-seeing firms don't get caught making just one product'. A third urged a Government scheme of public works, while there were one or two further variations on the theme of a voluntary insurance fund so that 'the redundant men can be sure of a living wage'.

Chapter 9

CONCLUSION

As stated in the Introduction, the object of this survey has been to investigate the actual experience of redundant workers, and the following pages summarize briefly some of the main findings which have emerged from the inquiry.[1]

1. As a percentage of Birmingham's total insured population, the redundancies examined were not significant. Nevertheless, they gave rise to problems unlikely to have been created by an analogous amount of 'ordinary' unemployment.

2. This is, first, because of the dominant position of the motor industry in the Midlands; all engineering and several other industries are geared to it to a greater or lesser extent, and it is generally regarded as the most important single factor in the maintenance of employment in the region. Secondly, at the date of the 1956 discharges there had been no precedent—in so far as the post-war period is concerned—for so large a number to be dismissed on a single day, the shock being heightened by the nature and suddenness of the announcement. In a sense, therefore, the redundancy produced something akin to a confidence slump on the Stock Exchange; a further factor was that the operation took place shortly before the industrial holidays when recruitment is in any event at a discount.

3. The amount of difficulty experienced by the men—259 of the 447 respondents, or 58 per cent of the sample, considered that it had been difficult to get work after lay-off—was thus greater than might have been expected in the light of the official unemployment figures. At the same time, having difficulty did not necessarily mean a prolonged spell of joblessness, 54 per cent of respondents being actually settled in a new post within a fortnight of dismissal, though 15 per cent were unemployed in excess of two months.

[1] The reader may like to compare some of what follows with the short but informative review of 'Redundancies Reported to the Ministry of Labour, October 1961—September 1962', *Ministry of Labour Gazette*, February 1963, pp. 53–4.

4. Another reason why the redundancy gave rise to problems unlikely to have been generated by an equivalent dose of ordinary unemployment is that the temporary character of the recession aggravated matters in the short run. Thus a significant number found that employers were unwilling to engage them—on the ground mainly that the men were expected to return to the motor industry as soon as the opportunity presented itself, lured by the higher wages available there. Though these misgivings proved correct in respect of just over one half of the sample, in so far as any one individual was concerned reinstatement was by no means a certainty in the immediate post-R period, while its timing was in any case unknown. Hence it was essential for the men to seek alternative employment, but the possibility of subsequent re-engagement was a hindrance in this context.

5. The reluctance of would-be employers to take on ex-employees of the motor industry was indeed a major factor delaying the securing of a new niche after discharge: one-third of the 259 men with job trouble spontaneously adduced such 'anti-RJness' as wholly or partly responsible, the only cause of difficulty more frequently mentioned being the recession and general scarcity of openings. In so far as the former reason is concerned, one cannot of course blame employers for their lack of enthusiasm in filling permanent vacancies with what might well turn out to be temporary labour. In such circumstances, however, individual bargains with the men—under which the latter would have committed themselves to a minimum period of service—might have prevented those who had decided to break with the motor industry from being unnecessarily penalized. Such a course would, at the same time, have enabled firms to choose their workers on merit without worrying unduly about their subsequent defection.

6. That the assumption that money was the chief consideration weighing with the redundant men was, at best, a half-truth is demonstrated by the fact that about 70 per cent of the sample did *not* turn down an offer of employment on grounds of inadequacy of reward. Even more 'telling' in this context are the meagre pay standards of the jobs actually accepted by the men after dismissal.

7. Of the 259 respondents encountering difficulty in obtaining work after discharge, only six had met with 'closed shop' complications.

8. Though the numbers are far too small to warrant any wider conclusions, the 13 coloured respondents interviewed were at a special disadvantage in finding a job at the time, even though they were much the most mobile sector of the sample.

9. Age was a distinct handicap after discharge, while skill was not the golden key that opened all doors irrespective of other considerations. Though skill was no doubt of help in securing employment, and while age was not an insuperable obstacle, as a broad generalization it was youth rather than skill which was an asset after redundancy.

10. The percentage commencing work within a fortnight of lay-off was 48 for the single but 56 for the married, the proportion placed in this short time-span rising with the number of dependent children.[1] At the same time, only 10 per cent of the single were unemployed for more than two months, though the corresponding proportion for the married was 17 per cent.

11. Taking all the evidence together, pressures and preferences on the supply side, no less than the requirements of employers, can be said to have had a bearing on the relative speed of absorption. Thus although unemployment otherwise lengthened with age, it was the 31–40 rather than the 30-and-under category which had the highest proportion settled in a new post within a fortnight of discharge. The men in their twenties, that is—a considerable number of whom were single—were able to bide their time to some extent, while their comparative lack of know-how may have been a contributory factor on the demand side. The 30–40 year-olds, on the other hand, tended to have family responsibilities and were thus more anxious to get fixed up without delay; they were also not yet handicapped by their age, while they were more experienced than their juniors. However, while domestic circumstances made obtaining work quickly a matter of special urgency for the family man, this differential factor no longer operated as regards extended unemployment, and the difference here between single and married seems to have been one primarily of age.

12. Twenty-four per cent of the sample made—or needed to make—merely one attempt to procure a new niche following dismissal, although at least 15 per cent pursued more than forty would-be openings. In general, the number of posts applied for diverged

[1] Except in the case of those with three or more dependent children.

widely—from nil to over 300. In this as in other respects, the elderly tended to exert themselves less than their more youthful ex-colleagues.

13. As regards the methods used in seeking employment, the great majority were not content to rely on one agency only. The most important single means by which work was actually secured was to make applications on the 'off-chance', 32 per cent of all first post-R jobs being found in this way—followed by 19 per cent obtained with the aid of relatives, friends or 'connections'. The method leading to the speediest absorption, however, was to have known someone in authority willing to offer work—such as an old boss—12½ per cent of the sample having a first post-R job with a former employer.

14. Seventy-three per cent of the sample registered at an employment exchange after redundancy, while 26 per cent did not. Although the overwhelming majority of those not placed within two weeks of lay-off signed on, the brevity of unemployment is not the whole explanation for over one-quarter of respondents not registering at an exchange at the time.

15. Only 15 per cent of the sample—or 20 per cent of those signing on —actually obtained their first post-R job via an employment exchange. A further 10 per cent of those registering stated that the exchange helped, or was or tried to be helpful, though 57 per cent said that it did not help. Nearly 35 per cent of registrants found that the exchanges had no vacancies to which to refer them, while the total advised of either none, no longer vacant ones, or unsuitable openings only—but not, that is, of any potentially suitable ones—was almost certainly substantially larger. A considerable amount of very outspoken criticism was expressed about the exchanges, and the feeling that the latter only have inferior posts to dispose of—both as regards type of work and remuneration—was widespread.

16. Since all the men did, sooner or later, secure a post, it is evident that there were vacancies at the time, but that these simply had not been channelled through the exchanges. In other words, it is plain that many firms must have been disinclined to intimate their requirements to the exchanges, while it is highly probable that, were it not for the latter's 'dole-paying' activities, many more of the present sample would have ignored them following dismissal. Though, as explained in Chapter 4, several exonera-

ting circumstances must be taken into account, if the *raison d'être* of a national system of employment exchanges is its potential efficiency in bringing together those offering and those seeking work, then the performance of the service in the present instance must be adjudged to have been inadequate.

17. One intriguing question raised by the foregoing is why employment exchanges should enjoy—as this investigation, at any rate, suggests—a so much lower reputation than other state agencies. More generally, an independent inquiry designed to throw light on employers' use/experience of exchanges, as well as that of workers in a 'normal' context, might yield useful information.

18. Getting placed immediately or very soon after lay-off was not invariably tantamount to a painless transition to a new niche in the labour market: one-quarter of the 244 respondents who secured work within a fortnight of redundancy had given or received their notice again within three months of commencing duties.

19. Nevertheless, the dismissals did not result in a vast number of short-duration jobs nor did they, overall, have any grave after-effects in the shape of recurrent unemployment. Thus though 323 out of the 447 respondents (72 per cent) were, when seen, no longer in the post first taken after redundancy, only 26 per cent had two or more such 'interim' jobs in the interval between discharge and day of interview. Further, while 18 per cent of the sample had—over and above that experienced immediately after lay-off—undergone some further unemployment by the time of interview, mostly this was of fairly short duration; only 5 per cent had suffered *additional* spells of joblessness totalling more than one month, though these included several instances of real hardship. Fifty-seven of the 447 men (13 per cent) were actually made redundant again in the 'interim' period.

20. Just over 15 per cent of the 323 first interim posts were in labouring, etc. occupations. Though this 15 per cent is not strictly comparable with the 5 per cent of the total sample graded as unskilled prior to dismissal, it is fairly clear that the 'labourer' element increased in the immediate post-R period.

21. This same period was likewise marked by very long working hours and a substantial drop in wages. Thus for 31 per cent of those having a first interim post, hours averaged more than 50 a week, while for 17 per cent they exceeded 55. Forty-three

per cent of the same group earned, on average, £10 a week or under,[1] while 3 per cent were making not above £7. Thirty-six per cent of first interim job-holders received a weekly income of more than £4 below, and 13 per cent of more than £7 below, that earned in the six months preceding redundancy (when more than one-third of the sample were on short-time). And as the analysis in Chapter 5 makes clear, the deterioration in hourly rates of pay as between RJ and first interim jobs was even more dramatic than that in weekly remuneration.

22. Almost one-fifth of the sample (19 per cent) had definite or serious financial difficulties after dismissal, 14 per cent of the 87 men concerned resorting to National Assistance in the period following lay-off. However, of the single only 4 per cent had serious financial problems, as compared with 23 per cent of the married.

23. The overwhelming majority—94 per cent—of the same 87 respondents also had a rough passage securing employment after discharge, three-quarters considering the search for work to have been *very* difficult. By contrast, of the 259 persons who found it hard to obtain an opening, only 32 per cent had definite monetary trouble. It follows that long unemployment in itself was not co-terminous with pecuniary complications of the more grave kind; thus of the 68 respondents in the sample out of a job in excess of two months, only one half had serious financial difficulties.

24. Twelve per cent of the sample fell into arrears on a contractual commitment, hire-purchase being the biggest single cause of such arrears. However, 'falling behind' did not invariably spell pronounced financial trouble; in some measure this depended on the ease with which accommodation could be secured from the dealer.

25. Forty-seven per cent of the 447 men drew on their savings after redundancy, though recourse was had to these not merely for 'subsistence' requirements, but also simply in order to maintain customary living standards. Savings were resorted to both during the period of post-R unemployment, and to augment the frequently much-reduced earnings once a job had been secured. An interesting point is that a slightly larger proportion of the single than of the married drew on their reserves, although a distinctly

[1] All earnings figures in this paragraph are *gross*.

smaller percentage of the former than of the latter were in serious financial difficulties.

26. In general, savings were a material help to the men after discharge, while a good many confessed that the dismissals had brought home to them the value of putting something by for such contingencies. The question of whether such voluntary savings are being given sufficient encouragement might repay attention.

27. Further, the chapter on financial and family adjustments showed that it is not the case that in the welfare state men have lost all sense of responsibility, leaving their fate to the mercy of the state. Indeed, both from a financial and from a 'job-finding' point of view the machinery of state played a relatively insignificant role in so far as the Birmingham dismissals are concerned, though it is fair to add that these were not sufficiently grave to have taxed the state's potential contribution to the full.

28. In all, whether or not serious financial embarrassment ensued after the 1956 lay-off depended on a variety of circumstances, the main factors in the equation being the fall in income resulting from unemployment and/or reduced earnings, commitments in the sense both of number of dependants and contractual obligations, and the resources available to meet any imbalance—such as the wife's wages or savings. In general, the data show that even a comparatively mild redundancy causes a not insignificant degree of hardship—a finding which lends urgency to the question of making financial provision for the more drastic manifestations of redundancy that are now upon us. It will be clear that it was not the purpose of the present inquiry to make a study of the wider—and highly intricate—problem of monetary provision for redundancy as such. But no great subtlety is needed for arriving at the negative conclusion that the present level of unemployment benefit, plus the voluntary arrangements existing for a small minority of workers,[1] are woefully inadequate.[2]

[1] See 'Redundancy in Great Britain', *Ministry of Labour Gazette*, February 1963, p. 50 ff.

[2] For a brief discussion on the subject of financial provision for redundancy see G. Goodman, *Redundancy in the Affluent Society* (Fabian Tract No. 340, 1962); National Economic Development Council, *Conditions Favourable to Faster Growth* (H.M.S.O. 1963), pp. 12–13; and S. Please, 'The Economics of Redundancy Compensation', *District Bank Review*, March 1963.

29. At the date of interview, 226 respondents or 51 per cent of the sample were back with the company by which they had been dismissed (RJ) in mid-1956. Of the 221 men who were 'not back', one had meanwhile retired and five were unemployed, though all these had had some work since redundancy.

30. About 78 per cent of the sample either were back at RJ on the date of interview, had been back since discharge but left again, or had at any rate received an offer of reinstatement. Another 14 per cent approximately had not been back, had had no offer, and had not themselves taken any steps to secure one. A further 7 per cent of the sample had not been back, had received no invitation to return, and had been spurned when themselves taking the initiative to this end; these latter include a number of real hardship cases, many of the men still 'hankering after RJ' when interviewed.

31. The three most important factors responsible for a return to the company were the receipt of an invitation to do so, a high level of pre-redundancy earnings and age (youth). Several others were involved—such as the dislike of the shift system at RJ and the fear of further redundancy—but, overall, the three cited had most weight.

32. Of the 215 'not backs',[1] only 49 per cent were still in the vehicles, other engineering, or metals industries by the date of interview. Even therefore allowing for the 51 per cent of the sample who had rejoined RJ, the 1956 discharges can be said to have resulted in a fairly sizeable industrial redistribution of the men involved. It follows that, where the phenomenon of 'returning to RJ' is absent or less prominent than in the dismissals here investigated, redundancy may be expected to lead to a much more substantial redeployment of manpower, though the causes of any such contingency, the state of the industry, the industrial structure of the locality etc. would clearly all have an important bearing.

33. On the subject of geographical mobility, the unemployment generated by the mid-1956 lay-off was not severe enough to impel more than a small minority to seek their fortunes away from home: only 46 of the 447 respondents extended their inquiries beyond daily reach from their home town, while a mere 15 men actually had their first post-R job in such distant parts. However—though it is currently not polite to say so—there is

[1] i.e. 221 minus the 6 not in employment.

some indication that, having been mobile in this particular instance, was not necessarily the best policy.

34. At the same time, in so far as the place of employment is concerned, the redundancy did lead to a distinct shift away from Birmingham, though the 'permanent' drift from the city was well below that occurring immediately after dismissal. Thus 83 per cent of all present jobs were located in Birmingham, as against 62 per cent of all first post-R jobs.

35. If we confine ourselves to the 215 respondents who had not returned to RJ, the proportion employed in Birmingham at the date of interview was likewise only 66 per cent. This exodus from the city on the part of one-third of the 'not backs' did not, however, entail moving house for the purpose: it was a case of a proportion of those living outside Birmingham at the time of redundancy accepting openings nearer their homes.

36. Though the question of leaving their home town altogether was rather hypothetical for many respondents in 1956, it is of interest that, when asked whether they had considered the matter and whether, further, they would contemplate such a move in the event of any future redundancy, some of the comments made pinpointed the conflict implicit in official policy in seeking to encourage both home ownership and labour mobility.

37. The great majority of the 215 'not backs' received no training from their present employer, while that given on all first post-R jobs is unlikely to have been any more extensive. However, in so far as the men had served an apprenticeship or participated in other forms of instruction earlier on in their industrial career, or had previously acquired the requisite experience, or belonged to a group of semi-skilled mass production workers for whom formal technical teaching is not necessary or usual, there is really no reason why they should have had a fresh training after lay-off. The scantness of training received becomes a matter for comment *à propos* of redundancy only, if it can be shown that respondents had relatively more difficulty in finding work because they were not trained, but in the present investigation the skilled were not necessarily better off than the less skilled, while as the men themselves saw it, lack of training and experience were only of minor consequence at the time. This is in no way to imply that the question is of no import—either in general, or in the context of a wider redundancy policy: it is merely to say that training is not, *ipso facto*, the crucial factor.

38. Forty-nine per cent of the 'not backs' thought that the official skill grading of their present post was the same as that of the occupation from which they had been dismissed, 9 per cent stated that their current ranking was lower, while 23 per cent believed that their present calling enjoyed a superior classification. It is also revealing that more than twice as many of the 'not backs' were, at the time of interview, utilizing experience accumulated prior to joining RJ than were drawing on know-how gained at the latter.

39. Another interesting point is that those 'not backs' drawing on their pre-RJ experience were well over twice as numerous as those who had found their way back to a former employer. Over and above the 42 'not backs' who had rejoined an old boss i.e., a good many others had returned to a trade or occupation in which they had spent some part of their earlier career.

40. For those who had not returned to RJ, there was a substantial switch from night/shift- to day-work, although hours were more arduous at the time of interview than before redundancy—longer, that is, as compared with the boom months at RJ in (the second half of) 1955. As a result, however, of the large-scale substitution of days for the pre-R régime entailing nights, 54 per cent of the 'not backs' regarded their present hours and shifts more convenient than those before discharge, as against 19 per cent adjudging them less convenient.

41. In so far as present job earnings are concerned, those who did not return to the firm lost heavily, despite the lengthening of their working schedules and the general upward trend of remuneration in the interval. Thus fully 61 per cent of the 'not backs' had incomes in their present post below those earned in the boom period at RJ (last six months of 1955), while nearly 48 per cent were worse off as compared even with the lean months immediately prior to lay-off.[1] Although, by the time of interview, the level of earnings had recovered from the depths reached immediately after redundancy, there is no doubt that non-return to RJ involved a sizeable pecuniary sacrifice.

42. Of the same group of 'not backs', 61 per cent preferred their current post to that from which they had been laid off. Twenty-two per cent expressed a preference for RJ, while for 14 per cent

[1] In the case of the 'backs', the corresponding proportions were 29 and 15 per cent.

it was a case of 'fifty-fifty' etc. A considerable number were thus declaring for their present employment, although it was yielding them an inferior, or much inferior, income. At the same time, a more substantial majority of the 'backs' than of the 'not backs'—91 per cent as against 78 per cent—wanted to remain in their present job.

43. Eighty-three per cent of the sample were members of a trade union at the date of discharge. When interviewed, 62 per cent of these were still (or again) in the same organization, 17 per cent were then in a different body, while 20 per cent no longer belonged to any union. While the dismissals thus had a marked impact, by and large this was not in consequence of activities or policies pursued by the unions at the time; it reflects rather the change of employment to different/less highly unionized undertakings. Though some hard feelings were certainly voiced by those no longer in membership, on the whole these were of pre-R vintage, and as the data in Chapter 8 bring out, both the switch of allegiance to another organization and the cessation of membership altogether did not, in broad terms, flow from any specific dissatisfaction over the unions' handling of the redundancy.

44. Thirty-nine per cent of the sample felt that the method of selecting those to be laid off in 1956 had been fair, 43 per cent considered it to have been unfair, while 18 per cent thought it was fair in some ways but unfair in others, etc. The precise mode of selection, as far as the present sample is concerned, varied according to the identity of RJ, though broadly speaking length of service was the main guide. What this survey *inter alia* underlines, however, is that 'last in, first out' is potentially something of a shibboleth, for it can be applied in divers ways—with very different results. It can actually be a fairly meaningless exercise, in that while it may deprive a firm of some of its best workers, it does not necessarily ensure any real equity between those of the same seniority. One might here comment that, where redundancy lists are compiled on a length-of-service basis, the sector of plant used as the unit of calculation ought to be at least as large as that over which workers are normally deemed to be mobile.

45. As for the principle of selection favoured *à propos* of any future redundancy, just over 62 per cent of the sample suggested length of service, 49 per cent mentioning no other method. Thirty-four

per cent cited skill, ability, time-keeping, etc., 22½ per cent again doing so exclusively. All other alternatives—including that of 'family commitments'—were put forward by an insignificant number only.

46. Questioned whether, in the event of a future lay-off, certain categories should be requested to leave irrespective of their length of service and similar considerations, 88 per cent of the sample thought that married women should be asked to go first, 63 per cent that men over 65 should, and 45 per cent that coloured and foreign workers should. It is clear, therefore, that the majority of the men were prepared to see their basic criterion of selection put into cold storage when it came to these special groups.

47. Although 'last in, first out' was the most popular single basis proposed, the majority of those commending 'L.I.F.O.' but no other method declared, when specifically questioned, that skill, time-keeping, etc. should also enter into the reckoning, some conceding with distinct enthusiasm the claims of these latter criteria. Despite certain inconsistencies revealed by the material, the data in Chapter 8 suggest that the demand for redundancy lists being based on seniority only may not be as widespread among workers as is sometimes supposed. It may well be that some kind of a 'points' scheme designed to do a degree of justice to both length of service and good workmanship etc. would enjoy considerable support.

48. Forty-seven per cent of the sample were of the opinion that redundancies are bound to happen, 27 per cent thought that they could be avoided, while 19 per cent felt that while they could not be prevented altogether, their frequency or scale could be reduced. This lends little support to the view that the British worker is unaware of the economic facts of life. It further prompts the reflection that, if he nevertheless tends to put up stubborn resistance to many a threatened redundancy, there is no need to attribute this to his lack of economic sophistication: it can more reasonably be ascribed to the inadequacy of national provision—both absolutely and by comparison with other countries[1]—for dealing with the various facets of the problem.

[1] *Cf.* e.g. 'Redundancy in Great Britain', *Ministry of Labour Gazette*, February 1963, p. 50 ff. and 'Redundancy Abroad', *ibid.*, April 1963, p. 148 ff. See also International Labour Office, *Termination of Employment (Dismissal and Lay-Off)*, Report VII(1) (Geneva, 1961).

49. One of the special features of the dismissals here investigated was the lack of notice given to (the majority of) the men. In one way, of course, the lamentable action taken by the British Motor Corporation in 1956 has been beneficial, in that it vividly brought home the state of collective neglect in certain spheres of job security, thus no doubt giving fresh impetus to attempts at remedial action. But though a concrete step forward has since been taken in the shape of the Contracts of Employment Act, 1963, the minima actually laid down by that measure would seem excessively timid. It is questionable whether a minimum period of notice of one and two weeks can be regarded as conferring 'status' on the worker in the second half of the twentieth century, while it is unlikely to lessen the both socially and economically harmful consequences of the fear of redundancy. It is also pertinent to add that as the incidence of the latter increases with the accelerating tempo of technological and organizational change, the proportion of short-service employees in the population will rise, so that it will become correspondingly harder to earn the entitlement to four weeks' notice—available under the 1963 Act only for those with at least five years' employment with one firm.

50. Quite apart from other considerations, a more appropriate minimum period of notice—say, of one month once the probationary spell of service has been completed[1]—might also induce a more economical use of manpower. The view has been widely expressed that the 1956 discharges were merely a rationalization of the industry's labour force, which had become unduly swollen in the preceding years. The knowledge that workers cannot be turned out 'over night' might lead to a more careful initial budgeting of scarce human resources while, given the requisite forecasting of manpower requirements, it need not necessarily entail a collective 'twiddling of thumbs' during the period of notice.

51. Consideration might also be given to whether it should become a statutory obligation upon firms to notify all redundancies (to be specifically defined for the purpose) to their local employment exchange. Such notification might take the form of a prescribed period of advance notice of the total likely to be discharged, with

[1] This is not to imply that long-service workers ought not to receive more generous treatment than this; it is also agreed that certain categories such as seasonal workers require special treatment. Our aim here is simply to say that the minima laid down by the 1963 Act are, even *qua* minima, inadequate.

subsequent particulars of the figure actually dispensed with. Among other things, this should help employment exchanges to function more effectively, while from the point of view of the individual concern, such a requirement could hardly be regarded as specially irksome. Nor does it establish any new principle, having regard to the several series of statistics already compulsorily supplied by industry under the Statistics of Trade Act, 1947.

52. The foregoing proposal would also serve to provide some long overdue statistics. Seeing that redundancy is now almost universally acknowledged as a major public issue, it is rather odd that we should lack the most elementary quantitative data on the subject. Even as late as 1963 the National Economic Development Council had—alongside its 100 specific tables on other topics—to content itself with the statement that '. . . a broad estimate of 200,000 for the average number of workers who become redundant each year might not be too far out'.[1] As the N.E.D.C. adds, this could be remedied if employers were obliged to notify the Ministry of Labour of all redundancies.

53. Another question posed by the present investigation is whether, where the total number of workers to be made redundant is of the order of several thousand individuals, the Ministry of Labour should have the power to request the company concerned to phase the dismissals over a certain time-span, where this seems desirable in the light of the local employment situation. To grant these particular powers to the Ministry would involve a departure from present policy—though no more radical a departure than has recently been made in analogous spheres of labour and industrial policy. In any event—depending on how 'certain time-span' is defined—it would not necessarily constitute a major infringement of managerial prerogative.

54. Though this inquiry represents a case study of a particular redundancy which took place in a particular area at a particular point of time, the dismissals which occurred in Birmingham in mid-1956 may nevertheless be regarded as a classic example of one type of redundancy that may well recur in the British economy—namely that due to a temporary, but major, contraction of demand occurring against both a general and regional background of full employment. This is not to deny that

[1] National Economic Development Council, *Growth of the United Kingdom Economy to 1966* (H.M.S.O. 1963), para. 143.

some features of the lay-off may prove to have been unique in so far as the post-war era is concerned—above all, the abruptness of the exercise in the case of the bulk of the sample—but, by definition almost, any case study is *sui generis* in some degree.

55. Though there appears to be no reason to regard the 1956 discharges as containing more than the inevitable element of 'uniqueness', the findings of this survey are, plainly, more fully relevant to any future contingency belonging to the same species of redundancy than to one belonging to a different variety of the genus. Thus where a major lay-off takes place at a time of general slack in the economy, or in a depressed region of the country otherwise fully employed, or where the operation is due to a permanent contraction of an industry, or caused, say, by automation or other technological change, the problems which arise and the impact of the dismissals must be expected to differ in varying measure from those thrown up by this inquiry. For example, the phenomenon of 'returning to RJ' is unlikely to figure so prominently in other brands of redundancy, though it may be noted that, according to the Ministry of Labour's recent survey, of the 371 private companies which have adopted some kind of redundancy policy, about two-thirds offer priority of re-engagement to former employees made redundant by them.[1]

56. One of the crucial questions raised by our findings is whether, seeing that the redundancies examined were not, overall, a 'major tragedy' for those involved, it is legitimate to infer that redundancy can therefore be viewed with equanimity, or even be actively encouraged in the interests, say, of greater economic dynamism or in order to help rid the economy of inflation. Some might, for example, feel disposed to use the data dealing with the present jobs of the 'not backs' in support of some such conclusion for, as we saw, about three-fifths of the latter preferred their current post to that from which they had been laid off.

Basically, however, what these particular data do is to underline the well-known fact that wages, etc. are only one of many elements making for job satisfaction; in giving 'the big money' pride of place when deciding to join RJ in the first instance, some men evidently underestimated the importance of non-monetary factors in their own scale of values. In other words, so long as job satisfaction is below its optimum level, any extraneous occur-

[1] *Ministry of Labour Gazette*, February 1963, p. 50.

rence, including redundancy, may be instrumental in augmenting it, but this in itself does not 'legitimize' the latter as an appropriate tool of policy. Similarly, while redundancy clearly may help rid the economy of inflation, it can be argued that it is a massive indictment of our economic know-how if we cannot devise less crude methods for this purpose.

57. It is also here relevant to point to two further 'results' of this inquiry which have not so far been reported. These are that almost seven in every ten men interviewed felt that the redundancy had been a 'blow' or a 'great blow' to them at the time.[1] Further, about 27 per cent of the sample stated that it had made a permanent adverse difference—of varying degrees of severity—to their private or working life.[2] Of this last group, more than one half mentioned a sense of insecurity or other psychological effect.

58. Taking all the evidence produced in this report together, the present writer would conclude that perhaps its main lesson for the future is not that the 'fuss' about redundancy is exaggerated, or that its occurrence can discreetly be discounted. It is rather that, even when buttressed by an employment situation as auspicious as that of Birmingham in 1956, redundancy causes a significant amount of dislocation as well as a far from negligible degree of hardship, even though it may also occasion certain favourable results for some of its victims. The obvious corollary is that, in the absence of such a propitious economic background, the repercussions of redundancy must be expected to be correspondingly graver—unless adequate preventive measures are applied.

59. In so far as such measures are concerned, there is one general point worth emphasizing, even though fortunately it is one which is now increasingly appreciated. This is that a national full employment policy in terms of regulating the overall level of demand—wholly essential though it is—will not suffice: the period of notice to which a worker in a civilized community should be entitled; the principles on which those to be discharged are to be selected; the question of monetary compensation and other financial arrangements; how to distinguish between avoidable redundancies due to faulty manpower budgeting and those which ought to occur in the interests of the economy; the functioning of employment exchanges; the

[1] Q. 56 (*b*) of schedule. [2] Q. 56 (*a*) of schedule.

respective role of statutory and voluntary provision or the respective responsibilities of managements, unions and the state—these are only some of the complex problems directly or indirectly coming to the surface in the course of this survey and as yet largely awaiting solution. No claim is here made to have provided these solutions—such was not the writer's brief—though she hopes to have done 'her bit' in the relevant direction.

Redundancy is an issue where a balance has to be struck between the social and the economic good, for some redundancy is inevitable if the economy is not to stagnate. Hence it will not do to succumb either to the attractions of an 'economically hard', or to the blandishments of a 'socially soft', set of remedies. What is significant, however, is that while social and economic desiderata undoubtedly may pull in opposite directions, this is by no means invariably so. The subject of regional planning is a case in point; so is that of industrial training; and so is that of redundancy policy. In the latter sphere, should our twentieth-century wits enable us one day to eradicate the fear of redundancy, a substantial contribution will have been made alike to social and economic welfare. But only when we have evolved a multi-pronged comprehensive programme, adequately covering all aspects of the problem and generously protecting all those liable to be affected, can we reasonably expect a measure of tolerance from the potential victims of redundancy. Only then—and not because a particular set of major dismissals proved less grave in the event than was feared when they were first sprung upon the nation—are we entitled to view redundancy with something approaching equanimity.

Appendix A

TABLE 86

Numbers Registered as Unemployed, Birmingham and Midland Region, 1956

	Birmingham		*Midland Region*	
	Men, 18 *and over*	*All Workers*	*Men*, 18 *and over*	*All Workers*
1956	*No.*	*No.*	*No.*	*No.*
January	2,576	3,635	7,500	12,931
February	2,331	3,237	7,976	13,322
March	2,725	3,703	8,567	14,197
April	2,983	4,413	8,829	15,285
May	6,539	8,337	14,838	21,938
June	7,659	10,145	17,402	25,655
July	15,622	19,384	29,530	40,548
August	17,013	21,706	33,104	44,525
September	4,630	7,623	14,022	23,610
October	4,305	6,955	13,193	22,035
November	4,249	6,787	12,168	20,758
December	4,186	6,602	12,627	21,553

Source: *Ministry of Labour Gazette*. The figures—which relate to the day of the monthly 'count'—include the 'temporarily stopped' as well as the 'wholly unemployed'.

Appendix B: Copy of Letter Sent to Men to be Interviewed

THE UNIVERSITY OF BIRMINGHAM

BIRMINGHAM REDUNDANCY AND RE-EMPLOYMENT SURVEY

FACULTY OF COMMERCE AND SOCIAL SCIENCE,
THE UNIVERSITY,
EDGBASTON,
BIRMINGHAM, 15.

Dear Mr.

One of the problems at present worrying many people is that of redundancy, and the University here is making a Survey to study its effects in the Birmingham area. As you may remember, by far the largest lay-offs were those in the motor-car industry in the summer of 1956:[1] we are therefore trying to find out what happened to the men concerned, what difficulties they had in getting jobs, whether they have now returned to their old firm, and so on.

We should therefore very much like to hear how you personally were affected by redundancy, and one of our staff will be coming to see you during the next few days to have your opinions and answers to a number of questions. If you should be busy, our interviewer will be glad to call another time, but in case you are out, *could you perhaps leave a message, suggesting when it would be convenient for him or her to call back*? (If it would suit you better to have the interview at the University, this can easily be arranged; in that case we shall be pleased to make you a small payment of 15/– to cover your expenses.)

This is an independent University inquiry and will not in any way affect your job, while any information received will be treated as absolutely confidential. The Survey has the support of the various trade unions, and we hope that its results may help to make things easier for those affected by some future redundancy. We feel sure that we may count on your co-operation, for which we thank you most sincerely in advance.

Yours truly,
HILDA R. KAHN
Head of Research.

P.S. Just in case you are wondering how your name was chosen, we have been supplied by the firms concerned with the names of *all* men laid off in mid-1956. As we cannot manage to interview everybody, we have picked names at equal intervals from this list: the selection has been made by *us*—as it were, by lot. We can assure you that there is no other reason why you are included.

[1] For those laid off from the two non-B.M.C. firms, the wording of this sentence was slightly different.

Appendix C: The Questionnaire[1]

University of Birmingham
Faculty of Commerce and Social Science

Birmingham Redundancy and Re-employment Survey

Confidential

Interviewer: ....

No.: .... Date of interview: ....

TRAINING AND EARLY JOB HISTORY

1. Place of birth: .... 2. Place of education: ....

3. Age when leaving school: .... yrs.

4. What sort of school was that?—technical/sec. mod./elem./grammar?

---

5. A. On leaving school, were you apprenticed to a trade? Yes/No
If 'Yes':
C. To which trade? ....
D. Industry in which served: ....
B. How long did it take to complete apprenticeship? ....yrs.

---

6. Have you at any time attended	*I. night school?*	*II. day-contin.?*
A.	Yes/No	Yes/No
If 'Yes':		
C. Subjects taken:		
B. Length of course:	..wks/mths/yrs.	..wks/mths/yrs.
D. *Addit.* to apprent. (if any)?	Yes/No	Yes/No

7. Time, if any, spent in the Forces: ....yrs. (*If nil, turn to Q.* 8)
A. Did you receive any special training there? Yes/No
C. *If 'Yes':* Type:
B. *If 'Yes':* Length of course: ....wks/mths/yrs.

---

[1] *Key:* R = redundancy; r = redundant; RJ = firm/job from which made redundant.

8. (*a*) *Details of all jobs held since leaving school up to time of R:*
(List in chronol. order. If impossible, list main jobs)

Occupation	*Industry* (include firm, if given)	*Town* (if not clear)	*Number of yrs.* (or dates)

(*b*) *If not clear:* Total no. of firms with whom worked up to time of R (excluding RJ):..........firms.

9. (*g*) A. Did you receive a formal *on-the-job* training from any of above firms before joining RJ? Yes/No
B. *If 'Yes':* Occupation(s) for which trained:

JOB FROM WHICH DECLARED REDUNDANT (RJ)

10. (*u*) When did you first join RJ?

Date	*Job(s) during period*
From..........till..........	....
From..........till..........	....
From..........till..........	....

(*f*) Total time with RJ up to time of R: ....wks/mths/yrs.
(*c*) *If not clear:* Occupation from which made r:........................
(*d*) *If not clear:* Time in do.: ....wks/mths/yrs.
(*e*) How was that (occup. from which made r) rated by firm as regards skill? S/SS/U/DK
(*g*) A. Did RJ give you a formal training for (any of) job(s)? Yes/No
B. *If 'Yes':* Length of training: ....days/wks/mths/yrs.

11.	*I. In 6 mths. immediately before R:*	*II. In last 6 mths. of 1955:*
(*h*) In ... (col. I or II), were you mainly on short-time, overtime or a standard week?		
(*i*) What shifts did you work in ... (col. I or II)—days? nights?		
(*j*) In same 6 mths. (specify), how many hrs. a week did you work *on av.*, when on .... (*h*), and doing .... (*i*)?	..hrs. gross/net	..hrs. gross/net
(*k*) How much did you make—what were yr. av. weekly earnings—when working.. hrs. (*j*), in ... (col. I or II)? A. Gross earnings: B. 'Take-home' pay: (i.e. A. less 'stoppages')	 £ . s. p.w. £ . s. p.w.	 £ . s. p.w. £ . s. p.w.

12. (*a*) What made you join RJ in the first place?

(*b*) If you had not been made r, would you have wanted to remain with RJ?

13. (*a*) When the lay-off was announced in the summer of 1956, were you surprised that you were involved?

(*b*) In general, had the redundancy been expected in the works?

14. (*a*) Do you think the method of selecting those to be laid off was fair?

(*b*) Have you any other comments about the firm's handling of the R?

15. (*a*) Were you a member of a trade union at time of R? Yes/No
(*If 'No', turn to* (*j*))

If 'Yes':
(*b*) Which union?..
(*c*) Were you a branch official or shop steward at time of R? Yes/No
(*d*) *If 'Yes':* Office held:..................................
(*e*) Did your union take any steps to prevent your being laid off?
(*f*) Did your union pay you any benefit after R?
(*g*) Did it help you in your search for work or any other way?
(*h*) Have you changed your union since R? Yes/No/No longer belongs
(*i*) *If 'Yes'/'No longer belongs':* Reasons:

If 'No' (i.e. if *not* a T.U. member at time of R):
(*j*) Have you joined a union since? Yes/No
(*k*) *If 'Yes':* Why have you now joined?

16. Have you any *general* comments about trade union activities or policy at time of R?

17. (*a*) When made r, were you told you might be taken back?
(*b*) Since your R, have RJ at any time sent you a letter/message offering to re-engage you? Yes/No
(*c*) Are you now back at RJ? Yes/No (*If 'Yes', turn to Q.* 18)

If not back, but re-employment offered:
(*d*) When did you receive invitation to return?........................
(*e*) Why did you not go back?

If not back, and no offer of re-employment:
(*f*) Have you yourself at any time applied to RJ for re-employment?

18. (*a*) After leaving RJ, did you find it easy or difficult to get a job?

(*b*) *If difficult* (*or not sure*)*:* What, do you think, made it difficult?

19. (*a*) When you were told that you would be laid off, how did you actually set about finding work?

(*b*) Can you remember about how many jobs you went after?
(*c*) Did you (also) try any of the following methods in order to find work? For example, (*Omit items already mentioned*)

	Yes	*No*
A. Did you follow up newspaper adverts?	....	....
B. Did you follow up factory gate notices?	....	....
C. Did you apply to firms on the 'off-chance' (i.e. without advert/gate notice)?	....	....
D. Did you ask relatives/friends to tell you of jobs?	....	....
E. *If a T.U. member at time of R:* Did you apply to your T.U. for details of vacancies?	....	....

(*If made no effort whatever to find work, apart from one successful attempt, turn to Q.* 22)

20. (*a*) When made r, in what areas (towns) did you look for work?
A. In Birmingham? Yes/No
B. *If 'Yes': Anywhere* in Birmingham, or only in parts convenient to get to?
C. Did you look in other towns? Yes/No
D. *If 'Yes':* Which?
E. *If 'Yes':* Were there any jobs you could not accept because of the lack of nearby housing?
(*b*) Did you turn down any jobs because of excessive travelling involved?

---

21. When looking for work after R,
    (*a*) Did you turn down—or not follow up—jobs because pay too low?
    (*b*) Did you have any difficulties because of closed-shop agreements?
    (*c*) Did your age affect your prospects in any way?

---

22. (*a*) When made r, did you register at an Employment Exchange? Yes/No
    (*If 'No', turn to (e)*)

    If 'Yes':
    (*b*) Was the Exchange of help to you in your search for work?

    (*c*) Did the Exchange offer you any jobs which you thought unsuitable?
    Yes/No/Had nothing to offer
    (*If 'No'/'Had nothing to offer', turn to Q.* 23)

    (*d*) *If 'Yes':* Were they unsuitable

	Yes	*No*
A. Because the wages were too low?	....	....
B. Because the work was unsuitable?	....	....
C. Because they involved too much daily travelling?	....	....
D. Because they would have meant your moving to another district?	....	....
E. Other reasons/comments:		

    If 'No' (i.e. if did *not* register at Exchange after R):
    (*e*) Why did you not register?

---

23. *In general*, do you think the Exchange could have done more to help r workers?

---

24. Had you experienced any unemployment prior to R?

---

25. *Ask, (i.e. recap.), even if already clear:*
    (*y*) How long after leaving RJ did you actually start your next job?
    ....days/wks/mths. after leaving RJ*
    (*If within* 6 *days of R, turn to Q.* 26)
    (*a*) Did you spend any of this time having a rest, taking a holiday, etc., during which you did not try for a job?
    (*b*) *If 'Yes':* How long was that? ....days/wks/mths.

---

* If *unemployed* since R, turn to Q. 36; if *retired* since R, to Q. 37.

26. (*z*) *If not clear:* How did you actually obtain first job after R?

JOBS HELD AFTER REDUNDANCY (*excluding* present job)

	27. *First Job**	28. *Second Job**	29. *Third Job**
(*c*) Occupation:			
(*b*) Industry (and firm, if given):			
(*t*) Town:			
(*s*) Time, if any, previously worked for firm:	..mths/yrs.	..mths/yrs.	..mths/yrs.
(*j*) How many hours a week did you work—on av.—while in this job?	..hrs gr./net	..hrs gr./net	
(*k*) What were your average weekly earnings, when working ..hrs. (*j*)? A. Gross earnings: B. 'Take-home' pay: (i.e. A. less 'stoppages')	 £ . s. p.w. £ . s. p.w.	 £ . s. p.w. £ . s. p.w.	
(*f*) Time in job:	..wks/mths	..wks/mths	..wks/mths
(*x*) Reasons for leaving:			
(*y*) Time unemployed before starting next job:	..days/wks.	..days/wks.	..days/wks.

30. *To be completed only if at least* 3 *interim jobs:*
   (*a*) No. of jobs between third interim and present job:........
   (*If nil, turn to 'Present Job'* (*Q.* 31 *or* 32))†
   (*b*) Industry and occupation of fourth and any subsequent interim jobs:
   (*c*) Were any of these jobs at RJ? Yes/No
   (*d*) *If 'Yes':* For how long were you back at RJ? ....wks/mths/yrs.
   (*y*) Details of any further unemployment between third interim and present job:†

* If this is 'Present Job' (*not* back at RJ), turn to Q. 31.
If this is 'Present Job' (*back* at RJ), turn to Q. 32.
If all interim jobs noted and now *unemployed*, turn to Q. 36.
If all interim jobs noted and now *retired*, turn to Q. 37.

† If now *unemployed*, turn to Q. 36; if now *retired*, to Q. 37.

31. *PRESENT JOB* (*not* back at RJ)

(*If back at RJ, complete Q.* 32 *instead*)

(*a*) Name of firm:...................... (*t*) Town:.................
(*b*) Industry:.................... (*f*) Date of joining firm:..........
(*s*) Time, if any, previously worked for firm:......wks/mths/yrs.
(*z*) *If not clear:* How did you obtain job?

(*c*) Occupation:...
(*e*) How is that rated by firm as regards skill? S/SS/U/DK
(*v*) Are the skill and experience gained at RJ of use to you in your present work?
(*w*) *If 'No':* Is any of your other experience?
(*g*) A. Did firm give you a new formal training? Yes/No
B. *If 'Yes':* Length of training: ......days/wks/mths.

(Now Q. 33)

32. *PRESENT JOB* (*back* at RJ)

(*f*) Date of returning to RJ:..........................
(*z*) Exactly how did you get back to firm?
(*a*) Are you doing precisely the same job as before your R? Yes/No

(*If 'Yes', turn to Q.* 33)

If 'No'/Not precisely the same job:

(*c*) Present occupation:...................................
(*e*) How is that rated by firm as regards skill? S/SS/U/DK
(*v*) Are the skill and experience gained at RJ *before* your R of use to you in your present work?
(*w*) *If 'No':* Is any of your other experience?
(*g*) A. Did RJ give you a new formal training? Yes/No

33. *PRESENT JOB* (contd.): *All respondents* (i.e. whether back at RJ or not)

(*h*) During last 6 months (or since joining present employers, if less), have you been mainly on short-time, overtime or a standard week?

(*i*) What sort of shifts have you been working in this (same) period—days? nights?

(*j*) Again taking the last 6 months, how many hours a week have you been working *on av.*, when on ... (*h*), and doing ....(*i*)?

....hrs. gross/net

(*k*) How much do you make—say, what have your average weekly earnings been during the last half year, when working ....hours (*j*)?

A. Gross earnings: £ . s. p.w.
B. 'Take-home' pay: £ . s. p.w.
(i.e. A. less 'stoppages')

34. (*a*) All in all, how would you say your average earnings now compare with those (at RJ) before your R?
(*b*) Do you find your present hours and shifts more convenient or less convenient than (at RJ) before your R?
(*c*) *If not back at RJ:* In general, can you say which you prefer—your job at RJ or your present one?
(*d*) *If back at RJ:* Apart from what we have already discussed, are there *any*/any *other* differences between your job now and that before your R?

35. (*a*) Do you want to stay in your present job? Yes/No/Not sure
(*b*) *If 'No'/'Not sure':* Are you actually planning a change? Yes/No/DK
(*c*) Comments, if any: [(*a*) or (*b*)]:

(*d*) Do you think your job is likely to last?

(Now Q. 38)

36. *To be completed only if now unemployed:*
(*a*) Date since which unemployed: ....(*If since R, omit* (*b*) *and* (*c*))
(*b*) What steps have you taken to find a new job?

(*c*) Reasons for any difficulty experienced:

(*d*) Have you thought of trying a new line?
(*e*) Would you consider moving from this area? Yes/No/Not sure
(*f*) Reasons/comments:

37. *To be completed only if now retired:*
(*a*) Date since which no longer working:........................
(*b*) What were your precise reasons for retiring?

(*c*) If not made r in 1956, would you have stopped work at this time?
(*d*) Any other comments:

38. (*a*) What do you feel has been your main occup. in your working life?

(*b*) Would you say that you 'belong to motor cars' rather than to any other industry?*

39. In the course of your working life, have you been kept at home much through illness or accidents?

FINANCIAL AND FAMILY ADJUSTMENTS

40. Marital status: Single/Married. 41. Date of birth:..................
42. *If married, etc.:* Respondent's household (i.e. living at same address)

	Now:		*Immediately before R:*	
	Work./contr.†	*Wholly dep.*	*Work./contr.*†	*Wholly dep.*
(*a*) Wife	....	....	....	....
(*b*) Children (S)	....	....	....	....
(*c*) Children (M)‡	....	....	....	....
(*d*) Relatives	....	....	....	....
(*e*) Lodgers/Others	....	....	....	....

* For those laid off from the two non-B.M.C. firms, the question read 'Would you say that you belong to any one industry in particular?'
† Include here anyone *not* wholly dependent on respondent.
‡ Include family of married children in brackets: e.g. 1(+3).

---

43. *If single:* Have you any dependent relatives?

	Now:		*Immediately before R:*	
	Partly dep.	*Wholly dep.*	*Partly dep.*	*Wholly dep.*
Number:	....	....	....	....

---

44. (*a*) Taking the time just before your R, did you (or a member of your family) have any additional income from a casual job, running a shop, property, or some other source? Yes/No
(*b*) *If 'Yes':* Details:
(*c*) *If 'Yes':* Did this continue after your R?

---

45. (*a*) When made r, did you *take on* any odd jobs to make some cash? Yes/No
(*If 'No', turn to* (*e*))
If 'Yes':
(*b*) Type of job done:..
(*c*) For about how long did you work at this job? ....days/wks/mths.
(*d*) About how much were you able to make per week? ....p.w.
If married, etc.:
(*e*) Did any member of your family take on either a *regular* or a *casual* job because of your R? Yes/No
(*f*) *If 'Yes':* Details:

---

46. (*a*) When declared r, did you collect unemployment benefit? Yes/No
(*b*) *If 'No':* Why not?

(*c*) Have you drawn unemployment benefit at any time since? Yes/No
(*d*) Details/comments:

---

47. Did you make any use of National Assistance facilities
(*a*) Immediately after R? Yes/No
(*b*) Subsequently? Yes/No
(*c*) Details/comments:

---

48. Following your R, did you draw on any savings to tide you over?

---

49. (*a*) When made r, did you have any regular commitments such as rent, mortgage, H.P., or similar weekly/monthly payments? Yes/No
(*If 'No', turn to Q.* 50)
If 'Yes':
(*b*) Did you—because of your R—fall behind with any of these payments? Yes/No
(*c*) *If 'Yes':* Details: (Type of payment and extent of arrears)

---

50. All in all, taking, say, the first three months after R, would you say you had *some*—or *serious*—financial difficulties?

---

51. (*a*) *Journey to work:* (*Omit A., if unemployed or retired*)
    A. Now:..........mins./hrs. B. RJ:............mins./hrs.

    (*b*) *Mode of travel:*
    A. Now:.................. B. RJ: ....

---

52. (*a*) Have you moved to new accommodation since your R? Yes/No
    (*b*) *If 'Yes':* Precise reasons: *(If 'No', turn to Q.* 54)

---

53. *To be completed only if move connected with respondent's R:*
    (*a*) Date of moving:....................................
    (*b*) Did you find it easy or difficult to find new accommodation?
    (*c*) Did your move mean
    A. Change of school for any of children?
    No change/Change for ....children
    B. Loss/change of employment for other members of family? Yes/No
    C. *If 'Yes':* Details:
    D. Separation from relatives/friends, giving up of clubs, etc.?
    E. Any fresh financial problems?
    (*d*) All in all, is present accommodation as satisfactory as previous?

---

54. (*a*) When made r, did you consider leaving your home town altogether?
    Yes/No/Not sure
    (*b*) Reasons/comments:

---

55. *Omit, if unemployed or retired:*
    (*a*) If made r again, would you consider moving from this area?
    Yes/No/Not sure
    (*b*) Reasons/comments:

    (*c*) *If reluctant to move:* Are there any circumstances in which you would move?

GENERAL

56. (*a*) Apart from its temporary effects, do you feel R has made any *permanent* difference to your private—or working—life?

    (*b*) Would you say it was a great 'blow' to you *at the time*?

57. (*a*) Where a redundancy is declared, what do *you* consider the fairest method for selecting those to be laid off?

(*b*) Do you think any of the following should also be taken into account?
(*Omit items already mentioned*)

A. Length of service?
B. Skill and quality of work?
C. Time-keeping?
D. Number of children?

(*c*) Do you think any of the following should be asked to go first, irrespective of length of service, etc.?

	Yes	*No*	*Comments:*
A. Married women?	....	....	
B. Single women?	....	....	
C. Single men?	....	....	
D. Men over 65?	....	....	
E. Coloured and foreign workers?	....	....	

58. Do you think redundancies could be prevented altogether, or would you say they are bound to happen from time to time?

59. Where a redundancy does take place, can you suggest any measures that would make them easier for those affected? Is there anything that the Government, firms, trade unions or anyone else could do?

60. Further comments, if any:

NOTE: *In the printing of 'open-ended' questions on the preceding pages, it has frequently not been possible—for reasons of lay-out, etc.—to reproduce the actual space allowed for the noting of answers on the original schedule.*

INDEX*

[Compiled by MRS B. M. D. SMITH]

* *Key:* R = redundancy; RJ = firm/job from which made redundant

For Product Safety Concerns and Information please contact our EU
representative GPSR@taylorandfrancis.com
Taylor & Francis Verlag GmbH, Kaufingerstraße 24, 80331 München, Germany

www.ingramcontent.com/pod-product-compliance
Lightning Source LLC
Chambersburg PA
CBHW071850270326
41929CB00013B/2168

* 9 7 8 1 0 3 2 8 1 7 0 1 9 *